WHAT DO YOU WANT ME TO DO?

13 years of Online Harassment

Lindsey Goldrick Dean

CHAPTER ONE
Online Dating

"My love must have taken your breath away. I wonder what else would take your breath away, my Golden Girl?" were the last ominous words that the perpetrator emailed directly to me. It set the scene for what was to follow.

Backtracking. I had moved back home to England after living in America since my early twenties. Divorced for two years now and ever romantic, I joined an online dating site, lured by the site's tagline - 'Meet someone like-minded'. It was 2004. The concept was still novel. It felt exciting. Getting to know someone online before meeting them felt safe. It appealed to the romantic, old-fashioned side of me. I could pick up whether someone was kind with a good, humorous outlook on life, by what they wrote. Through writing first, compatibilities will reveal themselves, I thought.

I so longed for a relationship where communication was paramount because that was one thing that had been lacking in my marriage. Interesting that 17 years ago, I thought that if someone wrote well, they would be good communicators verbally in real life, though. Lesson learnt. One really shouldn't presume.

I didn't disclose where I worked or lived online. I merely put *'In the Southwest'*, my name, my photograph and words of *'Perfectly happy 34 year old lady seeks a messed-up psycho. Looks not an issue. Deranged personality an absolute must!'*.

Actually, it was something wholly unoriginal like *'Genuine, Life-Loving Lady seeks Genuine, Life-loving Gentleman for talks, walks and fun adventures'*.

At the end of summer 2004, I wasn't connecting with anyone and it wasn't quite what I had imagined. Some wanted to meet as soon as possible 'just for fun'. I didn't want that. Regardless, I was beginning to think that online dating was not for me.

Approaching the end of my free trial, I was about to delete my account when Saul Furran contacted me. Somehow, his nonchalant emails drew me to reply. I detected a flippant, cheeky humour and it made me smile.

He wrote and asked me how I was and that he was looking forward to hearing from me. Immediately afterwards, giving no time between his emails, he wrote another. And asked if I would hurry up and reply because he was on a break and he didn't get them often. This made me laugh and I wrote back to 'Mr Impatient' and signed it off with a kiss.

I guess it was the kiss that I signed off with (why, oh why?) which gave him the intro to his next message. It began: along the lines of '*You mad romantic fool! We hardly know each other and yet…and yet…I feel as our relationship moves on and after a night of contemplation, we can swap personal emails and come back…stronger?*'. The exaggeration of the sentiment made me smile again and I felt compelled to want to know more about him.

He was a freelance technical writer and travelled around the world on contracts, whilst I was the editor of a huge corporate company's magazine on a year's contract. I was intending to set up my own business under my name after it had finished. So, we had things in common. We liked to write and it turned out, to each other: comedically and nostalgically.

My initial hopes were met! We shared stories of similar magical, happy childhoods. Loving our families and our abundance of wonderful, close friends. We had mutual interests in music, books, travel and poetry. I told him why I had joined an online dating site. I wasn't asking for much, I jested. I wanted to meet someone that was a good communicator. Someone who was positive and kind, openhearted, honest and grateful. A good sense of humour and being adventurous were super important too. He seemed to be all those. He also wrote poetically, intelligently and romantically.

After a few weeks of emailing though, he admitted that he had joined just to write to somebody. Disappointed, I asked him if he was hiding something like being married. Or whether he was in prison. He insisted he wasn't. Then alluded that it concerned him that on doing a search of me, there wasn't anything about me on the internet. I explained about the importance of my privacy. The dating site was the only account online I had created, other than my Yahoo account.

Also, all the writing work I had ever done wasn't electronically available. My career had began in the antediluvian age of writing with a pen or typing on a typewriter, using a fax and putting things in an envelope to post to a client. I had a stack of magazines that I had published but nothing had been uploaded online. I concluded that he would just be my online friend, at that point. Yet, I wondered why he had joined an online dating site.

It was amazing to be back in the UK after almost a decade in the US, which I had absolutely loved. I was having incredibly special times with my Mama, family and old and new friends. I was free to do anything I liked. Free of worries. Free of commitments. I accepted offers of any adventure, any day, for however long, in any county and any country. I lived life and loved life to the full.

Anyway, I didn't renew my dating site subscription after the free trial. I decided being a pen friend to someone that wrote in a way that captivated me was fine. Despite feeling seduced by emails that started out with.. *'I awaited your next missive and felt a 'rush' when I saw that you had replied'*.

And tickled by the ones that ended… *'Do write soon. You can't know the suffering I endure waiting for your sweet words'*. No alarm bells rang when he wrote that he was now using my image as his screensaver.

3

Then proceeded to tell me that he had also printed off a copy, laminated it and was carrying it around with him. It stopped me for a moment. I facetiously mentioned that I didn't find it *'scary, weird or the slightest bit stalkerish'* at all.

That moment of doubt was overridden by being flattered and thus, I made excuses for his behaviour. After all, I had built an image in my head. I considered that one day we may meet. But in the meantime, I pointed out to him that he should have joined penfriend.com not soulmates.com.

Three whole months of writing back and forth. Sharing stories and news of our days. Sending bits of poetry prose and snippets from songs. I was having a lovely time - writing to my pen friend. He responded to everything I wrote about, as I did him and it was fun. The feeling of getting an email from a stranger that I had already decided that was caring, funny, kind and handsome, set my heart alight. I had created this perfect man in my mind, who communicated beautifully. We may never meet but what was the harm when I was really enjoying our communication?

I was enraptured with my fantasy, I have to be honest. I saw no red flags that I had knowledge of wafted in my face. Nor were there any obvious signs of him being unhinged or obsessive. He made me feel like I was the highlight of his day.

So many emails were passed back and forth before he wrote and said that as part of his visa, he had to leave Saudi Arabia every month. Last time, he visited Dubai but this time, he wanted to come back and meet me.

How exciting!

We were meeting in Oxford, on a Saturday, in a cafe on a busy high street in October 2004. He took the train and I drove there. It had been almost three months of writing to each other and my stomach kept flipping.

I imagined turning the corner and there he would be - standing handsome yet looking humble. With a wide smile, long

4

wavy hair and tall in the bohemian way that I had imagined him to be. I almost pictured the guitar swinging from his back, for he had indicated this much. It was a busy day but it wasn't hard to see the person standing looking at me as I crossed the street, dressed in a smart black suit. He was still, midst the bustling crowd. On the corner outside the cafe. As I got closer, I felt surprised by how he looked. I cursed myself for being such a fantasiser.

He looked nothing like his profile picture, which had been rather obscure on hindsight but he had 'scanned it in' (it was 2004). Again, no alarm bells - I put it down to shyness. He didn't match the creation that I had made in my head, either. Apart from the colour of his hair, which was dark. Where I had imagined or seen a strong jawline and a big nose, there was a weak one and a small one. Where, in my mind, there was stubble, the actuality was a face that was smoother than mine! Small eyes took the place of the large, almond shaped green ones from my imagination. His height though, that was spot on and I congratulated myself on that! The build, I lost points on! My imaginary man had a wide build not a thin one (he had told me that he was overweight). When he spoke, I hadn't expected a low voice. He was to have a voice that was strong, clear and without accent.

Of course, I didn't fall for how he looked but I was disappointed that I didn't really feel the magic that I had anticipated that I would feel. I had barely slept the night before with excitement. Still, it was going to be a great day I decided because we got on so well with our emailing, and who knows what could happen? I met him with a huge hug and greeting. And chatter, chatter, chatter in my old style of filling silences and not giving a pause like I used to do, we went inside the cafe.

A crowded place was a good idea but I hadn't anticipated my hearing tone issue (I had to keep asking him to speak up). I also have selective hearing.

Anyway, as he picked up his cup, I noticed his bitten down nails that looked so sore. I heard myself feeling concerned about his anxieties. Then reassured that despite anything, it was just a day. Perhaps writing to each other was where it would stay for us, I was thinking. We both chatted and laughed in all the right places, as we walked around Oxford High Street. That was my interpretation. It could have been that I was doing all the talking. I realised that I knew very little about him, only feelings and images that I had conjured up from my imagination.

The physical connection that I had desired wasn't felt in person but the way he looked at me was intoxicating. I hadn't been looked at like I was the only person in the World before. It was surprising me how attractive that was and that made him more attractive. I liked it. He was charming. We agreed to meet again, feeling positive and optimistic because even though sparks do matter, they were there electronically. Subsequently, we met another two times.

Emails when he was back in Saudi Arabia didn't concern me at the time. Romantic, old-fashioned and quirky, albeit sometimes a little cheesy. Read in the aftermath though, are very creepy. That is entirely due to what subsequently happened, of course. Likewise, I did not feel concerned that he told me things like changing his log-in passwords into my name.

It is difficult not to analyse what was going through my head. I wasn't unhappy or bored. Quite the opposite. As engaged as I was with the fabulous people around me and as busy as I was with my ambition though, I did yearn for connection, love and desire. What I saw in his eyes was exclusivity. Longing to be the only person that someone saw was incredibly important. I felt that it wasn't ever going to happen. I didn't feel exclusive to my ex-husband. I had dated someone before that had eyes for others, too. This was the first time in so many years - in fact, ever, that I had been the only person in the room that they were occupying. It was fresh for me.

It was attractive and exhilarant. It overrode the initial lack of physical attraction. And enhanced the email personality attraction. The appeal of the way he looked at me on those three dates ruled. He wrote poetry and travelled around writing for a living. There's the seduction.

Far beyond any sensibilities, driven by romantic notions and despite my reservations, we began organising another date! Again, as part of his visa requirements to leave Saudi Arabia, his next visit would be in February 2005.

Then, he told me something that was incredulous.

He told me that he had created a website under the domain name: www.lindseygoldrick.com. My domain name. My future business name. My name!

On there was an ode to me, as a gift, he told me. I felt dumbfounded with disbelief that I had heard him correctly and then annoyed. He had no right to buy my domain name. I told him to close it down and delete it immediately.

The email that came back from him started with the lyrics to 'A Thousand Miles' by Vanessa Carlton, telling me that it was how he was feeling and ended with a promise to delete the website:

'Cause you know I'd walk a thousand miles, If I could just see you tonight. And I don't want to let you know, I drown in your memory, don't want to let this go....'

The website idea perturbed me. It wasn't creative or unique; just freaky. It was a strange thing to do, I felt and left me feeling so very uncomfortable. The website name belonged to me and for him to buy it meant that he owned it. Not knowing how domains and subscriptions worked in 2005 and not thinking about anything sinister either, it hadn't occurred to me that he would have bought my name (as a domain) for at least a year - the minimum time.

It also hadn't even occurred to me that anyone else would or could, or even want to, buy my name as a domain name either, hence why I hadn't already bought it. I hadn't pondered the process of buying one's own name as a domain name as having any challenges. Why hadn't I purchased my name already? Fifteen years ago, this wasn't something that would have generally been considered. Of course, it is wholly advisable to buy your name in domain form now, even if you do nothing with it.

What transpired during the trial and later when I was gathering everything together, was that at this point, he had premeditated the attack. He had purchased my name as domain names under several permutations, after the third date.

There was no chance of owning my name to host my business website at this point and I did not know. I had talked in length about my plans. It sickens me that I had doubts about him but didn't act on it. It sickens me that he was working on his crimes, at this very moment and had invested a lot of time and money with his creations. I was oblivious.

It sickens me that he also stole things from me to use that were evident later, too, at this point. Creepy to think about mementoes stolen from a bag or a bin. I am feeling bilious wondering what else he did that wasn't unfolded. With a bodacious lack of regard, he hinted that we may have missed things in his Witness Statement.

1,025 pages of exhibits in the court may only have been a fraction of what he did.

CHAPTER TWO
If in doubt...

If you heard that someone had serious doubts about another date and still went ahead, what would go through your mind? You may wonder whether they were lonely, vulnerable or just reckless. But I am none of these things. Quite the contrary.

I see myself as level-headed, independent and back then, I didn't struggle with confidence or low self-esteem. Seeing the best in people, yes. Optimistic, yes. I cared about people's feelings, so I wouldn't string it out on purpose, so what was going on? Was it because I was adventurous, free and open to opportunities? I certainly had joined the online dating with good intentions. My head was perhaps too full of romantic, optimistic notions. I had dashed instinctive thoughts that I should have listened to. I know that many of us do things and can wonder where our heads were at the time. I am no different.

So yes, it is hard to grasp that I decided to still meet him for Valentines Day, 2005, in the New Forest. I suppose I would not be analysing it now, 15 years down the road, had the other person not proceeded to do what he did.

The day I was meeting him in the New Forest, I woke up not feeling too great but I didn't want to let him down. He had travelled so far to see me and decided that whatever I had may clear by the time I got to the New Forest. I had bought him some books and had made him a copy of a CD that I had in my car that he liked and he gave me a gift like no other.

It was a long see-through babydoll nightie with matching underwear. I let out a nervous screech because it was so ghastly that I thought it was a joke. It clearly wasn't a joke, so I took it gracefully, not wanting to hurt his feelings, yet wanting to run at that very moment.

I felt nervous that he had sought out something that felt so loaded, cheap and creepy. Almost dirty (in a different sense). What was he expecting? It was the opposite of sexy to me. Of course, sexy is all in the eye of the beholder but it was verging on kinky. It was also a huge assumption that I would wear anything. It was so hideous. Had we met on a fetish site or discussed the love of see-through polyester, I wouldn't have felt so sick with the distaste. It was a fourth date. I felt uneasy and rather sleazy, and feeling more ill as well as struggling with hearing him. I realised that it hadn't been a good decision to come out, after all.

We hadn't been in the pub for very long but it was so uncomfortable with the sinus aches, alongside feeling particularly disturbed about the nighty and the website. I was also conscious that he was talking but I was in a world of my own: troubled, not quite so enamoured and optimistic, and with a pounding head. I had spotted the football match on TV in an adjoining room. I suggested that he should go and enjoy it, feeling that would be preferable for both of us. That way, I could sit (with my pounding head and pounding, perturbing thoughts).

He got angry. He looked so cruel and that, right there, was the clincher for me that there could be nothing between us. I couldn't talk myself out of the way he looked. His eyes were devoid of sympathy. The person that sat in front of me was so far away from the person I had fallen for.

It was enough for me to make the instant decision that I needed to get home, pretty fast. On telling him so, he seemed perplexed. His face contorted and he snarled, asking me why I had bothered to come. I felt hasty about leaving, all the more. Once at the car, I told him we were not right for each other, it wasn't going anywhere and that it was over. I climbed in the car with urgency. As I reversed, I looked up briefly to see him stood there, his face intense with anger.

The drive home was long. I thought about the mean look on his face. My head pounded and I felt dreadful. Thoughts were going around my head: I thought of him snarling and how mean and cruel he had looked. What had I been doing? I wasn't

10

attracted to him physically but I had loved his online personality. Which, on hindsight, was so different offline. I had been fooling myself, creating this person in my head that wasn't a reality. I had conjured up a special, romantic relationship with someone creative and kind. He wasn't kind, after all. I shuddered. The website was downright weird.

Then I remembered that he had told me that he was overweight. He was on a strict diet where the only food he could eat in Saudi Arabia was delivered to him in tiny pots! He was the leanest person I had ever seen. The horrific see-through nightie which was stuffed in my bag, out of sight - Ugh! I wish I had given it him back. It made me feel cheap and hideous.

I felt silly for my romantic notions and lyrics and poetry and sharing dreams and stories - and time, with him. He was quite socially awkward. I was irksome and ill. All sorts of thoughts were firing at me, as he had been so unsympathetic. I couldn't wait to get to the safety and warmth of home.

Later on that night, I had too many hot toddies. I was so spooked by him that it numbed my thoughts and blanked him out. I was soon wrapped up in bed with a book. The remainder of that night still holds uncertainties for me because I am not sure whether I dreamt about receiving a chilling email or whether it happened for real. If it was a nightmare whilst I was asleep or whether it was a real occurrence is still not clear because it was so vivid.

I opened an email from him. Whether that was in my dream whilst asleep or whether I got up, unable to sleep and looked at emails, I don't think I will ever know. It is too fuzzy, aided by the amount of alcohol I had drank, possibly. The email said he was watching me at every possibility and had filmed me when I was undressing through my bedroom window. Did I get this email from him or was it a part of a terrible, vivid dream, invoked by alcohol and feeling that my life was unravelling?

In my dreams or reality, I re-read it and then was physically sick and had to run to the bathroom. I went back to the email and deleted it. I want to believe that it didn't happen. I

11

don't have any evidence of it ever happening. Just a memory and whether that is a memory of a nightmare or reality, my mind cannot reveal any truth to me. But subsequent events suggest that there is a great possibility Furran sent me the email.

Regardless of whether it happened or not, it had an effect on me. I wondered whether he had planted anything on me and checked my bag, checked my clothes. Sounds far-fetched now but his behaviour was having an effect on mine, very early on. I changed my routine of undressing from then on and became rather inhibited. Which is quite the opposite of how I used to be, which was so carefree, looking back. Never again would I undress with quite so much abandon.

By the end of February 2005, he was calling me incessantly on my mobile phone throughout the day, whilst at work. When I picked up the phone one day, he was frantic, asking where my emails were. I reminded him that I had said that it wasn't going anywhere when we were in the New Forest and it was over. He hung up. It unnerved me how, despite what I said, it is as though he didn't hear me.

He really hadn't. He sent another email that asked if everything was okay. He told me that he felt like 'Ahasverus condemned to walk in limbo'! He was seriously creeping me out. I emailed him again, for the last time I thought, about not wanting to see him but wishing him well. I hoped he would get bored, if I ignored him.

It was around a week later and having returned home from work, Mama met me at the door, looking concerned. She had just that moment got off the phone with him. He had found our number and called her! She said he sounded frantic and had asked her where he stood with me. He asked her not to show me the package that was due for delivery at any moment. Of course, she had taken in a delivery of a box and with apprehension, gave it to me.

I took the box to my room and noticed that there was a strange smell emanating from it. I put the box on the floor and began opening it, timorously. I grabbed a coat hanger to pull back the top and to delve inside and the smell got stronger. It reeked of smoke and something else that I wasn't sure about. I couldn't quite put my finger on the smell. Was it metallic? I had a thought that if anger smelt, that is what it would smell like. What the hell was this? I didn't know whether to carry on looking in the box, or not. Mama shouted up the stairs, asking if all was okay and I shouted that I was and I would be down soon. All the while, I felt in a state of surrealism.

It was starting to feel macabre and sinister. A bilious taste was in my mouth as the acrid smell of the box was all encompassing. I proceeded. I needed to know what he had posted and had second thoughts about, to attempt at getting Mama to intercept it. What was in there? I should put gloves on, I thought. The next stage was in slow motion.

I couldn't believe what I saw inside. The first thing that I saw were rather a lot of ashes. I wondered if they were a warning, since it wasn't clear to me what they had originated as. I only know that they sent shockwaves up my spine. Then, I saw a CD broken into pieces and burnt around the edges and presumably it was the one I had given him. The books that I had given him were in there and also, a tiny piece of torn note that said on one side:

'Not sending me a valentine's card was the final biscuit!'

The other side was a request to send every single thing back he had given me. He had met a girl at the Embassy, he said, who had promised to 'wear the lingerie properly'. Had I sent him a valentine's card, this wouldn't be happening, he concluded. It completely threw me. He hadn't heard anything I had said.

I was shaking as I picked up a crushed up ball of paper. As I unfolded it, I saw the familiar sight of my lipstick blotting. I had discarded it in a waste paper bin somewhere - or so I had thought.

Wholly unnerved and frightened, and even though I didn't want to cause any concern to Mama, I needed a talk and a hug. Nothing else would happen, we hoped (and prayed). That will be enough now. After all, he had called Mama and had asked her to intercept the box, so he was having regrets. I decided to keep the accumulating evidence of his strange behaviour. Even though throwing the box away, deleting the emails and not think about it all again, was my inclination. I had already deleted many threatening emails from him.

Then, a succession of emails that were menacing and threatening, fired one after the other, like in the beginning. I had accredited him with so many qualities, hadn't I? In the beginning, the impatient email? That wasn't that funny, was it? I highlight this because people have told me that I am not on my own imagining that someone online was compatible by the way they wrote.

I wondered whether I should respond. I didn't quite know whether it would ignite him to send more if I ignored him. Who knew what his intentions were. I opted to write him a pleasant, firm response, severing all ties and wished him well. A clear message might do it, I decided.

How wrong could I be? More ensued. Just before creating a new email address, I received an email after I sent his belongings back, in March 2005 (that sent shivers right through my body). It was equal to four A4 pages. It is hard to read and I think if you have got this far, I feel that I would lose you if I included it. Suffice to say, he sounded manic, irrational, psychotic and obsessive, so I have omitted it. It felt so puerile and menacing. I have included the ending, since I think it is important as it contributes to understanding my fear:

'My breath has been literally caught in my throat. Do you know what that feels like?

I wonder what would take your breath away, my Golden Girl?

You have shown me love.

14

Then you changed.

You showed me HELL.

BE SAFE AND BE HAPPY'.

Stupefied, I read it. It felt ominous, threatening and sinister. He sounded crazy and twisted. It suggested that something was going to happen. Of course I wouldn't know what but it most definitely felt like he wasn't finished. His cruel face flashed in front of my mind when I felt ill. I shouldn't have gone but then I wouldn't have seen that side.

Quoting 'Be Safe and Be Happy' suggested that I wasn't to feel safe or feel happy but I didn't know anything, yet.

CHAPTER THREE
Be safe and be happy

For three weeks, I didn't hear anything and felt relieved that it seemed to be over. It was a huge relief. 'Goodness', I thought, 'I wouldn't want to go through that again. Scary stuff'.

Mandy (my colleague) and I were working late one Friday night, and she suggested we went for a cocktail after work. It had been three weeks since the last threatening email and I felt so relieved that it seemed to be over. I had planned on a bath and an early night to be up for a Saturday jaunt around Bridport market with my friend Debs, so I almost said no. Then, I thought about the huge relief of not hearing from Furran and how I wouldn't want to go through that again and thought, 'Why not?'.

Whilst out, Mandy introduced me to a chap that worked with her husband. I was rather surprised that after the evening and throughout the whole weekend, I couldn't get this chap's face and smile out of my mind. Considering that I felt like I had been put off men for a long time, anyway.

On Monday at work, Mandy had told me that the chap that worked with her husband had called her for my number. So, she had given him my mobile, my work number, my email address - both private and work's and I stood with my jaw dropped. Could she not have asked me, first? The last thing I wanted was a date!

I felt like I would have a very long, perhaps eternal break from dating. I was so put off but she was insistent and said it was a waste not to, stating how lovely he was and that I should. She didn't know anything about what had been going on, since I am very private. She just thought we would be a good match. I decided to just go ahead and meet him.

When I met Steve and saw his lovely, handsome face again and big, beautiful smile and gentle demeanour, I was rather pleased with my colleague. We began seeing each other. A lot. It was soon forgotten that it would be a long time before I bothered with the dating scene again. I didn't know anything about him but it felt good, safe and happy.

My instinct knew that this man was good, pure and honest. He was real. This wasn't a fantasy. I hadn't conjured him up, for he stood in front of me, as majestic as I thought him. I was smitten. There were no niggles, doubts or issues. He was kind and thoughtful. The perfect antidote to my recent experience with online dating. The old-fashioned way worked for me, after all.

We met up as much as possible through the spring of 2005. He was thoughtful and he made me laugh. He was everything that I had longed for. He was the antithesis to Furran. I loved being with him. Mum loved him. He had to go away a lot with work, though and this time it bothered me that someone I was dating would be so far away, for I wanted him close, all the time.

Reaching 8 weeks without hearing from Furran, was reassuring. It was all in the past. Thank goodness. I thought that I would be affected by him and not date for a very long time. Certainly not venture online for a potential one, ever again. This was a new chapter and a fantastic one at that.

In May 2005, I was still on a contract as a magazine editor. This was information that I hadn't shared with Saul Furran. All he knew was that I was on a contract and was going to set up a business.

Checking my emails at work, I worked through them one by one and then, in disbelief, I read:

'Thank you (see, it's not hard is it?). It's not so hard to find you, either! Even your Mum knows how nasty you are! Be safe and be happy.'

Gasping, I pushed back my chair. I was aware that I had created a noise and people were looking over, as I ran to the bathroom with my phone. I could hardly tap in Mama's number for shaking. It was ringing and ringing and she picked up in her usual cheerful manner. Was she okay? Where was she?

'*Are you okay more like?*', she asked. '*You sound flustered,*' she said. She was fine. She had her friend over for lunch they were going to go a garden centre afterwards. She wouldn't be home until late and might do a spot of grocery shopping.

'*Please be super careful, Mama,*' I said and I could feel my bottom lip quivering and tears rushed to my eyes. She asked again if I was okay. I didn't want to alarm her. I prayed to the Universe that Saul Furran would stay far away from my Mama.

'*Say hello to Ethne,*' Mama was saying as my ears started popping and I said I would later. '*Cheerio,*' Mama said, '*Love you*'.

'*Love you so much, Mama*'. We ended the call and I sobbed in the bathroom, suppressing a howl. I wanted to scream, wishing that I had never, ever responded online to Saul Furran.

I sat for a long time in the loos. I wondered about going home. After I had composed myself and walked back to my desk, people asked me if I was okay, saying I looked ashen. Too shell-shocked to be my usual jovial self, I stayed at my desk, attempting to work through my tasks. All the while, my heart pounded and a dread bubbled up inside. I couldn't concentrate. I felt invaded, vulnerable and unsafe. I kept wondering who else had seen the email. I deleted it. It disturbed me that he knew where I lived and had found out where I worked, too. He had also gone to lengths to find my work email address and what were his intentions? What else was he going to do?

My mind raced. Mama and I have a precious and rare relationship. We are more like close sisters and treasure each other. So, despite the false declaration in his email, he had caught my attention and hurt me. I had no doubts that my mother would not say anything negative about me. Quite the opposite, since she always praised me and showered me with affection. If the contrary is in jest, it wouldn't be to a stranger.

The issue here also was that he had found out where I worked and got hold of the email address. I started to feel scared.

What was he going to do? Or was he trying to intimidate me? He lived thousands of miles away in another country. He had invaded my privacy yet again. I couldn't hide from him and wondered how he had found where I worked. After I had deleted my online dating account, there wasn't anything online about me. Only my outdated address and phone number in America.

The receptionist at the head office informed me of an odd telephone call that she had received that morning. The caller, a male, asked her what department I was working in. She asked him if he wanted to see if I was available to talk (it was 2005, before breaches). He sharply responded with, '*No!*' and proceeded to hang up. Flabbergasted, I knew it was him.

Reliving this time, I realise that it was now that the vigilant scanning started. I didn't go anywhere before scanning the outside from inside the building, before I left. Then, the scanning when I arrived anywhere. It became second nature to sweep areas with my eyes. As was the habit of running to the car, locking myself in and driving, checking the rear view mirror. All drivers were him. Was he behind me? Was he following me? Is that him in that car or over there? Is he outside? This intense feeling of invasion soon developed into my wondering if he was inside. Being besieged by the consequences of a stalker's conduct was borne over 16 years ago. I still have remnants of the procedures that I developed, lingering.

The phone woke me one of many mornings of a perpetual ringing, around 6am. The volume was usually down. My stomach was in knots. I knew that it was him. I let it ring and ring and willed it to stop (no option of reject or decline in 2005). It didn't stop. I was about to turn it off and decided to shout at him to stop calling.

"*But you are the love of my life!*" he said, in a robotic, sinister voice. I hung up, pulled the covers over my head and wept, praying for him to stop. I considered staying home but a fire inside me said that there wasn't anyone like him that was going to change my plans. It was my day; my plans and I was going to live it like this wasn't happening. I had the power, not him. I felt defiant that I was not going to scream out the obscenities that were being introduced in my mind, either. If I did that, that was changing me, by losing control, and then he had power. That is how I saw it.

He continued to bully and threaten me through a succession of menacing emails and calls. I had not even considered going to the police, figuring that I didn't want to inflame the situation, which sounds crazy. I prayed that he would stop and presumed that it would soon.

If I am honest, I have to say that I was also embarrassed about it. I hadn't set foot in a police station in my life. It wasn't that desperate a situation, I kept telling myself.

Just a spot of stalking!

CHAPTER FOUR
Hacked off

It was summer 2005 and I was about to have a flying lesson in a glider with a friend of Steve's at the local airbase. The phone just rang and rang and Steve asked me why I wasn't picking up. I didn't want the moment to be spoilt. This was a thoughtful surprise from Steve and we were almost ready to go. He wasn't going to be part of that memory, I told myself. I knew that it was Furran, invading. I willed the phone to stop but it didn't. On Steve's prompting, I picked up.

"*If you don't send the underwear in the post*', he shouted, '*I will come down and get them myself. You are a* (I didn't catch it)… *and I know that you wouldn't like* (didn't catch that, either). *You won't like it*", he threatened.

It was quite simply outrageous, perverted and weird. On hindsight, I should have called his bluff. That often happens with bullies. As soon as you tell them to carry out their threat, they can lose their nerve or interest. Although on saying that, Furran wasn't curtailed by anything, as I was to find out.

Moments before, I had been so excited about flying but as Steve's friend said he was ready, I walked over to the glider, containing the tension, smiling and expressing my excitement. Meanwhile, worrying about what Steve must think of it all and not wanting him to be troubled by it, and actually wishing I was hugging him instead of the lesson.

Before I knew it, we were taking off…the noise blitzing out thoughts about Furran. We climbed higher and higher, finding pockets of air and peacefully transcending in the thermals, I felt free. As a bird, incidentally. The slow spiralling thermal, the buoyancy and the freedom. It was transforming those anxious feelings. The instructor asked if I wanted to try some manoeuvres and we did a loop the loop. Oh my goodness. I screamed. He took that as my loving it. We do two more. More screaming. What an escape. A perfect transcending of thoughts and feelings. 90 minutes in the sky. By the time we landed, I was fit and ready to tackle the ordeal of going to the police. It really was an arduous task and I did feel shameful but the freedom of flying had shifted my balance. 'Going to the police will be okay. I have just been loop the looping, for goodness sake. I can do anything!'.

I was trying to remember every detail for the statement at the police station, which is difficult to do. Especially under the circumstances. I felt very shaken. I was slightly coy about where we had met. There was an element of desperation about it, I felt in that moment and I whispered through the details, fearing judgment. Back then, it was very much a separate world from now and not as understood either. I had ventured onto the online world and look at what had happened. I stated that he wouldn't leave me alone; he was stalking me and that I was scared. I wasn't sure how else he had got information about me, I told them. Other than using his computer skills.

They asked for a description of him, his UK address and anything else that I knew about him like his Birthday. I knew it was the end of January. I knew so much about him from emails and yet, I didn't know anything about him at all. A futile hope of a romantic liaison, a desire to get to know someone first and here I was drawing up a harassment order in the police station, just months later. I would never, ever chat so extensively with a stranger online, ever again.

It would be passed over to Sussex police, they said, since they were his local police, and to expect a call from them in a few days. And I left and wondered if the lone person that was running up the street, was him. Lurking around and running away, not able to confront me, face to face. A coward and a bully.

On return home, I called his father. I was frantic. I thought that a father might talk some sense into his son. '*Doctor Furran*', he answered. Oh, a sensible man, I thought. Actually, that makes no sense at all but I was clutching at straws, remember. I told him briefly and then said that his son would be in big trouble if he continued and I added that I had moved to Scotland. I know. That was news to me, as well. Completely unplanned. His father barely said a word.

Later that month in June 2005, I had trouble accessing my Yahoo account. I gained access eventually and I don't remember the details how but it was frustrating and lengthy and goodness, it looked different. The 'To Keep' files deleted. Information files were gone. Photograph files were empty. All the while, my heart pumped faster.

I did not share my password with anyone but had I tapped it into Yahoo when someone else was around? It's possible. Or saved it by accident on another computer? Had I used another computer accessible by someone else? Had I taken my laptop with me anywhere? Any of it was possible.

My mind raced, as my stomach flipped over with dread, trying to unravel my memory. I couldn't be certain that I didn't save a password on another computer or tapped it in with someone else watching. I felt violated.

Eleven years of private and confidential emails on there. My Yahoo mail was a trove of private communication from 1994. I joined it as soon as it came out, when I lived in America. Bookings, tickets to future events, appointments, memories, private thoughts, confidential information - not only of mine but others; my family and friends. A journal of mutual, invested trust.

I thought about my contact list, my inbox, my sent list. Acquaintances. Clients. Past employers. Potential new ones. Children that I had cared for. Relations. People around the world that I had met on my travels. The sent emails making enquiries to a million places about a million things. So many precious friends and their private thoughts to me.

Dear oh dear! Ames and I had been writing daily since we met in the Adirondacks in 1999, with very personal, minute details, often twice a day. Therapy. Holders of each other's daily journal. Oh my goodness. Why hadn't I exported them? So much information on there from my cherished people, each of us keepers of each other's secrets. Confidantes. All of our private thoughts and stories, encroached and invaded. My stomach flipped over and over.

In light of what I was experiencing, it had to be Saul Furran that had hacked into my private email account. He wasn't stopping. Compromising my email account, compromising my life. I emailed everyone with a heavy heart. This was ridiculous. I was changing my email address because it had been compromised, I told them. Be wary of any more emails from me, I wrote.

Four months of invasions wherever I looked; wherever I was. This was too much, though. A complete privacy invasion. There were possibly hundreds of privacy invasions now and it would all be my fault because of some stupid four minute date with a disturbed person. I wondered what else was going to explode in my face. No good to warn anyone about what might not happen. It had to be him, though. It was too coincidental. Why wasn't my memory giving me clear records of what happened when I was with him?

It seemed to be getting bleaker.

CHAPTER FIVE
Life would never feel the same

I remember the day when I felt like what was happening was too large to comprehend; too shocking to believe; too alien to anything I had experienced, heard about, read about and thus, knew of no guidelines for what to do about it. I had nothing to compare it to; relate to and I also knew that life would never feel the same way again.

It was a day in the summer of 2005, I was driving home from a breakfast with friends. Steve and I were getting together in the afternoon and I couldn't wait to see him. Still rattled about the email hacking, though. It was utterly disconcerting. I couldn't seem to live as freely anymore, without wondering where he was going to turn up.

As if on cue, my phone on the passenger seat started ringing incessantly. It rang, ended and rang again and then a few moments later, another call. Taking deep breaths, I mentally begged him to give up. The calls kept coming. As the signals dipped in and out, whilst driving through the villages, the ringing did too. I pulled over. I had had enough. I was going to take my phone to the police to show how many missed calls I had from him, for the report. Then I was going to change my number.

Trembling in the car, in the middle of the countryside. Fields of sheep for company. I picked up my phone and looked at the missed calls. There weren't any from him, withheld or any anonymous numbers. I knew everyone that had called. It was Ian, Debs (both were close friends that I had met on return from the US), one of my lovely Brothers, Mandy and also Stella, both of whom I worked with. I listened to the messages. Each of them told me to ring them as soon as possible.

I called my Brother first. He sounded serious. I felt frantic. *'What is it, Darling?'* I was shaking. He was angry, *'I got a note in the post to check out a website in your name, Linz and I thought it was unusual because you would have told me about it but I checked it out. You need to take a look at it and tell the police. Where does the bastard live?'*. *'What is on there?'*, I pleaded. He said, *'Get to the police'*.

Dear Goodness! The Yahoo hacking! I am going to explode!

Debs: *'Darling. Where are you? It is the most distressing thing. I came home from the horses and there was a message on the answer machine. It must be that weirdo, Saul, but he sounded robotic, like he had used a voice changer. So, so scary. It was the strangest experience. It has completely freaked me out. It said to check out lindseygoldrick.com and I did and it is just horrendous, Darling. So many horrible lies and details. Where are you? I'm so worried. Let me come with you to the police'.*

I was crying as I called Ian. He too knew of my plans and he told me that he had screamed out, 'At bloody last!' when he had seen the note. (Ian and my Brother had received notes in the post, they said and it simply read: Check out: www.lindseygoldrick.com).

He told me that he had felt excited for me and had instantly checked the website and his elation for me soon turned to worry. It was a vindictive site, he said, full of emails from my email address with my photographs on there.

Although he didn't want to, knowing that it was created by someone else, he couldn't help but read some of it, he said. The fabricated emails from me that were on the site were very sexual and had quite titillated him, he said and that I had gone up in his estimation! The laugh was a welcome interlude in my now frantic state of mind. *'On a serious note, get to the police now, Dear Girl and do you want me to come with you?'*.

Mandy and Stella stated that they had received emails to check out lindseygoldrick.com. *'There's a lot of people talking about it at work,*' Mandy said. My stomach dropped lower. He must have sent the message to lots of people.

Everyone that had received some sort of communication from him were people that were all part of my everyday; in thought, physically or when at work. And in my email contact list! This was explosive.

Thinking more about it, my colleagues were not in my private email list. Nor would Debs's landline number be listed there. Ian's email couldn't be identified as his. Oh but his emails had his address at the bottom. No addresses were attached in my contact list. I just wasn't that organised. Was there relief in knowing this? Not really. It didn't mean anything because to try to comprehend anything about or predict the acts of an unbalanced person was pointless.

I was befuddled, trying to piece it together, though because I had a big network of friends and family not listed in my email, too and there had to be more people calling. I had most likely shared many tales about many events and trips with many people but never revealing last names or addresses, of course. My Brother's was an obvious easy one, though. This was a time of pre-social media, too. I didn't have anything accessible about me or my contacts online, that I had submitted myself.

With foreboding feelings, I tried to comprehend what was happening. It felt surreal. For everyone that had received communication from him, it was the email hacking or he had to have gone to great lengths to get their information. It would have taken in-depth research and money to find out addresses and phone numbers, unless he followed me to places. How could Debs's number be explained? It wasn't listed in public records. Had he very discreetly accessed my phone?

He was a technology expert, as he liked to tell me, so there would be many avenues that he could follow, on top of the hacking. There were websites that were offering information but you had to pay for their services. I have to reiterate that the internet wasn't like it is now. Information wasn't so free and abundant. You could tap in a person's name and see everything that the internet held on them but you couldn't access their contacts or history or any link whatsoever, unless they had submitted it somewhere.

As I stated, my information was limited. He was clearly investing a great deal of time for research. So disconcerting. How many more people would be receiving notes and phone messages? What was Steve going to make of this? Need I bother him? I wished with all of my heart that I hadn't used my real last name when I had joined the dating site.

Feeling sick and frightened, my whole body was trembling. I sat in the car, in a remote spot in the middle of Dorset, urging myself to pluck up some strength to start it up. I needed to get home to see the internet (phones were just for calling people in those days), as safely and as calmly as I could. At the same time, I didn't want to. My legs were trembling. I turned the key and great big tears were streaming down my face. What was on the world wide web about me, for everyone to see?

I must have looked dreadful by the time I got home. Mama was concerned. I had to look at the internet as soon as possible. Tapping the website name, my name, was hard, since this moment was a day I had dreamt of. It would have been exciting; a new venture. Possibilities. Prosperity. Not this feeling that my life was dismantling. He was stealing my identity.

In disbelief, I watched the website pages loading. It was slow. With added intensity, my image was seen first, bit by bit. First my hair and then my head. The email was still in my mind about watching me undress and of course, I thought the worse. It wasn't a sigh of relief when it was just a head and shoulders because there could be more.

There, under www.lindseygoldrick.com, the website name that Saul Furran promised to delete back in February, was a rather different website than just one ode dedicated to me. I really couldn't believe what I was seeing. It took me a while to fully take it in.

Foul words, nasty statements and hate speech jumped out at me in mixed size text. It was so crudely designed. Blood-boiling disbelief was an understatement. It wasn't just one page, either. There were lots of pages.

The first page had photographs of me on there from my Yahoo albums and the Soulmates online dating profile picture of me in a car. The second tab took me to fictitious quotes from me with sexual connotations.

The third page was full of hyperlinks to click through to another page: '*Click here to read My Sexual Fantasies by Lindsey / Linzi*' which linked to putrid, unspeakable 'sexual fantasies'. Then, more pages containing a large number of materials about or relating to me. Including a mixture of offensive and private and confidential information.

Defamatory statements dotted around in the ugliest font that you have ever seen, (which made it even more vile) about my alleged socially unacceptable conduct. A lot of lies. A disgusting mass of emails exchanged between us during our relationship, including more sexual subject matters and statements of how needy and clingy I was.

In bold, mixed ghastly fonts (no, a lovely sans serif would not have softened the blow), there were false quotes about how besotted I was with him, begging him to love me because nobody else could. The so-called copied emails had been embellished to make their content and style more sexually related than what had been originally written by me from what I could see. All of this was ascertained by only scanning the pages. I couldn't take it all in as I clicked through - it was too repugnant.

I felt so sick as I hit the print button and the printer started counting the pages of the website and I thought it wouldn't stop. Until it hit 52.

52 pages!

Then, something caught my eye.

CHAPTER SIX
At the police station

The background design to the website, when I looked behind the text and images of me, was a repeated graphic image of my lipstick blotting and strands of my hair. On every page I checked over. It was really eerie, weird…chilling. I wanted to scream. I needed to get the website off the internet as soon as possible. He needed to stop. The police needed to be involved now and help me. My ears started to buzz and with big sobs and my heart beating fast, I waited for the website to print off all it's 52 pages, which seemed to take forever.

Scanning the pages as they printed out, I sought evidence of private emails to anyone else or to me. I was terrified about anyone else's privacy rights encroached by someone that I had met. I never understood the word 'uncontrollable' before this moment.

On hearing the afternoon post arrive, Mama calling up the stairs with concern in her voice, 'What is this, Linz?',

I knew that she too, had received the same note, to check out: www.lindseygoldrick.com.

Through tears, I explained the website but she didn't need to see it and I was going to get it taken down as soon as possible. Mama being worried would have consumed me. I had to reassure her that everything would be sorted out as soon as possible. It had created a nasty taste in my mouth thinking about him contacting my Mama, too. How dare he! He wasn't going to get access to my Mama.

I took the posted note and the print-out of the 52 paged website to the police and I gave another statement. They took every detail that I could think about. Plus the evidence of the emails that I had asked my colleagues to send me as well as the note that Mama had received.

In the small interview room at the police station, the police constable tapped my name into the internet…

Not just one website appeared in the search engine results.

Four websites were live and on the world wide web:
www.lindseygoldrick.com
lindseygoldrick.co.uk
lindseygoldrick.net
linzigoldrick.com

All at the top of the search engine results after entering my name.

The room started to spin, as I lost composure and could feel horror bubbling up inside me. It was incredulous. Tears were running down my face. I could see flashes from the other sites, all with large pictures of me and derogatory, fantastical quotations. Purportedly from me.

'*You are the apotheosis of man*' which means Godlike and the ultimate, if you are not familiar with the word, '*I will die without you, Saul*' , '*You are more Godlike than God himself, Saul. I am the luckiest girl in the world*', '*You are my Moses…walking on water…*' and, '*How did little ugly me get to be with someone so handsome?*'.

Flashes of me….pictures of Oxford…the Southwest of England…maps and images of places I frequented…lies…fictitious quotes from me…embellished emails and not so embellished that I would ever want shared and private information about me and yet again, the lipstick blotting and strands of hair as a background. Sexual fantasies…round and round, I was spinning. I felt like I was passing out in the little meeting room.

'*Shall I get victim support for you, Miss Goldrick?*' The pc asked. '*Can they take all the websites down?*', I asked.

'*No*'.

I felt persecuted. '*Then, no thank you*'.

He had invaded my feelings of safety and security. He was hijacking my precious life and he wanted to ruin my reputation and get revenge. To what extent? And for how long? Would it and could it end? What is around the corner? What will he do next? Every vein pulsing with alert and danger and dread.

I had a flashback. My chest felt like it was burning as I thought about the lipstick that I had thought I had lost. What else….what else? It hadn't been mislaid, had it? There had to be more mementos that he had kept. What else did I discard in a bin? For someone quite savvy, I really had been clouded. I felt ridiculous for convincing myself that he was a regular, rational person. On the contrary. I had thought he was quite the opposite only the year before. I cursed my silly romantic, optimistic self.

This was a horrific intrusion. I sat in disbelief, with a noise that I recognised as a voice of the police constable in the background to my thoughts. Whilst my ear drums throbbed and my vision became tunnelled, in this consultation room at the police station.

I had everything firing around my mind. I felt nauseous and wondered if I may be physically sick. I was looking at the police constable and was aware of her speaking but I wasn't sure what she was saying. I hoped she wasn't going to ask me to stand because I knew that I couldn't move.

If anyone searched for my name online, as more and more people had started doing, they would find these pages of fabricated and private information about me. They were offensive, maligning websites, depicting me as someone who had low morals, no values, mental health issues, insecurities and bad manners.

According to the site, 'she is unreliable, very sexual, a liar and a tease'. Harrowing. I couldn't help but ponder what I had lied about, since I take the note that you trip yourself up with untruths and they come right back at you, tenfold. Unreliable? Sexual? A tease? The memory of these words associated with me, plastered in Comic Sans (I have a thing about fonts, you might realise), on the largest media platform in the world makes me squirm!

I imagined all of my family and their friends, old friends, old employers, new employers, neighbours, potential clients, colleagues, peers, anyone curious, anybody seeking information on our family name…all finding the sites that were full of vulgar diatribes and embarrassing emails.

Fake or not, the websites were very real. Small parts of the emails were my words and they were private. Being so very private, this felt crucifying. Having my reputation attacked felt life-crushing.

Somebody else's words from a weird mind, attacking my character for all to see, condemned me to self-conscious discomfort and shame.

Everything had stopped. I was alone in that room with tunnel vision. My ears were ringing, having drifted off into a realm of shock and dread - for how long, I am not sure, and I apologised. The police were speaking to me and had to repeat themselves. The constable told me that there wasn't anything they could do unless he had physically harmed me. *'We will pass it over to Sussex police and someone should be in touch with you soon. We will keep the 52 pages as evidence, though'*, they said.

It was all so blurry and surreal and I could not have appeared too coherent in my state of shock. I don't remember leaving the station and I don't remember the drive home.

I do remember hugging Mama so hard when I got back and feeling pitted, frightened and violated. I hadn't seen any signs of madness, just that we were not right for each other after 4 dates.

Sitting at the bottom of the garden on a bench, drinking wine like it was water, staring up at the moon through the trees, I wondered how long I could take this for. Would it be for another week; another month? Both were excruciating amounts of time. I had to work out how to get him to stop, get them removed and get through this without losing my mind.

I knew that life would not feel the same again.

CHAPTER SEVEN
Time to arrest him

When a female constable from Sussex police called me the next day, it was perfect timing. I had the day off work and I had been up cleaning since dawn. I was scrubbing my anxiety away on the floor on my hands and knees, thinking that if this carries on for much longer, I had better get myself some professional kneepads - and the shine on the cooker had me reaching for my sunglasses.

Anyway, they had received the crime report from Somerset and my statement, she said and asked me to start telling her everything from the beginning again, along with the address and a description of the perpetrator.

I had a flash of how my interpretation of his description, coupled with my imagination had turned out and I almost said, 'Nothing like I had imagined!'.

It is funny what you remember with clarity, at certain times of your life. That phone call stands out as fresh in my mind because the word 'victim' kept being mentioned. That 'victim' was me. I hadn't had the police call me before.

As I listened to her prompting me to talk and to repeat myself, I was pacing up and down in every room. Polishing light-switches. Scratching at some paint on the door architraves. Picking at bumps in the walls, slumping down in random places. Confessing everything that I remembered, again with a breathless whisper. As though the quieter voice took away the embarrassment I felt for seeking a date online. Shameful for what had happened, and perhaps judged; that she thought I was naive and desperate. Or deeming it the price to pay for going online, as I so often heard afterwards.

It was time to arrest him and give him a caution, if he was at the UK address, she said. It was a full course of conduct of harassment since I had reported it twice. I hadn't actually heard 'arrest' because there was only half of me in that moment. Someone was being arrested because of what they were doing to me. What a calamity. Nerves buzzed through my ears.

When I had got off the telephone to the police, Mama's friend Ethne called me. *'I've received a hand posted letter Linz, addressed to my full name without an address on it. There was this note inside that told me to check out the website which is your name spelt the proper way that you were born with and a dot com. Of course, I did look at it'*, she said and my ears started to throb again.

'I thought that you were setting up your company or something and I couldn't believe...' and my tunnel vision came back and I couldn't hear her anymore.

A letter posted by hand? Which only meant one thing. Ethne was not listed in the telephone book and certainly not online. Nor was she in my email contacts list. If I had briefly mentioned her to Saul Furran, it would not have been her full name. She had an unusual last name.

Saul Furran had to have watched Ethne leaving Mama's and followed her home. There wasn't any other explanation. I wanted to scream. Then where did he go after he saw where she lived? Did he come back to Mama's, sleep in the car and follow me to work the next morning? Was he watching us both now?

Sixth sense told me that he was following me. I wish sixth sense had bloody turned up before I had responded to him on the online dating site!

I ran and locked all the doors and windows. Then told Mama to be extra vigilant but tried to remain calm, so as not to cause too much distress. Nobody's last name was ever mentioned and nobody's address digitally. Gosh, I put my mind through the wringer, trying to remember, trying to untangle it all. I didn't carry an address book. My mobile phone!!!

That explains Debs and Ian and even the colleagues at work, too. Last names and landlines only, though. Nothing else. Smart phones were not invented. Regardless, I had to prepare myself for an even larger amount of people telling me about messages to check out what he had so laboriously done. It was astounding me, the extent of his revenge.

My dilemma was whether to tell Steve. He was leaving for a while for work and I didn't want to worry him. Did he really want to be with someone who was now in the thick of receiving harassment from someone, not knowing what hurdles I would have to jump? Did he need the added worry whilst away, too?

We had such a wondrous relationship and I loved having him in my life. It would be extremely unfortunate if Furran's actions would have power over that, too but I had to be open and I would hope that he would be supportive.

He turned out to be incredibly supportive. He would persecute him if anything else happened, he said. He and his friends wrote to him at his parent's address and told him to stop or they would find him. Which, I was to find out, was no deterrent.

Going into work was worse than expected (and I thought I may have blown it out of proportion as you can do when expecting the worst). The embarrassment was intense. When I walked in, there were lots of hushes, ahems, coughs and several coy looks. I didn't have it within me to address it there and then. And blow me down, someone else's conduct had me hanging my head in shame (like I was guilty!). I felt myself redden, I sat down and Mandy whispered to me: *'Gosh, Linz. How are you coping? Are you okay, Linz?'*.

Eyes penetrated on my back but I couldn't hold it in. Tears were now streaming down my face. Mandy's comforting words opened up a waterfall of tears… a string of emotions. I didn't have anywhere to hide and I hadn't done anything wrong. They were his creations but I felt crucified by his actions. It felt like a nightmare. I composed myself and told myself that I had money to earn and work to do and a bloody lot of it and I had to crack on. He could not break me.

I called my Cousin Teen the next morning. I knew that her wisdom, calm manner and sense of humour would steady me and she was as flabbergasted as I was. I knew that she wouldn't worry but would be supportive and say all the right things at the right time.

I told her to expect a note in the post and asked her to not look at the site. It flummoxed me how everyone else had been found with no social media account with friends and followers. Nor were they found from the email hacking. So there was no reason for her not to get one. I thought I would be having the same conversation with my other cousins, aunties, uncles…in the next couple of days.

I made the decision not to cause anxiety and do call arounds and tell everyone, since I hoped that it would not be necessary. I would deal with it, as is. I also thought that he wanted attention and that would give him some, albeit indirectly.

As the days passed in August 2005, I feared that there would be a succession of people that would be alerted to the websites. When my friends and family called me, I would pick up the phone in anticipation, take a few breaths and wait to hear about something sinister. Then, I would learn that they were calling me, as before and we had our regular conversations. I tried not to appear stressed and scared because his conduct was consuming me.

To have a respite from talking about it and hearing cheery little stories were brief comforts.

Considering his extensive research so far, there would be a barrage. Or would they get them at a later date? Had the others got lost or had he got their last names wrong or addresses? My other Brother hadn't got his yet, either. Were some people untraceable? Perhaps people were getting them but hadn't checked the sites out, yet. I willed them to be uninterested if they had received one. I willed the notes to get thrown out with the recycling.

I sighed with relief that contacts in other countries would be harder to trace and hoped that nobody would be interested to know what I was up to lately. Then remembered the account hacking. I wasn't about to alert everyone to it. My mind jumbled up with these alarming thoughts. I felt like I was going crazy.

He was clearly attempting to sabotage my having any future relationship, Steve said, but he wouldn't let it and if anything happened, he would make it his mission to sabotage his.

Looking into his eyes, I hadn't ever seen Steve so steely-eyed.

CHAPTER EIGHT
Stealing my identity

Stealing my name as a domain name, rendering me with a quashed dream, I felt tortured as it sunk in. My business - my career - nullified. If anyone tapped my name into the internet, they would find these websites, prominent at the top of any internet search site. All four. One on top of the other! It was sickening. Preposterous and implausible things. Written by a psychotic, vengeful person. Anyone that knew me would realise that.

But it did not stop me feeling ashamed by the lies and wanting to hide. There wasn't anywhere to hide, though. It was on the internet. Everybody Googles every one and every thing but prior to this, there wasn't anything about me that was digitalised. Not my private details. Not my work. He was investing so much time and money. His determination to bring me down was unsettling. To what end?

Now, I have always been a person that just gets on with things. Pushing through with a smile, not defeated, thanks to the teachings from Mum and Dad. But some days, my energy waned. The escalation of violent behaviour towards me and it being displayed all over the world just felt seismic. And it was hard to dust myself down and crack on, business as usual.

Whatever his backstory or cause to lash out with revenge, I couldn't bear that his behaviour was affecting me. My zest and lust for life, diminishing. The lack of complete control was making me feel oppressed. Self-confidence took a nosedive. My verve was coming in fits and starts.

I didn't feel that I could expend any type of great energy to anything other than the basics of getting through a day, let alone any of my entrepreneurial plans. Doubts took the place of confidence. Worry took the place of creativity. I had two capable hands and yet I felt handcuffed and imprisoned. A big self-critical slump came to sit by my side at my desk.

He wasn't going to take my smile away, though. Nobody knew me without it and I didn't want to attract attention. My friends and family picked up on that I wasn't my usual self, so doing anything with them often raised questions: 'All okay?', 'You seem distant', 'You are not yourself'… but I didn't want to waste any of our breaths or energy talking about him and creating concern about me because of what he was doing. He wasn't going to invade any of my beloved's lives too. Not more than what I knew so far, at least.

Yet, I was letting other people down and I couldn't explain why. The various projects and opportunities in the pipeline that I had got involved in. The other team members - What must they have thought when I just bowed out after being so involved and passionate? I could just about manage paid work because I had to get paid.

Going from chairing meetings and building strategies to calling and cancelling involvement, had me low. Or turning up and being stumped with nothing to say. I felt unable to move. All creativity was crushed. Any excitement about possible new ventures and projects didn't feel that thrilling anymore. I wanted to crawl into an undercover space until it was over but I didn't see an end to it, either. There wasn't a date when I knew it would end. Just escalation. Nothing was stopping this madman.

My angst-ridden thoughts were overwhelming as I was becoming increasingly aware of lives being taken; stories of people killed by someone that they had dated; stories of the taking of one's own life, due to the dreadful impact of being stalked.

Experiencing such fragility was alien to me. I felt appalled that anyone who searched my name on the internet would find all the violative sites. So what if they weren't true? I dreaded them seen and being judged professionally and personally, despite the fictitiousness. It curtailed my desire to continue with my plans at that point. I would have to wait until it was over. Could I stand a few more months of this? What was his plan?

Whether he had one or not, I definitely needed one to stay in control.

CHAPTER NINE
My Reaction Plan

The only thing I could control was my reaction.

I needed to compose and follow a reaction plan. So I hatched one out at the end of August 2005.

I would focus on what I could control. I could control my reactions, my responses, my feelings, my thoughts and my behaviours. Not give energy to what I couldn't change but give energy to what I could change.

What I could control was not giving Furran what he wanted and not drive traffic to his sites. The only way I could do that was not to talk about the website's existence, since people would be curious and take a little look at what all the bother was about. Human nature. Hope that those that knew, would forget. The less I talked about it, the less attention, the less power.

I could defer the reality as much as possible until I got help. If I talked about it and gave it energy, it would consume me and it would affect not only me, but those that would worry. If anyone worried about me, that would cause more anxiety. This I could control.

I couldn't change his conduct but I would seek help, fiercely and leave no leaf unturned. Control.

I would not give up until I found a solution. Control.

When I had found a solution, talk about it then. See if there is anything else to do to maximum effect. Turn it into something good. Control.

I would stay true to my energy and personality; staying positive, energetic and gripping hold of any silly fun and happiness so that it doesn't spoil me and my relationships. Keep loving and keep being loved. And continue how life would have been regardless; organically. This I could control.

In the meantime, I told myself:

Keep your power
Keep your head up
Keep smiling
Keep finding humour
Keep turning up
Keep strong
Keep healthy
Keep exercising
Keep being kind to yourself, too
Keep your emotional balance
Keep being grateful
Keep your spirit
Keep being you
Keep the faith that it will be over one day…soon.

Of course, he did have some power over what I was doing with my life but I fought hard not to let it change my days as much as I could, knowing full well that it really was influencing my every move; my every day.

I had to believe though that my way of thinking was stronger than his conduct and that ultimately, the power of my thinking would prevail.

I was bigger than him.

CHAPTER TEN
His extensive research

It had been two months and ten days and that was so many days longer than I had predicted that it would be continuing, and my having to cope with it. August 2005 and I received a phone call from my ex-husband in America and we had not spoken for three years, so as soon as I heard his voice, I was puzzled. '*To what do I owe this honour?*', I asked him with a smile in my voice. A few pleasantries exchanged and then he said that he had received an email from a Saul Furran, asking him if he was the one that had been married to Lindsey Goldrick.

If so, he had written, then he had interesting news for him and to contact him as soon as possible. '*What does that mean?*' he asked. He told me that he hadn't replied and called me instead and asked if I was okay '*because he sounds like a weird dude*'. My ears were buzzing and I was aware of my ex-husband still talking but I didn't hear him. It was so deeply distressing.

My immediate thought was the email hacking and so, it felt like my head was being crushed because that meant that there were hundreds of people yet to contact me. If not the hacking, then how had Furran found his personal email address? He lived in the US, he had no acquaintance with him and the extent of research that would have been involved was incalculable. I had dropped my married name when we divorced. I had not shared exactly where I had lived. It was mind-blowing. My whole body just seized.

This intrusiveness left me feeling defenceless, as I had no idea what was going to happen next and what was possibly happening right at that moment. I heard my mobile phone going and my stomach dropped - Who else has heard from him? - and then I realised that I still had the landline phone in my hand. I had gone off on a tangent and remembered that my ex-husband was still on the line. '*Are you sure you are okay?*', he asked. '*I don't know, is the answer but I will sort it out*', I replied and '*Thank you. I would have loved to have known what interesting news it was*', I laughed. I felt grateful though that he hadn't played into his hands. I still don't know what was interesting though.

Despite knowing that most people knew me enough to conclude that the structure of the words were most likely not mine, or the quoted words themselves on the websites were definitely not mine, it didn't make it any less stressful.

What about everyone else? Anyone that could have been just checking me out, out of curiosity, would be met with that gross information and that would be attached to me. It was cheapening. It took away my dignity. It diminished my good reputation.

He invaded my privacy and he took away some control of my life. Two majorly important things to me. Two reasons why, at that time, I hadn't joined social media. This was torturing.

He was going through my contact list and finding people that I knew around the world, still and promising them information about me. What else was he planning to do? Feeling delicate, I wondered if he had intentions to physically hurt me, after all. In many ways, what he was conducting using the digital world and how it amplified and never went away, felt like a continuous beating of the mind and body. All of it was impacted. The mental strain was certainly manifesting itself in my body. I had never felt so ill.

Why did the police need to see physical evidence of a serious beating, when I felt so black and blue all over?

You may be thinking it already but I will sound contradictory and repetitive throughout. It was a long time. I had my plan to cope and my strong constitution but it still anguished me. I felt strong one day and then after a sleepless night with new evidence that he was persisting and no help from anyone, I would be less strong the next day; less able to cope.

Another day also meant another chance of people seeing the websites. If anyone's eyes lingered longer on me or if people looked twice in my direction, I would cower and cringe. No escape from online abuse.

Clearly, nothing was going to deter this person from carrying on his vindictive campaign because also that month in August 2005, I found another new website: www.myanamcara.com. I took a quick look and underneath it, a new version of www.lindseygoldrick.com had appeared.

Shock and disbelief somehow blocked my brain from actually processing what I was seeing for a time. It took me a while to actually realise what was going on with the new websites. I didn't look at the finer writing, for my eyes were stuck on the images. I didn't want to read what the words were possibly saying. It couldn't be true. It couldn't be! My chest started burning and I was glad to be sat down. I was rooted.

Both websites showed pictures of me and my home town and where I frequented, referring to me offensively and again, flourished with lewd sexual comments. Routes of where I went and addresses of friends and family were in bold text wrapped around images. He was actually inviting others to harass me, by doing this. He was informing other people about where I lived and where I went. I had heard of the term about blood boiling before and this was it. I felt like I was on fire. I needed air. What a despicable, twisted act. I didn't think the websites could get worse.

He was encouraging people with bad intentions to physically stalk me by telling them where I frequent. It was entering a new level of a horrifying realm. I was not to feel safe anywhere.

I could barely copy the URLs and paste them into an email to Google because I was shaking so much with frenzy. Something I was doing a lot of lately. So much so that my Brother asked me if I had taken to heavy drinking. It was something else for me to be conscious about whilst I was trying to continue appearing normal.

I eventually sent the links to Google and kept checking back for days. I sent them again and again. No response.

To know that I could not get help with taking those websites down, when he was clearly exposing me to attract more abuse had me stunned. Leaving me so vulnerable and so unprotected. Not knowing when that abuse would occur and how it would reveal itself, because it was there all the time for anyone to see, was petrifying.

And not that it would just be attacking my reputation with falsehoods and sexual references, which was excruciating enough but now, there was the added disturbance of a possible gang of abusers targeting me but how, and to what end? He was banging on about sex, provoking potential violent physical attacks, in reality. I had quelled that thought deeply, at the time. For survival purposes. It was true, though. He was devoting time to maximise the exposure of the sites so that they would be found. When found, I could be found. Everyone would know where I lived and worked, too. They knew where I frequented. I am having palpitations remembering this.

There was no way that I couldn't be affected by the intense anguish I felt, looking back. Yes, I kept thinking of my coping strategy and keeping my power but what a battle!

The whole of the first page of Google contained nothing but intimidating websites about me when my name was tapped into the search engine.

Blast my romantic notions.

All of those months, when I thought that I was playing it safe, I had been communicating with a dangerous human being that was now devoting his time to attempting to devastate my life.

CHAPTER ELEVEN
Desperately searching for help

In September 2005, frantically, I reported the new websites to my local police and to Sussex police. It was the day that a girl got shot at her desk in Harvey Nichols in London by someone she had dated for six months and told him that it wasn't going anywhere. He had shouted, 'If I can't have you, nobody else can.' Before shooting her and then himself. It was well known that he was stalking her.

That poor girl's family, forever tortured. A precious life lost. She could have been saved. Nobody had taken it seriously.

Sussex police arrested Saul Furran later on that day, so he must have been in the UK.

The arresting officer spoke with me the next day and said that it was odd because Saul Furran actually seemed to enjoy being arrested. He told me that he had smiled the whole time. This news was particularly chilling. They gave him an adult caution and he was told to take the websites down and to stop harassing me.

An adult caution is given to an offender where they have to admit to an offence and sign it, or face prosecution. It goes on their criminal record and can be used in legal proceedings.

Which incidentally, was a complete waste of time. He didn't stop. He subsequently created more websites. It was October 2005. He was not phased by his arrest or his caution. He simply fled the country, updated the websites that were live already and created more.

So, if a caution and an arrest only purported him to create more things for the whole world to see on the internet, what else was he going to do? This wasn't a deterrent for him. They only incited him to escalate his levels of harassment.

It is hard to believe that he was given a caution only. A caution is given when the police have determined that the harassment will most likely stop. He was optimising the sites and encouraging more harassment and there wasn't any way of measuring other people's intentions. He had basically advertised my whereabouts online and referenced sex!

I feel appalled that there wasn't any way of tracking when he was back in the country to arrest him and have him tried at Criminal Court. I needed the sites taken down. I needed him taken down. I needed a restraining order issued by the court. What he did to me was criminal and persecuting.

In the whole of the month of October 2005, people were still talking about it, despite my not discussing it. It was overwhelming how stressful it felt that it was on everyone's lips. Everyone talked about it, as soon as they saw me. There wasn't an escape.

Friends of friends offered to sort him out. *'Give me an address'*, they would say but I wouldn't have given it to them, even if I knew it. I only knew that it was Riyadh. They were livid. They would sort it out, they said. I did not want their lives ruined by this crazy person because it often doesn't fall in favour of the innocent. They would be in the wrong. I felt adamant that nobody else was to be affected by him, as grateful as I was for the support. I found out later that they did their own research in trying to locate him, to no avail.

I made a list of who I was going to contact to try and get help from and worked through them. I wrote to the Guardian Soulmates site to tell them about what he was doing so perhaps they could ban him and save someone else from going through the same thing. I don't know if anything was done.

I wrote to the company that he was working at in Saudi Arabia and told them that he was possibly using their equipment and time to create these sites and I sent them the links to them. I didn't get a reply. I wrote to Google and asked them to block the sites. Nothing.

I booked an appointment with a Lawyer's office in Somerset. After 30 minutes of explaining what was going on and that I needed legal help because the police could only do so much, with him being in and out of the country, they told me that there wasn't anyone in that field. In the country. That was it! *'Nobody in that field'*. They didn't have any suggestions on what to do, either. They dismissed me with, *'Nothing we or anyone else can do. Bye Bye'*.

I added the Bye Bye, myself, by the way. They were dismissive. What? There wasn't a lawyer in the country that could have helped me with any of it, they said. *'That's it, then?'*, I asked. Dejection embedded deeper as I heard, *'What do you want me to do when there is nothing we can do?'*.

Clutching at straws, I wrote to secret intelligence services but heard nothing back. It was exasperating how much energy I was putting into getting nowhere fast. The internet had been around for around 16 years and you could do anything that you wanted on there. Including using it as a tool to hurt and bully and commit crimes. Without penalties.

The police and lawyers were telling me that there was nothing that they could do. Harming me would bring a result, though. Perhaps when he had killed me? There wasn't any guarantee of the vengeful websites being removed though, even then. Surely the websites could not be on the internet forever? If nobody could stop him and block them, then there was the possibility that his pernicious and abusive bullying would remain for all to see, infinitely. Unfortunately, I had the feeling that he would be happy with that and may continue and devote his life to it. What the hell?

Despite my talking with close family and friends openly about everything and despite Ames and I writing and sharing details of our lives daily, it may sound strange to not talk about something so predominant in my life. Something so life-affecting. Something that was deeply concerning and escalating and impactful. But as explained, I had my reaction plan and my way of controlling, protecting everyone and not giving Furran visitors to his sites. Until I got help, I could not talk. And let's bear in mind that I figured that I thought at this point, it wouldn't take me too long to sort it out. I would soon be telling everyone, I thought. It wasn't a long term plan at all, of course.

I had a brief taste back in October when everyone seemed to be talking about it, of what that would be like and I knew, for sanity's sake, tempering it was containing it.

Ames was aware that I had met someone on the internet that had creeped me out but she had no cause to think that it was continuing. We wrote so many times a week for the next 12 years before I mentioned it again, when help was underway. My trusted and treasured friend, as those who I hold close are. Each other's confidantes, each other's cheerleaders. And I loved the distraction of focusing on other minute life details that didn't involve the horrendous ubiquitous trolling and impending doom, which were welcome respites.

I wanted everyone to still tell me about their stresses and any challenges. They wouldn't have, if they knew about it. They would always be considerate and mindful, and I didn't want to change the organic flow of our relationships and dynamics of our days because of that very unpleasant being.

The routine of sitting and writing every day with Ames and not spending good regular chunks of time thinking about the prevalent, escalating privacy invasion, stalking, reputation attack....whatever it was - was an integral part of my survival.

It kept me sane.

I knew that everyone that I loved and trusted would have been supportive but they would have also felt angry or worried about me. That created anxiety in me, the very thought. Their lives affected as well.

Yes, Teen and Debs knew that he hadn't gone away but they wouldn't bring it up unless I did and I hoped that they were not affected. Steve quite possibly felt differently. He didn't speak about it.

So far, nothing could be done and I wasn't going to give up until it could be but this is what saved me. Communicating with friends and family most days about other things were strengthening.

A distraction from the detrimental realities of his destruction and imperative for my mental health...to my coping. Clutching onto living organically.

After all, those moments in time were all we had. Now is all we have, I would say to myself. This moment, this time, is precious. Right now. Being in the moment is so strengthening and it is true. It is all we can be certain of. It is all that mattered.

Which is how I explained it after the event when everybody wished that they had known, so that they could help. My saviours. They were helping immensely. I was adamant that he wasn't going to get any more than he had and I gained strength from everyone that I was close to and loved. Just them being who they were, and just being in the moment with them, being how we would be, as it would be normally.

Silent support.

CHAPTER TWELVE
Power is with the website owner

As the season shifted into winter 2005, going from one place to another felt like a highly vigilant affair. Shorter days. Less light. I felt grateful that I had self-defence classes growing up and then recapped them when I lived in New York. Having some defence tools if I was attacked physically, was something. Wherever I went, I looked over my shoulder, several times. When I got in my car, I locked myself in instantaneously. I carried a torch and a loud beeper. I ran from A to B.

I changed my Yahoo password regularly. I was wary of anything that came in the post. When the phone called, it made me jump. I saw shadows. I had nightmares. I cringed thinking about having actually kissed this creep of a man. To think that he had written on the website that I had stated that he was the ultimate man turned my stomach. 'Sick and twisted man' was more apt.

It was November 2005 and I visited Google again, knowing that there would be another site and sure enough, there was a new creation: www.yesweknowyouknowlindsey.com. The focus on sex had upped a few notches. He was obsessed! The words that were supposed quotes from me were rather erotic, alongside fabricated quotes such as: '*He does walketh like a God*'. Crikey! I was apparently using speech from biblical times, now! I wish that he would walketh right outeth of my life noweth.

Pronto-eth!

On further thought about that quote, was it an indication that he was declaring himself so powerful; that he could do what he liked 'playing God' - that ultimately affected my fate?

It was also so embarrassing to see words that I had definitely written too because I had written about my day, who I had seen, what exercise I had taken, what music I was listening to, what I was reading, memories from many parts of my life and romantic gestures. None of his emails to me were published now. Never again would I have an expected level of privacy when writing emails again. I felt mortified and humiliated. I had typed words to him - not to a mass audience.

They were all chockablock with a mix of words from private emails and words from Furran's dark mind and were excruciating to read. They were crude. They were dirty. They were written by an unhappy soul; a disturbed person. Which was reflected in the mixed, garish fonts that he had used and blurry images, somehow making it all even more alarming.

The lies involved derogatory quotes about certain parts of my body from fake third parties which made it even more frightening. Although I knew that the people I cared about would know that the lies were just that, and the rest was clearly the workings of an unfit mind, it did not make me feel any less diminished. There they were, splashed all over the internet.

My career and dreams felt over. My confidence was shrunk. My sense of safety disappeared. My reputation attacked, ferociously and so publicly and far-reaching. Knowing that all of the sites were indexing and getting embedded deeper into the web made me want to sink into the ground.

I didn't want anyone to notice as I had planned, and so continued facing the World as though nothing was happening. I threw myself into work and filling every moment with distractions, as much as possible. If people wanted help with anything, I would be there. I knew what I was not entirely myself but I would show up, remain convivial, be diverted and distracted. Sleep would always be blamed for anyone making remarks that I wasn't quite myself. When I had moments alone, these were the moments when my stomach just felt knotted.

I searched online for any type of help. There weren't any support groups. There weren't any forums. There wasn't a lawyer listed. There was nothing! Online stalking and online harassment did not exist. There were reports of stalkers, killers and tragic endings. In the offline world. Two different worlds back then.

I had to keep focused and have faith that he would get bored, one day. At this point, it was 10 months since I had broken up with him. Maybe a year would be his cutoff point with this vindictive campaign and I consoled myself with the belief that he would meet someone else and he would focus on them and stop all of this.

My diary became my dumping ground because I wasn't going to burden anyone with my woes. I pondered not including them because many of the entries I list contain repetition of feelings and frustrations. I decided to keep them in. They are what they are. It is important to have an outlet.

I wrote in my diary, December 2005:

He is obviously delusional. What else is he going to do? It feels like he is using me to declare the love for himself and that his ego is so bruised because I have ended it. What else? I keep wondering. This was his response to me ending it after 4 dates? I have gone from feeling angry to actually feeling sorry for him.

I keep pondering, had I given him attention that he wasn't used to? I analysed my behaviour over that time. It is true, of a romantic nature and really wanting romance in my life, I had thought initially that the emails that we had shared were fun and engaging and I was only being myself when I met him. It is true to say that I am questioning how I had behaved and I feel guilty for that. I regret my romantic words and nature. I am sorry about this but don't all possible meetings and relationships start out excitedly and rather thrilling?

It is still glorious with Steve. No question. No doubts. Could I really take any responsibility for any type of harassment? It is wrong. Why can't he accept that I didn't want any more? He has to move on. I don't deserve this. Nobody would. A handful of dates, a lot of hope and a lot of emailing. I wouldn't have imagined anything like this, if it went wrong. How much is he spending on all of the research and website hosting and registering? Encouraging others to join him? What else?

I just wish the police would do more and quickly. I feel so worried and out on a limb, expecting more but not having help to deal with it. And Steve? What must he be going through? It is so discombobulating. I look dreadful and haven't slept for weeks. END OF DIARY ENTRY.

We travelled North for Christmas 2005, Mama and I. Visiting one of my Brothers and his family brought reprieve from Steve being away. A darling, toddling nephew occupied me in different ways, yet nothing could distract me from what was impossible to escape from.

The word 'internet' was just about every other word from everyone's mouth. Each time heard, a sickly twist would wrench my stomach. A constant reminder of requests ignored. I bombarded Google, imploring them to take the webpages down. Had I actually had back up, I would have felt able to bring myself to counting how many there were exactly. At this point, when gathering information later, I am so glad that I didn't know. It was explosive enough.

Website hosts and domain registry sites that replied to my appeals were as frosty as the ground we were walking on. The fog and the drizzle of the moody wintry skies added to my mood when we had all said our cheery goodnights. Moments alone. Nothing competing with my attention. Like a magnet, the internet drew me to it, imploring me to investigate and probe and find a reason; a logic...a solution.

Discovering that power is with the creator and owner of webpages intensified frustration. Hosts were sorry but they didn't control content. Sorry, but not sorry. Goodbye.

Anger and frustration took over. 'Goodbye, Furran. I said Goodbye to you almost a year ago. Stop!', I ordered mentally. It was infuriating.

I fired out angry emails to internet companies, pushing for answers and more information, whilst mourning my privacy and worry-free, free spirited holidays: *'Why are you allowing clearly harassing and unpleasant publications? Why are you assisting him? You are aiding and abetting a criminal. Free speech, you say? How can an unregulated place like the internet that doesn't feel safe even promote free speech? Nobody was safe on there'*.

I was having a hard time with free speech. Free speech and expression is an essential liberty. Without which, societies can easily slide into a culture of oppression, suspicion and fear. What if free speech is not doing its job and it is actually contributing to a culture of oppression, suspicion and fear? Could there be a reform to include 'thoughtful' and to encourage kindness?'. I get it. No rules. What happens on the streets? If people scream abuse, they get arrested. There has to be encouragement for behaving online as you would offline though. Surely?

Optimism stayed by my side, as constant as the anguish that hovered close by waiting. To swoop in to jangle nerves and make my heart tick quicker when something else unfolded. Optimism never wavered. Someone would help one day. Despite every exhausting request ignored. Every phone call left me hanging for hours. Every call with Steve truncated. Nothing diminished my worry.

As the new year was rung in, we drank to everyone's prosperity and health, and to those less fortunate, as we always did. I then cast out an extra wish for Furran to meet someone and be too happy to continue in 2006.

CHAPTER THIRTEEN
Ignored by pleas online

January 2006. I was inundated with flowers and cards from Steve. His love overrode someone else's efforts to bring me down. In my mind, of course. His thoughts to cheer me were mightier than the effects of defamation, I would tell myself. I looked at the freesias in a vase sat on the table by the computer. Such a lightness in contrast to the heavy burden that was there, lurking, ready to try and yank me down.

February 2006 brought Steve home. 'Concentrate on the now,' I would chant over and over as his arrival time got closer. 'It is all we have. Now. He would be gone again soon.' But I hadn't prepared for Steve coming back with fresh perspectives of wanting to hunt him down. No need for him to look far to see if the sites were still there and escalating.

He had an army of friends offering to help, he said. He wanted to take over and hunt him down. Our first heated words. I adamantly refused for that tiny, sad person to have power over Steve's life, too. He was not going to ruin his career or his life, as well. It would only make things worse. Hunting a bad man down would not go in a good man's favour.

DIARY ENTRY, APRIL 2006: *It is still going on and it has been 14 months. Nightmare. Then, the postman arrives with another 12 bunches of freesias that Steve had sent. Divine. Gosh, I love that man. I miss him so much. It feels like torture. He has to be away and he is reminding me of his love with the constant flowers. And I am to be reminded of the opposite of love with the acts of the pernicious sick Furran. Why?*

Currently looking for a regular paying job, so that Steve and I can get a mortgage and live together, which is lovely. Trouble is, with my name being used for the abusive websites, who would want to hire me? Yes, obvious that it was all vindictive and showcases a very strange person to people that know me but employers do online searches on candidates more and more. Who wants 'potential trouble' attached to their business name? Zaps my confidence, somewhat. Makes me feel low. Seeing sexually explicit words about someone when you are considering them for a project would not be encouraging. lindseygoldrick.com was meant to be showcasing my work and promoting myself, not pictures of me with the words, 'Who doesn't love a gangbang?'.

Even though untrue and unrelated to writing jingles and business communication for clients, those untruths won't do me any favours at all. The nullification of my good reputation. Humiliation on a personal level. Career stumped. All other creative projects stripped from my mind. I just had a cringing thought that mortgage lenders, property managers and house sellers may do a search on me and be put off, too. Stress is just bubbling away consistently and when I have a sudden revelation about the possibilities of someone seeing the sites, it is like I have reached boiling point and I might explode. It is a horrendous feeling. Can't be doing my ticker any good. END OF DIARY ENTRY.

Steve and I were successful and bought an old cottage in a lovely village in the August of 2006, that needed work. Most importantly, it felt safe and had a very joyful feel about it. Doing up the cottage was a brilliant distraction from Steve not being present and Furran's creations omnipresent. Mama and I went on trips, I visited my family and lots of people came to stay and I tried not to look at the internet.

Whether I looked or not, it wasn't like it was going to disappear or I could take a break from it, though. I had found a job and although not what I wanted to be doing, it had its challenges and I liked the people. It wasn't far away. I needed the money and the routine of regular hours was a good distraction.

Keeping strong, healthy and exercised was part of my coping plan and I couldn't let myself down. It was all conducive to retaining resilience and heck knows I wasn't getting enough sleep. Mama and I joined a gym and went every morning at 6am. Despite the days of finding it hard to get up at all, let alone for the gym, we kept it up. Each feeling like we would let the other down if we hit the snooze button, we turned up, we worked out and we felt good for it. Adrenalin and endorphins topped up for the summer of 2006 and beyond (for years), when I could quite easily have spun out. At a time when I could have taken to bed, called in sick and not left the cottage.

That said, there were bills to pay and we had this beautiful cottage to restore and live in and I had to keep balanced. I had to keep my power. I reminded myself: 'If you don't show up, you are letting yourself down more than anyone'.

It had been 19 months since the start of the harassment. The longing to provide writing services under my own name that I had was merely a longing now, and it went around my mind, most days. I didn't have a chance. My name was out there in a despicable way. If I picked up a client, they would automatically check out the internet. Oh, what joys for them to see. What chance did I have? Even though it wasn't true, I, nor anyone else it seemed, (since I kept on trying to find help) couldn't do anything. It was beyond my - or anyone's capacities.

If only the search engines would block the websites, I would think. I just couldn't understand why, on alerting these hosting sites or search engines about obviously offensive websites, why they paid no attention. Why they allowed them. Why, by allowing them, it wasn't deterring online abuse. Why they couldn't block any with my name attached to it.

Oh, if only I could take the URL addresses to the local court and have them block them by order of the government. I had all sorts of ideas that may not be possible. They must have looked at them. Many told me that it was up to the owner what they did with it. Frightening to think about. No limitations. No banishments. A free for all. It baffled me why that could not be done. Why could I not, if I showed my passport, have autonomy over my name and reputation on the web? The image and name

61

matched my passport. There wasn't anything complex about it. This was a bully's dream come true, the internet. How to expedite bullying in one easy step. Do it online! I repeat: I made the request to Google, over and over. I didn't ever get a reply.

Worry lay beside me in bed for most of the nights, mulling over what might be on the internet about me the next day. Then dread would kick in and keep me forcing my eyes to stay open because of the fear of seeing him sometimes in nightmares and wanting to stay alert in the wee, vulnerable hours. So I would often just get up at 1 or 2am and paint a wall or strip a door down, like any normal person does (!), working through the angst.

Then, dog-tired and feeling sick, I would decide on trying to find someone that could help again on the internet, fuelled by moments of feeling positive and determined - which was a great idea at the time. Crashing at 4am, only to struggle getting up less than two hours later, and dash about getting ready was the reality. And that is no way going to help with emotions. My adrenals must have been overworked with too much caffeine, too and I must have had super early nights where I crashed out (but I don't remember them, to be honest). It was a vicious cycle. I would work harder and longer and often bring things home to work on to overcompensate. In overdrive, I was tough on myself. All, with a smile on my face, inviting no concern to anyone - mostly.

All of it was a distraction, of course.

CHAPTER FOURTEEN
Tired of being turned away

As time passed through the 20th month and then the 21st month of harassment, through worry, fear and sleep deprivation, I became clumsier and started to feel muddled and forgetful. I was always rushing around outside, quick to get anywhere, not wanting to linger anywhere too long.

Mama continued to ask if I was okay. 'Just tired', is all I had to offer. I cannot imagine how it would have affected her, if she had known. She has a fertile imagination if I am late or hard to get hold of, that we often laugh about together! There wasn't any way that I was going to tell her what was happening. I didn't talk about it and had said that I was going to sort it out, so she presumed it was over. I had control over that, at least.

Instinctively though, because we are so close, she always knew when she needed to whisk me away for time out together; suggesting a holiday or a day out. That bond is so strong. Perhaps she saw it in my eyes that I needed some play time. Incredible really, looking back. Like everyone else in my life. Connections that we have with people. Knowing and not talking about it. Calling when you were just thinking of them. Dreaming of them and they knock on the door the next day. Having a memory with someone and they send you a text just at that moment. Precious indicators of what it is all about. Connections. Love. My people. My silent support. Lucky me.

It was November 2006 and I noticed that lindsey-goldrick.com had been changed. There were more quotes on there that had been made to appear to be exclaimed by me and what caught my attention were the words: '*He hacked into my account!*'. Where had he got those words from, other than a private email from myself to Ames? I called the police to tell them but had to begin again and explain from the beginning, to a new constable, who came around to see me at home. It was exhausting. I was sick of my own voice, repeating over and over but knowing that there was nothing they could do until he physically harmed me, I felt like it was all time wasting but when Sussex police called me a week or two later, I felt elevated and hopeful.

They asked for all evidence: The box and its contents, the notes from Saul Furran to friends and family and anything else to be sent to them.

Reading from the police reports that I acquired later on for evidence purposes, from this time...

November 2006 to November 2007, Saul Furran remained under investigation by Sussex Police. Sussex police contacted the Criminal Investigations Department and upgraded it to a Full Course of Conduct, which meant they could arrest him for harassment again, since he hadn't stopped even after a caution.

They ascertained that he was the owner of the websites and that they were regularly updated by him and that he lived overseas much of the time but he did make regular returns to the UK. They intended to arrest him in July 2007 and then it was moved to October and then finally after a year of attempts, they concluded that they just couldn't keep tabs on when he would be back in the country and their attempts had been thwarted. They told me it was out of their geographical limitations and out of their jurisdiction. They told me that they had sent him a strongly-worded email and told him to take them down or he will be arrested, which he didn't take any notice of. It only ignited him further.

Back to 2006.

In the December of that year, I was driving home from work and all of a sudden, somebody drove into the side of me at such a great speed, it had spun my car around and up the verge of the opposite side of the road on a dangerous corner. My head and neck were yanked. I picked up my phone and called the police. I needed help getting me away from the dangerous corner, as soon

64

as possible. The door was yanked open and it was the driver of the other car and he was clearly very drunk. He slurred and asked me what I was doing and when I said that I was calling the police, he ran and got back in his car and sped off. I was glad that he sought to see that I was okay but I worried about him being on the road. He must have been obliterated to have missed the Stop sign and just carry on driving from a side road, at such great speed.

Steve came to pick me up and as I waited for the police to come back to our cottage after sorting the road out, to take down a statement, Debs called.

She told me that there is a new site: soyouthinky-ouknowlinzigoldrick.co.uk. I wanted to scream!

A quick glance revealed more strange and weird words and clearly an embellishment on top of the other embellished websites. This development was excruciating to deal with and it further exacerbated my distress because the police's involvement really did not have the desired effect on him. He knew that he couldn't be arrested whilst being overseas. It was only encouraging him to create more and now there were seven websites about me. Ignoring the adult caution, arrest and email with the threat of arrest again when he was in the UK, made it clear that any involvement with the police was not going to stop Saul Furran at all.

I looked at the domain name and tried to make sense of the meaning of it, as nonsensical as that sounds, since where was the sense in any of it? Soyouthinkyouknowlinzigoldrick, though. Delving deeper - it suggesting people knew me or think they know me. Ahhhh, dear goodness....oh my goodness......would this website be full of the information from my hacked Yahoo email? Other people's private information? Oh my...my heart was exploding. Ears buzzing. I couldn't look. The police had arrived to take down the statement about the crash.

And I sat, stunned with dread and feeling deflated... sick, answering them, half-heartedly. Stunned. Wanting them to know about this new, harassing website that was more painful and life changing than a yanked neck and a knackered car but knowing that there was nothing they could do, I didn't bother. What was the point? They always told me that they couldn't do anything.

When they left, I forced myself to go back to soyou-thinkyouknowlinzigoldrick.co.uk. I needed to know that my friends and family's private information wasn't blasted on the websites, too. It was murderous the amount of time it took for the website to load. Each page was horrible. Each page was violating. No words 'belonging' to anyone else but 'from me but not me'. I shake my head.

My chest felt like someone was sitting on it. 22 months and no sign of stopping. Just signs of more and more and more.

CHAPTER FIFTEEN
Birthday treats

The whiplash from the car accident gave me an intense headache that lasted a month. We had my Mama, Ethne, my Aunty Maggie and Uncle Bob over for Christmas for a few days and we had also invited an elderly neighbour who was on his own. It was a fantastic distraction, despite my feeling ill and helpless about all the escalating websites. The strain that I felt was intense. Having gorgeous people around us stopped me from sobbing.

Just ten days later in 2007, on my Birthday in January, I was treated to a new website about myself. I would never be prepared for what I expected to see. Where were all these pictures coming from and why were there quotes on there that I only ever emailed to my friends? My heart pounded. 'Here we go', I thought. 'Private information from my contact's emails were going to start appearing. Other people's communication to me'.

I couldn't stand this. I could barely keep my hands steady as I searched Yahoo to change my password. I had been changing my Yahoo passwords every morning. The previous times, it was possible that he had learnt my password by watching me or my using a computer that he used, too and I had saved my password by accident but he had to be a hacker.

There were private, real emails that were on there but they were of no interest but extremely embarrassing to think that anyone could read them and think that my very private emails to someone were made available publicly. Excited emails of a romantic nature now looked silly and pathetic.

Optimism screamed from the emails and the thrill of sharing travel plans and recipes, thoughts, memories, things that made me laugh, chitter chatter chitter chatter. Silly hopes. Silly notions. There were the spiced up versions including fantasies of the carnal kind. My authentic pronouncements of *'Woweee!'* And getting carried away with silly little thoughts, were okay at the time, written to one person that I was imagining was a perfect match.

Then, another page would be hideous words of *'loving threesomes whilst having my toenails clamped'* or whatever weird things he wrote on those websites. I want to clarify that we didn't have sex talk emails. Romantic, yes. The rest? No. If anything was referenced, it would have been funny. It isn't my bag. *'Have a gorgeous day!'* and *'Have a smashing and brilliant evening'* were most definitely my colloquialisms, smattered around, which would give it authenticity, which again had me feeling subdued. Followed by his words of my looking forward to my day because I was having a skin wax and it excited me or something that would have been very tedious to read and equally mortifying.

These websites had my pictures on and my name as a domain name, under all of the variations possible. Despite them being obviously created by someone that was obsessed with revenge, they felt equally destroying.

It had been 3 years ago that I had fallen for this man's creative correspondence. It is what drew me into him and kept me interested - enough to meet him. The now angry and detestable words spilled out from the internet into my room; home; mind. I felt betrayed and foolish. It was approaching two years of this nightmare and not quite the few months of mental torture that I had originally predicted - and dreaded!. This wasn't an average, even-keeled person. He was irrational; a mad man; a psychopath?

'The works of an unstable mind evident to anyone that might stumble upon them, surely', I would occasionally rationalise, but it didn't stop me feeling weighted and oppressed. Those were my names that were being used and not just those but everything else that had happened and might happen, and what he was doing made me feel like never leaving the house but I had to. I had bills, I had a job and this 'regular' life to lead, so as

68

to not to draw attention to the workings of a madman and the hold he had over me. I had a reaction plan.

I fought with that a lot, as you will gather. I kept telling myself that he didn't have the power but I was adapting my life around the ramifications of his conduct.

April 2007, 2 years 1 month later. I stopped meandering to smell the flowers. I ran everywhere. I wondered if everyone noticed that I was always panting when I arrived! Little obsessions began and I started checking that everything was locked and then checked again to see if I had checked properly. Any little tiny noise became a huge noise.

The whiplash from the accident had given me tremendous headaches but there wasn't anything that could compete with the bouts of anxiety that I started experiencing.

At first I thought it was attributable to the accident because when the drunk driver smashed into me from the side, the impact was so hard. But it wasn't that. These anxious little attacks slowly crept in when the phone rang late at night from an 'anonymous caller' or 'withheld' or when I woke and heard noises in the night. Also in the mornings when I wondered what was on the internet about me that day. Or seeing him, or someone that looked like him, walking away from our cottage.

It was over 2 years since I had last seen him and I had forgotten what Furran looked like now, yet he was there all the time. I didn't see him, per se, but I saw his outline and his shadow everywhere I looked. I saw him in the street and in crowds but his face was blurred. The black wavy hair, thin stature and the way he moved was vivid and I stopped watching any film or TV programme if an actor had any similar visual characteristic to what he had.

The hairs on the back of my neck would stand on end if anyone spoke to me that had a remote hint of his tone and his accent. Reminding me of his nefarious activities and extent of harassment. Of the overwhelming, far-reaching threats to my sanity and safety as a result. Not knowing if and when he was going to stop was daunting. Not knowing how it would end felt terrify-ing.

CHAPTER SIXTEEN
Being watched from nearby

Some days I would torment myself trying to make sense of it and it kept going around and round, while I questioned my behaviour. It was almost like I was seeking justification; searching for something that I had done. As if finding an answer would assist in it ceasing.

I would be ruminating: 'I had wanted a great relationship, that's all and I moulded him to fit what I had in my mind. His writing about loving people, romance, music, books and travel were just mirrored from my emails. He moulded himself to fit in with me. He had charmed me'.

I ignored all of the alarm bells and incompatibilities. He had matched the image that I had created via email in the virtual world but the reality was so different. Goodness, if he hadn't have been unkind on the last date, how long would it have taken before I realised? How long is this campaign going to go on? Even if we had been together a lifetime, it is a preposterously crazy, vindictive thing to do. What else would this psychopath do? Over and over. Tortured with regrets, unanswerable questions and being associated with really bad fonts.

In between reporting his conduct to the police and having overwhelming feelings of anxiety and fearing for my life, I carried on as best I could without drawing attention to it. It was the summer of 2007. I went on trips with my loved ones and took breathers when I was alone. I visited and had visits from my favourite people and kept on writing emails daily all about my other everyday stuff.

Now and again, I touched on the sites with Teen, briefly. She would always say something comforting; something to remind me that I was more powerful than him, giving me reprieve and eventually having me laugh out loud. Contained moments of talking out loud about it with my cousin were enough and yet more.

The months went by and we received news that Steve was going to be away for a while. It was always heavy and disheartening. Quite out of the blue, in August 2007, he suggested that we got married quickly. I loved him so much. Why not? Two days later, with the help of a Royal Navy Commissioner, we married on the beach at Lyme Regis.

I liked to think that being married to me would give him fortitude and something as a distraction to think about whilst away, thus the power of the wilful thoughts (it wasn't working for me, though) would bring him back safely.

Neither of us really had any control over what was going on.

Soon after our marriage, in September 2007, an internet search with my new married name brought up all of the websites. Google had lists of horrible, offensive websites about me, as Lindsey Goldrick Dean. This highlighted that he had changed the meta tags behind the websites to include Goldrick Dean and not just Goldrick (which if you are unfamiliar with meta tags, they are content descriptors in the admin section - the source code area- of a website that help search engines find that particular website).

They had been search engine optimised to include that name, so there wasn't an escape at all even with a new name, albeit only slightly different and it was clear that Saul Furran was watching me regularly and he was tweaking the websites to reflect significant changes in my life. The thought that he knew that I was married (and we married quickly and without significant notice), in addition to the knowledge that he knew where I lived and worked, was more evidence that perhaps he was watching me from a closer vicinity still. He surely couldn't be hacking into my account on a regular basis, could he?

I need to reiterate that I was not on Facebook or any other social media site. There wasn't any information about me on the internet at all, offered up freely by me or any other company, so any information gathered about me would have had to have been extensively researched or paid for or from my email account.

Many of his emails to me had been deleted and I didn't remember, nor had saved any of his email addresses outside the work email that he used in Saudi Arabia. I had the notion that I might plead with him to stop but it might just ignite his deranged creativity further for who knew why he felt compelled to traumatise me. Showing him that I was distressed might be all that he wanted to receive vindication. It was best not to engage but what could I do?

DIARY ENTRY 2007: *I looked for his company today on Companies House online.* (Companies House, by the way, is a division of the UK Government which is registrar for businesses for regulation purposes and it makes their information public, so that anyone can monitor businesses, openly). *The reason being was that I was exploring the fact that he may have a partner that would have influence on convincing him that it wasn't regular behaviour. I noticed that the secretary bore his name and on another page, it had said that she had another name and this indicated that they had married in 2007, the very same year that Steve and I had married! It is the same year that he created www.soyouthinkyouknowlinzigoldrick.co.uk.*

I resent that he is running his business and continuing on with his life, (feeling quite sure that his wife doesn't know anything about his horrible hobby), whilst harassing me so much that he is impeding my life. I am thinking of confronting him but not sure how to go about it and whether it would be effective? I did actually ponder calling his wife, thinking that might stop him but instinct made me stop. What if she left him and it only aggravated him and inspired him to be more 'physical'?

I can't quite believe this is still happening. It is two years now! He might take pleasure in knowing it is bothering me, though and do something else. His wife can't know, can she? I wonder if there are others? I wonder if he has done it before? I couldn't imagine how

73

that would feel: finding out that the person that you were married to was spending time and money on creating nasty websites about someone else and paying for them to be live online, trying to destroy their lives and on further investigation, you found out that it was after 4 dates and a mostly online relationship!

She may wonder what the hell would happen to her if it went wrong because she had actually married him! I wonder if she would wonder if I was the only one that he was doing it to, like I do? He must be spending tons of hours away from her creating these websites and doing updates. She may just think he is working hard. I am feeling concern for this woman that I don't even know. She might be in on it! END OF DIARY ENTRY.

Mama recognised that we both needed another escape and suggested that we popped over to Morocco. She knew instinctively that the travelling, the moving, the change of culture, smells, colours, landscape and language would boost and spur me on. Great roaring laughs lifted us both from the moment we left home and accompanied us to the jostling, chaotic Djemaa el-Fna square in Marrakech that kept us alert and entertained. Lured and hounded in souks and the medinas.

Completely distracted and immersed in unfamiliar noise, smells, colours. Fantastic! We met many people who talked of hope, wisdom and strength on the streets of Essaouira and we were scrubbed and hosed down at the hammams in Agadir. Never been so near-naked and scrubbed so clean by a stranger before…ever!

Travelling through the arid, hot Atlas Mountains. Slowly we ascended, as stress descended, stopping for pictures with the goats on argan tree branches, as children ran out of nowhere with bags of almonds, chasing the tourists. The Berber freedom flag… so little, so much. The verdant valleys, the smell of juniper, finally blending in wearing djellabas, the sweet addiction of mint tea… Oh, it was so special.

It was necessary for a change of thought; a change of environment. The contrast from home and reality was enough for respite. The constant companionship of my precious, kind, warm and fun Mama. No real escape from the internet, for the internet felt like it was some invisible force all above and all around; always accessible and yet not when we were away. The only time. Nobody knew my name. A powerful visible and mental escape.

The call to prayer, throughout the day, through speakers wherever we were on land, took us to another world. At times we felt like we were trespassing and at the same time honoured to witness it. The symbol of God in the mountains whilst out at sea. Reminders everywhere about the necessity to not fall out of practice of believing in the greater good. That spiritual sound so transporting; so moving. I understood faith... and rituals of appreciation, belief and hope.

My own rituals of thanks throughout the day for the darling people in my life, their health and safety, clean water, a roof, good food, a job....were tremendously transcendental. Putting me in a sense of peace and love, which were so much bigger than anything, for a long while afterwards.

Trips were paramount to my coping. I knew it then and looking back, I see it even more. So lucky to have been invited on so many. What was also nice was that I was being invited - not because people felt sorry for me (because they did not know) - but because people wanted my company.

That perked me up, so much.

CHAPTER SEVENTEEN
Cracking up through the cracks

So, it was around 2008 that the police said that due to the geographical limitations, they really could not help me. Saul Furran lived in Germany now and visited the UK sporadically. Three years on, the internet was being flooded with these violating websites about me and nothing could be done to make him stop. I felt like I was slowly cracking up whilst slipping through the cracks. I didn't give him the quantity of site visitors that he was expecting but it seemed that the attention from the police encouraged him.

I imagined him in a seedy, dark room sniggling with having the control and getting excited by creating more, when he received the email from the police attempting to get help. I was still thinking about how he just enjoyed being arrested and how he made more websites afterwards. He was enjoying this attention and being so far away, felt invincible. He was a cowardly bully, who hid behind the internet and it made him feel good and bigger to be causing distress in me because he was weak and sad and hadn't had any attention before. Nobody would catch him now because he lived far, far away in internet kingdom obscurity.

I prayed for him to get a life. I prayed for him to focus on his wife and to be too happy to spend time on this campaign. I prayed for him to get new hobbies. I prayed that he would suddenly see it for what it was and it had ended and realise that he was being crazy and delete, stop and move on. I longed for him to realise that it wasn't acceptable behaviour to react this way (and for so long).

Even if he was in Saudi Arabia for a few weeks at a time and felt lonely. He had to keep coming back from there, as part of the visa. It wasn't like he was in the military or in prison. He chose to be there. He wasn't forced to go on behalf of his country. He was there on his own means. There wasn't a sob story. Also, if he just wanted someone to write to, then why join Soulmates? Why not: someonetowriteto.com or IdontactuallywantomeetyouorIwillbecomeastalker.com? Or: youwontlikemewhenImangry.com? It was emailing over 6 months and 4 actual dates. 'Move on', I pleaded, 'and just stop!!!'. I longed for him to just stop!

Some mornings, the alarm would go and I would listen to the bird's dawn chorus. I would think how delightful it was to hear and how I should be thoroughly chirpy too, as I always had been in the mornings. As I lay there and the light shined through the curtains and hit the crossing beams on the ceiling, I would watch the shapes and shadows form on the wall and I would start to feel the heavy reality.

I would have felt complete happiness had it not been for Furran's acts of revenge and it was now three years. So, I would then contemplate not getting up, as the reality of the web pages about me kicked in and the dread of what was new out there about me now and wondering if anyone had seen the websites and what the ramifications were, if they had.

Who knew how my employers would feel or my neighbours? Not many people truly knew me, did they, apart from my circle? Closing my eyes, feeling sadness wash over me, I wished the day away and I wished that I could wind back the clock and I wished that I could eradicate everything on the world wide web and I wished with all my might that Furran got a new hobby and mostly that I had never met him at all. I cringed at my optimism for romance back in 2004.

I am not sure what made me pull back the sheets and head to the shower. Was it the will to not be defeated? The will to not let him have power? It had to be. That and responsibility and conscience. I was expected at work. That and also not having anybody start scrutinising me and asking questions and noticing that I wasn't 'quite myself'. One huge cover up. The turmoil and pain would remain invisible. I had to keep living like I would normally live.

I knew all of this but some days, I wanted to hide and scream in a corner and stop having to put a face on. My life felt tarnished and ruined. I would have many moments like these and then the responsibilities of my life would usurp me out of the mode, and I would tell myself to pull myself together because there are people going through much worse.

CHAPTER EIGHTEEN
Back and forth

Throughout 2008, Steve was away a lot and I worried about him. He had so much to contend with with his work and he must have felt so angry and helpless about what was continuing. On top of all that he endured, he had the knowledge that there were escalating volumes of websites about me. Despite my not discussing them, he was always aware of them.

Instead of climbing the walls and wailing, I pottered about the cottage doing little repairs and changes and going to work and to the gym and having people to stay. Having chances to do menus and make feasts and pamper others, along with little breaks away, filled up my diary and the distraction lists.

Meanwhile, I would be constantly praying to the Universe that something would happen so that Furran would stop or that the police would help but it was so frustrating because there wasn't anything to cling onto and hope for. It wasn't like there was help and I couldn't afford it, in which case, I would have the hope and help there but needed to get the money. There wasn't anything at all that any amount of money could buy, so I was just left clinging on for some miracle to happen. I kept thinking of creative ways that could make it happen.

I enrolled to learn code. I conducted my own experimentation, using other businesses' websites, to their delight, not really knowing that there was a name for it (search engine optimisation) but I watched their sites climb as I changed the meta tags and linked in and out, and by looking at competitor's sites, I could see what they were using to boost their rankings. It became a game and I enjoyed it, considering how I could make it work for me. Pushing the negative items down and pumping positive items up. I needed to find the solution.

I would spend so much time online in the evening trying to shut him down. Or find someone that would help and all the while, in the light of day, trying not to let anyone know about any of the ordeals on the home front; Steve with his trauma about work and me with the trauma of the online harassment. Our communication wasn't tiptop at the time. It was more of a silent acknowledgement of stress recognition in each other and talking about it wasn't on the agenda, since it might tip us over the edge. There wasn't anything that we could control about our lives and we both felt desolate with the unwieldy burden of being unable to change things. It felt suffocating.

After so many years of generally being lucky to wake with happy thoughts, and now feeling my stomach churning with dread as my mind was enlightened with the dreadful reality, I decided that I had to do my utmost to retrain those thoughts somehow. It was over three years now, in the spring of 2008.

'*I couldn't control what Furran was doing but I could control how I dealt with it*', I had to keep reminding myself. 'All thoughts had a major affect on you', I decided, 'so they may as well be positive ones'.

I would wake up and be thankful for being able to wake up, that Steve was safe, Mama and everyone close was well and to have the stamina to keep a job and do it well, working for a really kind man. This morning ritual of feeling grateful for everything good in my life would be a good focus, I decided, even though I found it hard leaving the house some days.

Yes, I felt despondent about my dreams being put on hold and I lost a lot of confidence but I was going to give everything to the position that I was doing. The company I worked for were vociferous in the positive changes what I was doing for them and I battled with the torment of wishing it was my company that I was boosting and the gladness that my cognitive abilities weren't entirely blitzed.

Clutching onto the good, shifting thoughts of worry, tempering stifled and shirking the thwarted feelings every day on waking - or else my health would suffer. Reasons for keeping a grip. I had to stay healthy - mentally and physically. Only too aware of the fragility of losing one's mind. It was like walking a tightrope over a pit of sinking sand. Striving hard not to fall and sink.

Downhearted and resentful, he had robbed me of my name, my visions, my ambition, my reputation, control over my life and taken away the bliss of pure joy. He had snatched away my feelings of safety and had taken up camp in my nightmares and crushed my chest.

The fact that I felt insular and humiliated. Distraction was easier and less painful. I had jeopardised my reputation; my whole life by meeting a madman when all I wanted was to meet 'someone like-minded'.

Yes, I had moments of blaming myself, feeling sorry for myself, feeling isolated, worthless, helpless and left to fend for myself. Struggling along, working hard for someone else, wishing it was for us, striving with contradictory feelings of thankfulness for what I had and for my own strength and yet, dumbstruck with the lack of help, falling on deaf ears.

Feeling sick that I couldn't see an end to it because his bullying wasn't diminishing in any way. I didn't want to cave in because that would have felt like he had won. It was like playing tug of war with a monster that was getting bigger and uglier. It was exhausting trying to keep holding on. But I had to keep a grip until it was he that fell to the floor. Not me.

I would go back and forth with my feelings of being vehemently determined to not let him win one day to feeling like a crumpled heap the next. On the crumpled days, social invitations were declined. Impending parties cancelled. Curtains were closed. Paranoia came to give me company in bed.

Crowds would be avoided, lest he was there. Imagined conversations out of earshot wondering where my sparkle had gone. Tired, spiritless, diffident and murky and not as colourful as I thought I once was. I couldn't dance like nobody was watching anymore and I didn't want to attract attention to my listless self, invoke curiosity or invite questions. Dread. Afraid that I may scream out, '*I am dealing with a mentally ill stalker and nobody can stop him. I am hanging close to the edge of a breakdown*'. For the reality was - it was there, continuously.

I didn't want people to be reminded about my existence, to be introduced to anyone new or announce my name anymore to anyone. My name had to be hidden. Curiosity is rife. I feared anyone searching my name, online. '*Someone else has stolen my identity*', I wanted to scream, as loud as I could.

'*What do you want me to do?*' reverberating around my head. Trapped in a tank, treading water, too tired to stay afloat and despite my waving my arms around and knowing that there were lifeguards, they couldn't see me. Nobody was rescuing me. They would let me drown. Nobody is helping me and now I am drowning.

And then, like a phoenix rising, I would remind myself about the fight within me to keep my emotional balance and faith and power and that I, Lindsey Goldrick Dean was not any of those things that he was attaching my name to.

I was a powerful, strong woman and I would win this war.

CHAPTER NINETEEN
Ungoverned web

Training for something else that I was interested in and that would satisfy and distract me, came to me one night in the May of 2008, as I sat staring at something on TV. That would be something that I could control. I could learn something new and put something else in my thoughts and so, I enrolled for an online Nutritionist Degree; something that I could study for in the evenings. For, it was late at night when I had time to think (when I should have been in bed asleep but was too afraid of my nightmares) that I needed something else to fill my brain. Mama had ignited my interest in nutrition from being tiny, and so I thought that perhaps that could be a new career.

Studying all night and working all day through the week gave fresh perspectives; hope; possibilities. Much to do to achieve those goals. Deadlines. Exams. In between work, family times and running errands for neighbours. I was too busy to be stabbing around in the dark trying to seek non-existent help on the internet. Watching debasing words expanding across the search engines about myself only fed my anxiety.

It would have had crushing damage on my new routine to know that at that moment in time, Furran was emphasising my point, by publishing: www.anastylyingpieceofwork.com/Lindseygoldrick. (It was live from 2008 and continued until 2018, a month after the High Court of Justice and was updated during the litigation process, just after we received his Witness Statement admitting everything).

My mind started playing melodramatic tricks and I dreaded what hadn't appeared yet and that would be my face superimposed on a naked body in a revenge porn manner. I wondered whether he was saving it for some 'grand finale'. Who knows what else he had planned. I wasn't dealing with a regular person, was I? I am not sure what a regular person is but I am trying to avoid saying that I thought he was more than crazy). I had nightmares about something that may not actually happen and this is when I knew that paranoia really was kicking in, too.

At this point, three and half years later, the websites were my name under every permutation, all 16 of them with a dot com or a dot uk or a dot org or a dot co dot uk. www.lindsey-goldrick.com, www.LindseyGoldrick.com, www.Linzigoldrick-.org, www.linzigoldrick.com, www.LinzIGoldrick.com, www.lindseygoldrick.co.uk, www.linzigoldrick.co.uk, www.LinziGoldrick.com, www.lindseygoldrick.org.uk, lindsey-goldrick.info and www.lindseygoldrick.net, aswell as: www.myanamcara.com, www. anastlyingpieceofwork.com, www.yesweknowyouknowlindsey.com, YesWeKnowYouKnow-Lindsey.com and www.soyouthinkyouknowlinzigoldrick.co.uk.

I wrote to as many of the domain registry sites that I could find and got a reply from Nominet, the only one. I begged them to help me take the ones that they could, down from the internet. For four hours, the three .uk sites went off the air and I thought that it was a breakthrough. I thought that I would some-how find out the .com registry sites and they would disappear, too! But the .uk ones reappeared, the very same day!

Nominet then told me that they could not manage or monitor them and that the control belonged with the owner. Al-though it was brief and temporary, the help that I received from Nominet was the only help I had received in so long. I hung onto the poor chap's email address and wrote him a novella, explaining how I felt and presuming he was technologically minded, asked for his advice. Poor bloke. I bet he had wished he hadn't helped at all but he did reply, '*I don't have any advice at this time*', which gave me hope for the future and I hung onto his email address and felt so grateful that he had given me something with the words: '*at this time*'! Desperate, so I was.

It was clear that freedom of speech and lack of rules on the internet were applicable all across the net, and not conducive

84

to being a safe place to be for anyone. Domain companies that didn't have regulations invited a whole host of horror. And possible horrible creations by people with negative intentions. A whole different future for other innocent people because these companies were going to facilitate the abuse. That is exactly what was going on.

Website administrators saw what he had created and said that there was nothing they could do, which meant that they had no rules. Google was not doing anything. And their moderators must be able to see how when my name was tapped into the search engine, it resulted in three pages of filth. The sites were in no way anything but abusive and crude. They were allowing them to stay, which made me feel that unless this stopped, my case could only be one of trillions in the future.

I was astounded that there was this huge world that we had entered and used just as much as the world we had always known and it was all merging. Yet, this part that could amplify abuse and horror in nano seconds and enable criminals to do what the hell they liked and take it, spread it, access it, all across the world had no rules. It was bonkers and it was frustrating and my heart was heavy. It felt too huge to do on my own and I was exasperated what to do, anyway.

The police not being able to do anything and their lack of power over what happened on the internet made me feel helplessly alone. The police's lack of a dedicated technology team that could terminate Furran's actions on the internet bothered me so much. It all felt so old-fashioned. They could terminate harassment on the street but not on the net and yet we were all spending more of our lives on the internet.

I had an address for the perpetrator. In the UK and abroad. There would be an IP address. Surely I wasn't the only one going through this and needed help but it seemed that I was. I had trawled the internet for anything; something that would give me a glimmer of hope or a shimmer of support.

There weren't any support groups in the UK on the internet in the early 2000s. Nor were there stories of survivors of any online abuse that I could contact and seek comforting words from, knowing that they would understand. And that is all I wanted so many nights. I felt desperate to talk to someone or email anyone that might state, 'I know how it feels'.

CHAPTER TWENTY
Hijack

Throughout the summer of 2008, it all just felt ridiculous. 3 years and 5 months. I felt foolish for ever believing that it was going to stop soon but it was all I had. I had to believe that he would just stop, come to his senses and take everything down. Nobody else was going to do it but his persecution was escalating.

Some days I felt like this belief was crazy and far-fetched. I would be up all night trying to shut the sites down or trawling for support groups, in touch with the police the next day and working as diligently as I could. Meanwhile, always looking over my shoulder. And feeling so apprehensive but trying to hold it together.

Always finding distractions when I could and all the time, feeling myself sliding into this abyss of despair but on nearing the bottom, managing to scramble back up again a bit and then sliding slowly down again.

If I wasn't alone, it was all with a smile on my face, too. It felt like I was in a cruel farce and I kept trying to find meaning in it all and wanting to know what my lesson was. I know that it wasn't constructive and pointless but I was trying to be constructive and what else did I have but my wondering, ever-increasing anxious mind? The mind that was getting more paranoid about what was going to happen next.

Again, having had two hours sleep, I would be woken by the alarm. I would then listen to the birds' chorus and the bellowing tractors going down the street. I'd see the light coming through the curtains and hitting the beam where it crosses on the ceiling. And I would watch how the light caught the beam and it would make shapes that would dance across the ceiling and I would think, '*Do I really have to get up? Would I really be missed at work?*'. Shutting the world out would be easy. Cocooned and safe.

And I would play the game of the battle of the burden of dread versus the coping plan. As the vile things came into my mind, I would bring in pretty flowers and great songs. The vile things came back with a vengeance and I would boot them out with defiance and they popped back in as I made my way to the shower. And my face was already wet with tears long before the shower reached it.

And the notes I wrote were all over the house, wherever we turned, reminding me: *'Attitude is a big thing that makes a big difference'*, *'Focus on what you can control'*, *'Life happens. Reaction is everything.'* And *'Keep your face to the sunshine'* (no wonder my skin is like leather).

I couldn't turn a corner without being reminded that nobody has my full power but me. As hackneyed as some of them were, those encouragement notes were another momentary distraction; mind savers. Better to have them than not to have them.

Sleep would not last long because any noise would wake me. I would imagine that those creaks on the stairs was Saul Furran, coming to physically harm me and maybe this is the night when I would get help from the police because he was going to kill me.

One night, 3 years and 6 months since the start, the noise that woke me at 3am sounded like glass being smashed. I waited and listened further. A definite sound of glass. I ran to the bedroom door and locked myself in, barricading myself in the bedroom. The set of drawers went behind the door and then the bed.

I sat up in bed with my (26 inch solid wood) rolling pin, listening for more noise amidst the sound of my loud beating heart. I didn't have the landline phone with me and I usually did and I sat frozen, listening for more noises, my heart pounding and the rolling, churning dread in my stomach as I fought sleep.

In the morning, in the sitting room, glass from a window pane lay shattered. It had to be Saul Furran. Nothing like this ever happened in this village. Somebody's plant wilted in their garden last month and it made front page village news. Still, a glass pane shattered was such a tiny crime to the police but a huge invasion for me because it was him letting me know that he was moving closer.

This would be just a sprinkling of what else was to come over the years.

CHAPTER TWENTY ONE
The ultimate distraction

Then, it came out of nowhere in autumn 2008 and clung onto me and became an obsessive thought: the desire to be a mother. I was 38 and I was intensely broody for a child. I had always longed to have a child one day but at that moment, it was overwhelming; it was visceral - I felt like it was my last chance. Instinct was telling me that I was running out of time and it was now or never. I cannot explain how the yearning took over. If we tried and it didn't happen, then I would have to accept that but if we didn't, I know that I would regret it.

So much in my life seemed out of control and it seemed, this overwhelming desire to become a mum urgently felt like it was the only thing that I could control. Steve would be an amazing Dad. Oh but it would help if he was home. That year, he wasn't home much at all but he was home in November for several nights. I felt like I needed divine intervention.

I visited my super special and gifted Aunty Maggie and Uncle Bob, who were holistic health practitioners, before they retired. After my treatment, I left feeling renewed, recharged and really feeling like something had shifted; a powerful change had occurred. I had felt it instantly. I continued the celebratory feeling at Teen's with her wonderful family in the same town for the weekend and cousin Karen joined us. I truly felt good to go!

Steve came home for a few nights in November. It was bittersweet, for he was away for Christmas in 2008. So, Mama and I decided to visit Gambia and take supplies to the orphanages and schools there. Focusing on those less fortunate would be grounding but we inevitably felt humble and powerless. What could just us two do? We couldn't change their lives. We gave them brief, temporary pleasures with our suitcases of supplies.

I won't forget the beautiful children's eyes as they sang welcome songs. They had nothing. I hope that they had love. Our Guide Lamin had made a Juju for me, for good blessings and to keep bad spirits away. Before I wrapped it around my stomach, so it would be in the right place (a square piece of leather, wrapped by more leather and threaded on a long black lace), I whispered in it that I wanted to be a mother. We had great adventures around Africa but Mama was sick every morning, though and I came back with one huge virus. Or, so I thought.

It was January, 2009. The Doctor had asked me if I was pregnant and I said that I couldn't be. Steve was home very little prior to our trip. I took a test to cross that off the list and I could have fallen to the floor when it revealed that I was indeed around 8 weeks pregnant. Elation took its time to settle in because I was stunned and instantly worried!

I'd had the obligatory yellow fever, typhoid and rabies shots, strong malaria drugs and drank infected water by accident (some shops were selling their own dangerous water in bottles), going to Gambia. Of all the times! I had jeopardised my chance of having a healthy baby. I could not believe this. Aunty and Uncle's work! Wow! Steve was only home briefly in November. It felt like a miracle.

Dazed and amazed, I walked home and sat in the middle of the sitting room on the rug, as though I couldn't quite make it to the sofa, collapsing with gratitude. 'Thank you... thank you' and prayed for Steve to call me because he had to be the first to know. This was a long shot. He could only call me every four days or so.

It was astonishing that moments later, the phone rang and it was him. There's that connection thing that I talk about. I didn't waste any time telling him and he, shellshocked, said, 'Wow' but I sensed the worry.

Oh, this was going to be a long pregnancy. Looking back to Gambia, Mama was having my morning sickness for me (she's so good to me!).

What was also poignant, as if Dad was sprinkling little baby dust amongst us, my sister-in-law was having a baby, too. It transpired that our babies had the same due date! More magic!

Unfortunately, midst my most amazing, wondrous news, at the same time for my Birthday in January 2009, I was treated to another variation of: www.linzIGoldrick.com - in a mixture of upper and lower cases. It amazed me about how many variations you could get out of my name. Quite impressive.

I knew there were more but I just didn't want to count them. I could not handle it because there was no chance of getting them off there and he wasn't giving up.

I didn't know this then but there were 18 websites about me at this point. This one, that day, included more of the same nauseating and tedious untruths. I sat and stared at the large picture of me, wondering where that had come from, which stated in the largest, ugliest font:

'Even her mother knows how nasty she is'.

It rattled right through me. It was such a ridiculous un-truth and of course, he had purposely done that to get a reaction. I couldn't bear that he had succeeded there because mentioning my Mama was a huge violation.

The whole website, as with the others, was fabricated on lies and screamed that it was being created by someone with an unstable mind but it did not stop me feeling humiliated. It didn't make a difference. I felt tyrannised.

But then, I reminded myself that I had other bigger and better things to think about for a while. I had to keep healthy for the baby. Nobody and nothing was going to jeopardise that. And knowing when to bolster me further, Teen would send a text to me: *'Hang in there, Linz. Nobody gets to us Ladies. Come visit, this weekend?'*.

And the ladies that Teen was referring to are my family that I would choose as best friends and they consist of Mama, Aunty Maggie, Cousins Karen and Teen - the beautiful souls. My life-long nurturing, cushioning, belly-laughing ladies. My life-long rocks.

I carried on working through the day throughout 2009 and studied until as late as I could manage but pregnancy was making me just want to sleep more. The Juju around my stomach was getting so tight that I put it around my neck. I was yawning at my desk, the school I was studying with folded and despite being transferred to another, I stopped studying and the alternative career slipped by.

The most sublime project was keeping me occupied now and so, I didn't fight sleep and went to bed early every night. I had this undercurrent of worry, though and thankfully, I had the most attentive midwifery team, who had me regularly checked and scanned for reassurance.

When I was 7 months pregnant, we were invited to Clarence House in London. Steve was to receive a medal for one of his tours. When we were interviewed by the BBC, I was asked about how hard it was being pregnant whilst my husband was away and being alone. It caught me.

The tears just flowed, as it ignited the thoughts of feeling scared about being stalked whilst being pregnant and alone in our home. Amalgamated with worry about Steve when he is away. The cameras rolled and I blubbered through it! I had been asked how I feel! The floodgates opened. Viewers must have been thinking, 'Crikey! She really does find it hard!'

Despite that debacle, it was a proud, fun day and we fell into bed on our return to Somerset.

I got up in the night to get some water, heard a noise downstairs, stood at the top to listen more and I wobbled and fell down the stairs. I cried at the bottom and called my Midwife and was taken in for a scan, to check the health of our baby.

Whilst they were smearing on the gel and getting the sonogram to work in the right place, I was scanning their face for the delivery of bad news and it seemed to take forever.

The sheer peace from hearing the heartbeat made me sob.

CHAPTER TWENTY TWO
Blissful joy

The scare of the fall made me decide to take maternity leave earlier than expected. I couldn't stop the stalking but something had to give. I was so shaken up and I wanted to nurture and nest and wrap us up in cotton wool. This time was too important, too precious and Steve was away for much of the pregnancy. I didn't want to fight sleep at a desk and sitting at a desk with a computer only reminded me what was just a click away.

My allotment where I grew veggies and fruit was sitting, looking busy...waiting for harvesting, more digging, shouting out for more seeds, more weeding, more life, more growth....I could feed the land, feed us, feed my need for nesting, earthing, the necessity for being away from technology and for being outside. Fresh air. Fresh space. New perspectives. New times ahead. Preparation. Barefoot in the soil. As I watched the veggies grow right before my eyes, the sense of peace that I would soon be doing that with a little human was feeding me exactly what I needed at that time.

Nearing the end of pregnancy, I channelled my fantastic midwife doula friend, JoJo. She and I had met in New York. We found each other across a loud and noisy room. I heard a loud, infectious laugh and so did she. Instant friends. Both British. She lived in Connecticut. Me, New York. Together, we travelled the States. We married Americans. Neither of which worked out. But we did. Our friendship cemented and precious.

I felt absolutely fine and secure and had an amazing team and midwife and really, the best, but I missed her. I also greedily wanted extra medical expertise and protection. I still worried. About the vaccinations for Africa, about the fall, about my age...about everything. About having a stalker. I hadn't had a child before. She was too far away. Then, one day, a birthing pack of visualisation cards and music for a natural birth arrived from America; from her. Of course she was with me. Connections. Silent support. It arrived at the perfect time.

After digging and after walking for what seemed like hours, I would sit, sprawled in the sunshine in the garden, listening and studying. Feeling waves of love, protection and imagining what our baby would look like from staring at the scan pictures. A seahorse, apparently.

The maternity team were expecting a 10 pound baby from me, considering my size and so when he turned breech, they whisked me in for a c-section. Visualisation for a natural birth right out the window. Mama held my hand and held my gaze and focus in the operating theatre, as Steve turned green when they inserted the cannula. How would he be with a caesarian? He had to wait outside. Or stay fainted on the chair, more like. Our darling, healthy, beloved boy Rex was born 7 pounds 8 ounces and my body popped like a balloon.

The blissful joy of having a healthy, magnificent boy was indescribable. No description comes close. An intense feeling of immense happiness, relief and gratitude that won't go away. Flooded with oxytocin, my gaze had gone from staring into the beauteous soul of my Mama's eyes to our newborn's. I didn't think I could feel more blissful as the energy of unconditional love swirled, swept and weaved in and around us.

What lucky people Steve and I were and especially considering the vaccinations that were administered for Africa, in the early days and the tenseness that I felt. It gave Steve and I a new, fresh perspective. Our hearts grew - along with our overprotective instincts.

Glancing back at this time, I realise that Rex, was a saviour for both of us.
And his healthy, darling cousin was born too, before him. Sublime family news.

Being blissfully distracted by a baby throughout the autumn of 2009, breastfeeding on demand, having too much to do and being too tired to stay awake stopped me from reporting new evidence for a time. A huge chunk of energy on what was proving to be a fruitless exercise didn't make sense.

'Focus on what you can change', I reminded myself. Accumulating evidence was important but I could do that myself without having to deal with the excruciating exercise of talking to a brick wall, only to find another day gone. Another day wasted when it could be spent on cooing over our boy.

So, I avoided the internet for a while and really, just used my pc for emailing people and Skyping Steve when he was away. I couldn't cope with seeing what new creations Furran had made at this time because it would give me the feeling of the complete opposite of what Rex was making me feel.

My role in life had changed dramatically and I was elated with absolute jubilation and sheer blessedness. And a deep protection mode kicked in. I couldn't bear the scope of his bullying and how close to home it was, in all ways, and it having any effect on Rex. It hit me, now that I was a mother, how much it would have hurt my Mum, if she knew that someone was hurting her baby.

All engaged with this bundle of love and life. Every single movement was amazing. Every single thing he did (which wasn't a lot at that time), was incredible. This was the best baby ever to be born and I didn't want it to be marred by giving time to thinking about what was written about me on the internet. I would not be able to deal with such intense love interspersed with wondering what other horrendous things Furran had done and may do. This time was too precious.

As the gifts and cards and visitors with well-wishing came in and the cottage filled with flowers, my preoccupation didn't allow any room for what was going on outside the love and adoration of this new little perfect person in our lives. Steve was away when, one day, as I was rocking Rex in my arms and singing to him (poor Love is subjected to that a lot), the postman knocked.

A box had arrived and I so happily signed for it and then, I recognised the familiar obnoxious smell of acrid smoke. I dropped it and kicked it out to the street (and I do not know the fate of the box to this day).

All I know is that my perfect cocoon of oblivion and love with our new baby was invaded with the reality of the ugliness of Furran's conduct. Snapped to the reality of what he had published on the internet and his escapades offline, I screamed when I closed the door after kicking the box to the street.

Noooooo!

Furran knew about my baby!

CHAPTER TWENTY THREE
No escape from online harassment

I felt more threatened than ever because I had this beautiful baby and I needed to protect him. Rex had to be with me constantly. In a papoose, cradle or right by my side, never out of eyeshot. We were not safe anywhere. It would not have done any good telling anyone, other than worry others and what would the police do? They would ask me, 'What do you want me to do?'.

This would remind me that I had to show physical proof of harm before anything else could be done. He may not have been physically touching me but the impact of being stalked and publicly shamed on the net made me feel like he was brutally beating me up whilst shouting on a megaphone for everyone to come and watch - 24 hours a day, every day.

Feeling apprehensive about going online but wanting to email pictures of our perfect baby around, when I had little snippets of time, I would go straight to my mailbox and steer clear from the search engines. I had no inclination to know if there were any more creations by him on the internet, despite knowing that there would be and I didn't want to know. What could I do with the new information, anyway?

On opening up my Yahoo inbox, an email startled me: *'Thank you for registering for Made for Mums'*. I froze. I hadn't registered anywhere. Then, the emails were popping in, one after the other, welcoming me to websites devoted to being a mother. Websites that I had not visited or registered for. Also, with no social media presence on the internet, with regular life updates (other than what Saul Furran had put on there), it was more evidence that Saul Furran was watching me from a close proximity. It was also a possible confirmation that the box that smelt of acrid smoke was most definitely from him. What else was he going to do? I felt petrified for us and crying hard, I packed a bag for us both and headed to Mama's.

I remember driving to Mama's with Rex in the car and I had to pull over. My breathing had quickened and my chest was tightening. Anxiety had to come out some way. It was now 4 years and 7 months of hell. I looked at our gorgeous boy and felt adamant that Saul Furran was not going to get the best of me. I thought of my strategy plan. 'Focus on what you can control, focus on what you can control'. I had to be strong for my boy. I had to be strong for both of the boys in my life.

It was so magical, spending every moment with Rex and I wondered how more amazing it could have been without being stalked. I didn't want this time spoilt by thinking about Furran but what he was doing was continually there. Such a precious time that wouldn't be repeated. I resented Furran for that. I had waited a long time to be a mother and I couldn't believe how lucky we were. Then I would wonder what the hell I had done to be unlucky enough to be juggling with the extreme opposite of that exquisite joy, by having a psychotic man with a mission to try and ruin my life at the same time.

And my mind would go to the insidious nature of the internet assisting the escalation of his harassment. I pictured him optimising and maintaining the websites, so that the effects could be maximised. Ever refreshing defamation web pages, indexing and being linked to. The internet was the perfect vehicle in order for his embittered provocations to be as far reaching as it could possibly be because there was no escape mentally. All of this was whirring around in my mind on repeat until a text came in. Ping!

It was Teen, describing Furran in such a way that is unprintable and it made me snort with laughter. Then, I would be perked up for the next stretch of precious time and I would sweep Rex up in my arms and kiss his head and hold his tiny feet and marvel at his toes and fingernails. Perfect baby.

Once my mind was on the trail of the scope of harassment, it became overwhelming. I would start to think about people seeing the websites and feelings of sadness, violation and isolation started kicking in. And then I would yo-yo in my mind from the extra special time to the afflicted cruelty. Such a contrast. This stage, in particular, of escalating attacks on me were bringing out an annoyance in me because of the poignancy of the time - a brand new healthy blessing such as our baby. We were so lucky and it was a magical. A time to cherish. A time for us. A time I didn't take for granted. And I didn't want it spoilt in any way. We would never get back this time. I didn't want it in my memory attached to one of the most magical times in my life.

And I had this madman, disgruntled and vengeful, fighting with all his might to try and bring me down after 4 stupid dates because of his ego. I didn't want unpleasant feelings toward anyone in my heart. It just went against my nature and it was forcing me to feel unfamiliar and negative emotions. He could be angry and vengeful and all of whatever he was going to be but he wasn't going to bring it out in me, as much as I could feel it there, bubbling up to the surface.

This was our time. He had no place near us. I pleaded to the Universe to make him stop. I channelled my strategy plan. 'Keep your power. Keep the faith that it will be over soon'.

CHAPTER TWENTY FOUR
Alone on an island

Looking into the eyes of our gorgeous Rex - I embraced nurturing him, loved him with all of my heart and I would tell myself that nothing could penetrate those thoughts. This love was more powerful than anything that Furran was conniving.

Steve was away so often and for months at a time that my memories of him home were poignant and bittersweet. It was so hard for him to be away from his little lad and it hurt my heart.

We didn't have heating or hot water and only a wee kitchen in our little 300 year old cottage because renovations had halted for a while, since our baby had come along. We had this huge open fire. I would fill a baby bath with hot water from the kettle and cold water from the tap and I would bathe him by the fire.

Mama came over for days on end to help and enjoy our little chap. I had great faith in the restorative power of nature and we are blessed to live near an abundance of natural surroundings. So, we would take long walks around the countryside and village lanes, with him in a papoose or his pram. It was always sunny from my memory - walking with my Mama, smiling at our boy.

An influx of dear visitors would come and go and Rex took every ounce of energy I had. I devoted myself to him. I had to have him always by my side. Always, at the back of my mind, I didn't know what was on Furran's curriculum. Just the thoughts that one day, Saul Furran was going to get inside our home. Accompanying the tranquility not too far away, was the dread and fear of what was happening online, what had happened physically and what may happen any moment.

I say that Saul Furran didn't have power over my life but it would have been extremely difficult for it not to be affected, especially when I had a baby to protect and Steve was away so much. Fear and protection took hold of me even more so when Rex was born and being in fight or flight mode was the new norm.

The police emailed me back about the registrations that I had forwarded to them as evidence, asking when I wanted to see a police constable but I put them off. I really didn't want to go through the story again, only to be asked what I wanted them to do or be told that until he did something physically, there was nothing they could do. It only added to the feelings of despair and exhaustion.

So, it was now 4 years and 9 months of no help with stopping him from escalating his putrid creations. Along with constant reminders that he wasn't going away; insinuations that he was thinking all the time about how to go about persecuting me.

I tried the Citizen's Advice Bureau one day. Even though I knew that they needed guidance in order to understand me by way of previous incidences, it was a practical exercise to reach out for assistance. Albeit aborted. They couldn't rely on references to be guided by, because at that time, there was nothing about online harassment, stalking online, online abuse, cyber-bullying, online trolling and doxing and all of that.

There weren't support groups, forums, lawyers, solicitors, help and advice, guidance websites, stories of other targets and victims…nothing to reference at all, which always made me feel so isolated and like I was in another world. When they asked me to repeat myself, that familiar dampening of discouragement came over me. This would be another body of people that would be asking me what I wanted them to do.

I was put on hold and I could hear the lady asking someone else if they knew what to do and then a muffled voice and a shuffle back to the phone and the expected, *'Have you tried the police?'* response came. I suppose they cannot presume that I would have tried them first…and over and over?

Frustrated by the fact that nobody could help, I didn't have the energy or patience to explain again what I was going through.

It was rather complex, as it wasn't just one thing. Broken down, each thing was so convoluted that each thing required a lot of attention. So I thanked them and left it.

CHAPTER TWENTY FIVE
Explosions of intrusions

It was approaching five years now and Rex was five months old. Steve went off again for three months. It was so supportive of Mama to be there for us, as always and we booked a trip to Barcelona to celebrate my 40th Birthday in January 2010. I was excited for us to be going away. It always lessened the time that Steve was away, too. It snowed hard in England that weekend and all flights were cancelled from Bristol, so it wasn't to be.

Instead, we kept the fire going and cosied up until the storms passed but I ended up crying on my Birthday and Mama comforted me, presuming it was because of sleepless nights and Steve being away.

But the real cause was because I had just intended to log into Yahoo to get my Birthday messages from my friends and I had a brief optimistic thought that maybe it would all have disappeared. It was five years later, after all but no, on tapping my name into Google, I had received Birthday gifts from Saul Furran, too.

To my absolute chagrin, during a time of which should have held nothing but jubilations about reaching another Birthday, Furran had created another stinking website, along with refreshing existing ones:

www.anastylyingpieceofwork/lindseygoldrick.com, www.Nastylyingpieceofwork.com, www.lindseygoldrick.com, www.linzIGoldrick.com, www.lindseygoldrick.co.uk, www.lindseygoldrick.net and www.myanamcara.com/lindseygoldrick.

The content again: always able to slap me across the face with crass words, mocking and shocking. He had attached the same photographs of me and other low resolution pictures, that were obviously copied and pasted from somewhere online of where we had dinner and where we had walked. And the picture of the carpark where I last physically saw him.

The blandness of the images and the meaning behind them and the menacing pixelation, made them look even more sinister. The usual mixed bag of snarling remarks and encouragement to others to pile on some more harassment were there and I thought that he must be running out of material (and running out of steam, I hoped).

Then, devoting pages to some of my poems that I had written, was confusing initially since they hadn't been doctored by him but then I realised that it was control. As soon as I saw the title of one at the top: The Land of Milk and Honey, I gasped. I had shown him many. He had been interested. I must have been feeling daring, one day. My guard was down.

I expected a level of privacy when I emailed him. He had encouraged me to send some of those old poems and I had trusted that it would be okay to do that. Poetry was always so personal to me and they, like a journal, were words I didn't normally let go of. I had his word, yet remembered how I felt when my finger hovered over Send.

Worried about scrutiny and criticism. Fearing his thoughts would spoil my private pastime but I took the leap. I enjoyed our mutual sharing of things we appreciated at the time. He was another lover of poetry and words. Or was he?

It was only poetry and not a naked image, I know but… seeing those personal words in a place that was accessible around the world when I had been reluctant to share with one person, sent a volcanic rush of recoil through me. That shyness that I have. The privacy that I valued.

It doesn't matter that it wasn't defamatory and that it was my true work. It was all mounting up. The fact that he had now put my work in a public place alongside an explosion of pejorative diatribes about me that he had created, felt derisive and cruel.

Even the thought of anyone seeing or knowing anything about me, true or false - and the thought that people would express opinions, positive or negative, felt like I had lost a large part of myself that I would never get back. Something so precious, teamed with an attack on my character was violent. I had shared how much I valued my privacy with Furran. He knew this about me, so it was a determined, permanent, unforgivable act of cruelty. I couldn't recover it. Ever. It was irreversible.

I knew that my privacy was shot for life. I had protected it so much and so carefully, and it was gone forever now. It is hard to explain when you value your privacy so much. What I wanted to share was always in my control and only with people that I trusted. Always.

It was a continuous succession of intrusion explosions and exposure, to such levels of violation that I couldn't even begin to comprehend and I could not stop it.

Who knows what could possibly be going on in his mind? The background remained with my lipstick blotting and hair strand design that he so favoured and I shivered, thinking about what else he had taken that was mine!

What could be worse than my privacy, though?

CHAPTER TWENTY SIX
'Not a lot that we can do'

I knew how it would go when I called the police about the new sites; that it would be an arduous and fruitless exercise. On this particular day, I was feeling really quite depressed about it all. After five years of reporting it, I was hoping that something different would happen when I called them.

I really must have been the first person to be harassed online and certainly to have websites spread all across Google, I figured. Nobody knew what to do with me. The people that are meant to help everyone that have become a victim of crime, didn't know what to do because he was bobbing in and out of the country. So, they arrested him because harassment is a crime but they couldn't do anything because he hadn't physically hurt me. The bruising had to be seen for proof yet there was proof to see online.

Did they see it as different with it being online? For harassment to be committed, there must be two or more related occurrences that cause alarm or distress. Whether online or offline, the acts do not necessarily have to be threatening in nature. For as far as I could see, it was all harassment, no matter where it took place - and there was plenty of evidence everywhere. I got no sense through research and online investigations. I was exhausting all avenues and feeling desperate but also getting more despondent. No developments five years on.

I got the following information from my Crime Report in 2016 when gathering evidence and I had no idea that there had been an attempt: Avon and Somerset police passed it over to Sussex police, who then contacted the telecommunications unit with the aim of establishing how they could discover the IP addresses of the offending websites in an attempt to confirm the identify the creator of the websites. The telecoms unit, after checking out the new websites, said there wasn't any way of checking who owned them, as 'whoever had done it was technologically aware and had cleverly set them up so that they couldn't be found'. They said that a last resort would be to contact The High Tech Crime Unit or to seize the suspect's computer.

This wasn't pursued and there isn't anything to say why, other than suggesting that they may seize his computer when he returned from Europe. On reading this report when gathering evidence, I wish I had known that they had a High Tech Crime Unit that would deal with the internet. Nobody mentioned it. Of course it was reserved for the big stuff but I could have worked with them, given them my homework; told them of my ideas based on what I thought would work. It might have been easy work, had I had someone to work with. They may have known about disclosure orders, for instance, too which could have been used to confirm who owned the websites.

Anything was better than what was happening. Then it hit me - why had they not pursued it as 'the last resort'?

Wasn't there anything anybody could do? They checked with me that only the suspect, Saul Furran, had access to the emails and photographs that were on the website, other than myself. And was there anyone else that they could get a statement from? And so, Teen gave the police a statement. It felt so odd. It wasn't long ago that I had been telling her how excited I was about going to meet him. It felt rather pathetic, taking up her precious time as a result of my meeting a madman.

Reading more of the crime reports that dated back to this time in 2010, had me so confused. Sussex police stated that it was re-classified from a first time harassment to a full course of conduct in 2010. I had continually been reporting incidents related to the same case since 2005. So, after two reported occasions, it was a course of conduct of harassment. Which should have been in 2006, the second time of reporting... and not years later. Confused or not confused, I wasn't confused about how little anyone could do for me. That was clearly apparent.

Regardless, in April 2010 the police decided that, as they had found that Saul Furran was residing in Germany, the evidence related to the offence was probably 'beyond our reach given the geographical limitations for search powers' under the Police and Criminal Evidence Act 1984. Accordingly, the investigation was discontinued on 9th May 2010.

At that time that they discontinued the investigation, there were 18 websites under my name on the World Wide Web - at the least. It had been continuing, without pause, for 5 years and 3 months - and the investigation was discontinued. I felt deeply dejected, let down and thoroughly disturbed that there was no deterrent for Furran and no protection for me.

Was he in Germany though, right at that moment? He would have had to have come back several times to know that I was married and had a child because I wasn't posting my life events online. I was changing my email passwords too often for him to be able to hack again.

Why couldn't they be alerted by Border Control and that way, the police would know when he returned to the UK? All of that time going back and forth wanting to arrest him and then finally giving up. When a quick alert, email or call from Border Control would have saved so much police time. It didn't make me feel safer knowing that they had found him to be living in Germany.

DIARY ENTRY, 2010: *Tonight, Debs alerted me to two more websites: www.linzigoldrick.info and www.linzigoldrick.org. I thanked her for telling me and then dismissed it, changing the subject. I didn't want to ever talk about something that I was striving to get off to no avail. We were not seeing each other enough to spoil our time with him being in it. As if it degraded our conversation, somewhat. And he didn't get the honour of being part of our conversation. It was violating. 5 years of this.*

I haven't seen anyone's private information on any yet and each time, I expect it as well as always expecting more alerting phone calls. Because there wasn't any, I just presume that he is saving them for another time. Only he knows what his game is. He just doesn't want to let up on letting me know that he is still around; still vengeful; still trying to do something to me. What if I didn't have my constitution? If I didn't have the special people in my life? If I wasn't invited on holidays like we had just been?

We have just spent a couple of weeks sailing around the Greek Island of Paxos to celebrate Debs's Birthday. With her family, Rex and I. It was precious and meaningful, but like with everything, I cannot fully relax and it bugs me because life would be pretty damn sweet without his continual interruptions. Just the word 'online' jerks me back to the reality of his defamatory creations.

Oh and I was lying down by the water with Rex asleep on my chest and this lady commented on his blond curls. She must have asked where we are from and long story short, which is bonkers, on a Greek island, I meet the granddaughter of the lady who used to live in our cottage. She knew our cottage! She talked about the bread being baked in the inglenook fireplace and asked if there was still this and still that. She had loved our home, she said. Visiting Grandma. A stranger had loved our home long before we had, as a child and was talking of the poignant memories it held in her heart.

Only this morning, pictures that she had taken of us all swimming in the water, appeared in an envelope with a heartfelt note. Of course, she knew our address. Unexpected and sweet surprise. This morning, I was reminded that our home held a special place in many people's hearts. Many people had crossed our threshold, hearts full of good intentions. This evening, I was reminded about one person who had tried to cross the threshold with a heart full of bad intentions.
END OF DIARY ENTRY.

These two new websites had the same materials and the same format but just two new variations. He wasn't giving up. By now, any search of my name under any variation would show countless offensive and belligerent material about me.

111

I wrote to the chap at Nominet again that gave me a hopeful refusal '*at this time*' and reminded him that he had helped me temporarily last time but maybe something was in place now for a more permanent solution? I asked him to look at the sites. I really was clutching onto straws, and someone else responded, stating, '*There is not a lot that Nominet can do*'.

They explained that they can suspend and cancel domain names if they are not registered correctly but they were not internet regulators and cannot comment on how a registrant uses a domain name. They suggested the police and the citizens advice and Google, which I had done, of course but they also told me to try two other hosting sites' compliance departments, where they could see some of the sites were registered to. They may have regulations about the content of their websites, they explained. They gave me help. It meant a lot.

I wrote to those compliance departments and pleaded with them to remove or block the sites or ban the user and they didn't respond. I wrote again and again and told them that the owner of all of the website accounts was committing crimes using their services. I sent them links to the websites and I questioned whether it was acceptable. I didn't get a reply.

For six years, I had been asking Google to take down the websites, which I estimated at 6 times a year. So, 36 requests at least and after the first two years, they had turned into pleading emails. Nothing. I didn't have much hope but one day, they did remove two websites. I kept expecting the websites to come back again and they didn't.

So, why didn't they move all of them? Why those particular ones and how different were they than the others? There were sexually explicit ones still up. Was I only allowed a certain quota? I wrote to them, over and over and didn't get a response. However, I felt grateful for the two that they had removed, even though it flummoxed me. 2 down and 16 to go - at that point! Or so I thought.

CHAPTER TWENTY SEVEN
Remaining optimistic

During 2011, I plucked up the courage to tap my name into the internet with delirious optimism that they may have been removed based on my constant barraging to internet sites but sure enough, there would always be more websites. I didn't want the horror of them to cloud my elation of being a Mum.

So utterly blessed did I feel, sweeping my eyes over the divine child that Steve and I had created. I'd remind myself that he was more important; he had my attention now; he was the best distraction from all of that deliberately cruel stuff inflicted on me but at this point, there were 16 websites about me. What could I do? The police could not help. Who could help?

I couldn't cope with knowing what was on the latest sites because I was afraid to read any fresh news which confirmed that he was following us. I didn't go anywhere without Rex. I learnt to speed walk whilst looking over my shoulder whilst making sure I didn't trip with my child!

Anybody walking near us just made me so jumpy. Being in crowds felt horrendous. I would become breathless and I would sweat excessively. I could feel the beads of sweat coming from my boiling hot head. I felt like he was in the crowd and I wouldn't be able to escape. I would see him often but wasn't sure whether it was him or not.

Getting home when it was late always gave me a panic. I would dread getting caught in traffic or when the clocks went back and the shorter days. On return home, I would be holding Rex in my arms whilst checking behind doors, under beds, in the large cupboards and in the boot room. One room would have been sufficient to live in; not a whole house to check and worry about with lots of places for Furran to hide in.

There were too many areas to check and it would take me a long time, with my heart pounding and my stomach feeling like it was in my mouth. I felt so afraid, as I moved around checking around, with my massive, heavy-duty rolling pin in one hand and with the other, holding our baby's head protecting him from the possibilities of having to deal with Furran in the house. Remembering this, I shake my head at the extent of my fear and how four dates with a madman had led to this, where my whole life felt in jeopardy, for 6 years and counting.

When I had absolutely made certain that there wasn't anyone else in the cottage, I would then feel that it was safe to put Rex to bed. I would lie with him and put on some gentle piano music to soothe us both. Often, I would pitch up outside his bedroom door and to the background of music, I would open my laptop and start my search for help on the internet. Or practise yoga and do some deep breathing and meditation.

I knew what I had to do and that was to stay emotionally and physically balanced; to not buckle, to stay powerful and positive but it was all so very challenging for me - right to the core. With no sign of help on the horizon.

It was through no other basis than we needed the money that I was back at work part-time when Rex was 16 months old in 2011. I loved being at home with the precious boy and as you know, I risk contradiction by saying that we also went away as much as we could.

Switching from feeling that we needed to be having adventures ferociously and defiantly, living even more so, because Furran wasn't going to spoil our fun, coupled with the need for distraction. To then just wanting to feel safe in our four walls. Yet I didn't feel entirely safe, did I?

I had the knowledge that he knew where we lived etched in there, unfortunately. There was the fact that he was encouraging other stalkers and other abusers to join him in his tirade of terror against me. Who knew if he had succeeded in his recruitment? Any person that I saw looking at me or that were close by could have had ill intentions, having seen what he had published online. He published where I went and he published addresses. I felt sick, often.

Steve was away too often; too much.

CHAPTER TWENTY EIGHT
Upping the harassment

Mama had our little chap for the two days that I was at work and it would not have happened if she wasn't close by. She would love and occupy him, be watchful and be my substitute. He was in the safest hands, yet I couldn't switch off from worrying about the safety of both of them. My legs were like jelly the first few times he wasn't with me and I went to work with a perky look on my face and a peaky feeling about not being with Rex. It felt like real punishment. Thank goodness for my kind and obliging Mama, as always.

She would still often ask if I was okay, picking up on something greater than Steve being away. Seeing more than just my being on my own, being up through the night because Rex was a light sleeper and going back to work. Mama is a worrier, though. I couldn't tell her. I had to protect that beautiful heart and mind of Mama's.

Through sheer exhaustion, we pitched up one day and we stayed 3 days. Desperately needing some sleep and Mama being so utterly protective and loving us both, I could relax there. So cocooned and nurtured under Mama's care. So blessed and grateful, did I feel. Sleep. Glorious sleep. It was necessary.

We arrived and Rex was so excited to see Grandma and squealed with delight. Grandma was so much fun and loving and engaging. She played games all day long! And would sleep for hours when we left!:). Me? The same reaction as Rex but also tearful through lack of sleep and worry.

It was so easy to cry with so little sleep and a lot of anxiety. I think my hormones got blamed a lot. And I would cry more thinking about not talking about something so huge with my Darling Mum. We didn't have secrets. But this one wouldn't let her rest and there was no way on earth that Furran would have access to my Mama's heart, health and mind. He had already had too much, calling her and mentioning her on a website. As I type this, I get teary. I am so glad that I did not tell Mum. Controlling that was a really good plan.

When I couldn't fight it and sleep eventually took over, I would have nightmares about standing on the edge of a huge cliff and wobbling forward or even falling off. Sometimes I would be running but not getting anywhere or I would be locked inside a building but there wasn't a doorway or a window and no way of escaping. I would be chased down a never ending path by a man in a mask and wake up in a panic before he caught me.

To round off the year in 2011, to upscale his harassment, Saul Furran decided to utilise other websites to pile on the harassment. One in particular was called sexfodder.com. He submitted the newly embellished sites about me to this site in his endeavour to enlist a troll gang to join him in order to take the bullying to new heights.

My Brother found it one night and called me. It was a user-led website where users submitted sex sites. Other users and site visitors were goaded to analyse the sexual content and vote, with marks out of 10. Saul Furran had submitted www.lindsey-goldrick.com, soyouthinkyouknowlindsey.com and linzigoldrick-.co.uk. He had pimped them up even more, with the connotations that various copulation activities were a huge part of my vocabulary and my pastimes. I want to just add that they are not. I wish I had the energy. I jest - but the truth is, the webpages were sickening and gross.

According to his websites, I wore super short pvc skirts and long black latex heels. The image just makes me laugh out loud because they just wouldn't suit me. However, if I wanted to, I would have. Would that have made me provocative? Would that make me a good target for abuse?

The abuse had changed and shifted in that he was now intent on encouraging name calling and shaming to be targeted on me but he was objectifying women in short skirts that liked sex. This bothered me just as much. And he was encouraging bullying and ganging up. It was sexual violence.

He was given the highest score for invoking sexual arousal but a low score for format and design. You could leave comments online and on there, someone had written that I looked old. I said to myself, 'I absolutely feel it too. You should see me now…what's your name….Anne….what? ominous? Anne Ominous? Are you serious?' You can't make this stuff up, you know.

Lots of comments on there. It astounded me that anyone could produce any type of site, be free to do so and to be allowed to leave such lascivious comments on there. Which encouraged more from others.

Until someone had commented that it was obviously a psycho the person that had created them and someone else had responded, and I am guessing that a strong contender was my Brother, who wrote, '*What a sad wanker he must be that created this site*!'.

I talked it through with Teen. She would say all of the right things for me to ease my mind. She always had a different name for him that made me guffaw and wouldn't be as effective to read in black and white and like with many comedic situations like that, the moment in time couldn't be replicated. Her intent was to make me laugh and have reprieve. Nothing else mattered in that moment, other than having the usual good laugh with my cousin.

When I had put the phone down and I glanced at the site again, I had very unpleasant thoughts about Furran getting his comeuppance!

CHAPTER TWENTY NINE
Being stalked

As the police kept telling me that there wasn't anything they could do, in January 2012 (approaching 7 years), I decided to approach my local Member of Parliament. He took down a statement from me and then a few weeks later, I received a letter from him saying that having spoken to the local police, they said that there wasn't a case to answer to. Another let down.

If there wasn't a case to answer to, why had he been arrested and cautioned? The inconsistency was hard to bear. It was confusing and left me feeling quite abandoned by my own county police force.

So, I had a husband that must have felt extremely angry about what was happening, along with having work-related stresses. I had the joys of being a mother running parallel with the feelings of being heavily burdened with what the global public creations of horror were doing to me. I felt like I was in a vat of glue and I couldn't get out, desperately seeking air, life…escape.

If I didn't have the constant focus of our little fellow Rex, what would have happened? I felt like a shadow of what I could have been, I thought; a suppressed version of myself. I would write angry thoughts about him and then throw them in the fire. I didn't want anger in my life. I wasn't going to let that happen but despite being a gentle and passive nature, I knew that if anything happened to anyone that I loved because of him or his conduct, I would have hunted Furran down and not cared about the ramifications of what I did to him.

It was a struggle to leave the house some days and I became paranoid that it would not be long before Furran would call or email where I worked. He had done it before in the last place and he was monitoring me, so it felt inevitable. I only had to have

someone look at me twice or the phone ring at work and for
someone to look at me, whilst they were talking to someone else
on the phone and I would think it was him calling to prompt
them to check out the websites with the intent of bringing shame
to me and compromise my reputation at the company.

Even though I needn't explain that the websites were
created by someone as continuous vengeful acts of having finished a very short 4 date relationship, I was mortified by what he
had put on the net. People may believe elements of them, if not
all, I agonised.

My confidence took a regular nosedive and especially
when someone dear to me called that I wasn't in contact with
regularly. Like when Ian called one day. I was taken right back to
when he was telling me about the note that he had received about
the website, so my stomach knotted.

And it was just to invite Rex and I to his Chapel for
lunch because he hadn't met him yet. I said yes but I almost declined because I wasn't how he would remember me, I thought. I
put the phone down and reminisced.

I had met Ian on my return to the UK from America,
working alongside him at his Company. He was a leading figure
in architectural conservation and worked on many important
buildings in England. Soon after, I was assisting him, with a team
of building specialists restoring his home which was a chapel on
the Somerset Levels.

When work was done for the day and if he was home,
we would light the fire, have soup, share stories and play word
games or go out for a spin on his Ducatti. Or I would leave and
go home to Mama or Debs's for dinner in Dorset (I met Debs
when she was looking for someone to work with Ian and we
were instant friends. She invited me to take the job and she invited me for dinner with her lovely family).

Ian would ask for a lift to Scotland or London at a moment's notice for a party, a lecture or a meeting, so it wasn't ever
dull or predictable being in his company. I would listen to him
reciting sonnets that he had written for the woman in his life,

whilst I painted the walls lovingly with some distemper. Or angle grinding the lead off the altar railings to give him some privacy (or rather, incidental noise as background to his declarations of love).

Up on the mezzanine, where once people used to congregate to pray together, I would look out to the river that we often took his hot pink boat on. And across the levels through the windows, surrounded by the smell of damp wood, log fire, incense, old chapel and there would always be the smell of coffee bubbling on the stove and I would feel truly happy. I can smell that time now. Hectic and hilarious times.

I worried about seeing him because I wanted to remain as I was in his memory. I worried that the burden might be visible to him. But I missed him. He had been inviting us by email for a while. As I travelled there with Rex, I wondered what would have happened if I had taken the path of moving into his Chapel.

He had asked me to, just before I met Furran, purely for selfish purposes, he had said because I made it a happier place. I had gone over to discuss the possibility back in 2004 and we ended up not discussing it and watching cartoons, instead. I wonder what would have happened if I had moved in? I may have been too busy to join an online dating site, with his influx of visitors and parties.

Ian had invited other people that I hadn't met before that afternoon and it forced me out of my comfort zone. Rex was melting hearts and invoking laughs, as he ran around the Chapel. A thoroughly distracting afternoon.

We arrived home as it was going dark. When there wasn't anywhere to park close to our home at night, it meant walking down dark country lanes with no street lights. Babe in arm, bags strapped around my other and swinging off my neck, trying to walk quickly, turning around every few seconds, panting, quick steps, knots multiplying in my stomach and twigs breaking.

I recognise that this may all sound like paranoia but being stalked with constant shocks and surprises, that is what it made me feel like. Anything was possible. That is what the years of mental torture was doing to me.

Was he in the shadows? What was that noise? My pulse was rapid. The key wouldn't go in the door quickly enough and I had two locks to open. *'Please... Please let us get in safe'*. The keys would turn. My breathing laboured. We would get inside the house and I would think, 'Why is the landing light on?' And go and investigate, Rex clutching onto me. Trusting me. Relying on me to protect him from harm.

Shadows and noises were always there, if I listened or looked hard enough and whatever that noise is, it's the one that sounds like the one that I dreaded. I would eventually calm down, tuck Rex up and fall asleep, after a while.

I would wake in the night and want to nip to the loo but would spend ages wondering whether to take Rex with me. (Oh, those were the days when I could hold my bladder). Wake him or risk it? Dash and dare? That's so true. Then, I would speed to the bathroom and would run back quickly, regretting having gone and feel the same sense of relief he was still there, a mass of blond curls on the pillow, softly sleeping.

Again, there was a whole cottage to worry about with corners, shadows, alcoves, cupboards, tons of windows, doors, beds to hide under, lots of places to hide and places to watch. It all just felt too much. I would lie, desperately trying to hear noises over the sound of my audible heart beat, so protective of little chap, Rex.

CHAPTER THIRTY
A terrorising memory

Seven years on and I don't think I will ever forget this:

It is 9pm at night and I am on the rug by the open fire with a laptop on a cushion on my lap, in the sitting room, casting my eyes to the flames dancing in the fireplace and then back to tapping an email to my Husband Steve. I had just settled Rex, who was now 3 years old, having wrenched myself away from keeping watch by his side and double checking the doors and windows.

I wanted to let Steve know that we were fine, there was nothing to worry about and lots to be proud about with our son and send some brief cheery distraction. The fire was crackling but there is a noise in the other direction, coming from the front door and my heart pounds immediately, since dread and fear were never far away from thoughts and feelings.

The heavy velvet curtain that usually drapes across the door as an extra shield, had not yet been drawn across and I am just four metres away. My heart beat is so loud, playing alongside the pump, pump, pump of my eardrums pulsating. Sweat seeps out of my skin, making me feel clammy and I stare, waiting; knowing that something is going to happen but I am praying hard and willing it away.

Then, it happens.

The post flap opens and four gloved fingertips sit perched in the box. No! I am shaking and the room is whirring. It is happening tonight. This is the night when the police can help me. When I am dead.

As the door handle turns, sweat is dripping down my neck. It isn't my imagination. I can see the small paint splash that was at the top of the door handle move left. My hands are at my mouth and my breathing is audible and alien and so loud, it is as though someone else was by my side.

Did I lock the door? Oh my goodness. I don't remember locking it, even though I always check the locks. I didn't do it tonight, did I? The door is going to open any second now. He is going to kill me. He will be inside the house and that will be it. I need to get upstairs to Rex but I cannot move and my body is sinking into the ground rather than rising.

I open my mouth to scream but no noise is there. I try again - a strangled whisper. He can't hurt our boy. The pain that I feel at the thought, rips through me. Please Universe, protect Rex.

Fear is what I smell and taste next, I know. It smells hot…dirty….putrid, dry, urgent and intense and unearthly; something I haven't smelt before. It is not a smell that I expected to smell and taste time and time again.

But I did.

Amongst all of the smells, tastes, thoughts, ear popping, pumps of the heart and sweats and as my body would not stop shaking, my eyes were firmly fixed on the door, waiting. Deep breathing and silent prayers to the Universe. Please, don't open the door. Please don't open the door. Please go away.

How long I sat making deals with the Universe, I do not know but the door didn't open.

It had most definitely happened but I must have locked it, since I have been in the habit of checking at least ten times that I have locked it, when we are inside our cottage but I couldn't trust that. By the time I was able to move, I was shivering - the fire had died down and I could hear our boy rousing.

Shaking in the aftermath and feeling freezing cold, I dragged the sofa to sit behind the door, checked that the door was definitely locked and ran to Rex and kissed his cherubic powder sweet cheeks with tears running down my face. Extreme fear to extreme love in moments.

Then I dialled 999 and told the police, with what felt like cotton wool in my mouth, about what had just happened.

Again, I had to explain what had been going on, right from the beginning and it felt torturous for it was taking too long. They sent someone over later on that night and I could barely open the door, with the dread that I felt and I began telling my story again, to a female officer. Even though they had a report, I had to begin at the beginning.

I wasn't surprised to be told that there was nothing that they could do, so why had I bothered? Fight or Flight mode kicked in pretty darn heavily that night.

This night has been relived in recurrent nightmares for 15 years, in and out, over and over because it was so frightening. In those dreams, the handle would turn and a gloved hand would come through the letterbox and the door would be pushed open and a masked man stood in the doorway. The little sleep that I was getting was flourished with nightmares that would wake me up with a scream.

Feeling totally safe at home had been compromised definitely now and I took solace in the fact that we had many close neighbours that we could run to at any time of the day or night. In particular, our wonderful neighbours across the street had said many a time, if I needed them at whatever time of the day, or even want to stay over, we could. This was without them knowing anything and the feeling of reassurance brought tears to my eyes. It was precious to know.

Often, the phone would ring with 'Unknown Caller' and I would sit rigid, just watching it ring.

'Nothing we can do' just reverberated around my head.

It was now 7 years and 3 months since the start.

Just for the record, changing our number was the least of my concerns. The phone consistently ringing directly to me was nothing compared to the internet being accessible to anyone, anywhere all over the world, 24 hours a day.

CHAPTER THIRTY ONE
Lost keys

DIARY ENTRY 2012: *I was invited out the other night to a gig with Debs at the weekend and Mama babysat but it was hard work staying awake and being how I used to be; all lively and full of laughter, like I always was. I managed to still be that smiley, lively person that laughs a lot when I am not alone and dealing with this but on occasion, I just can't muster it up. Maybe I just felt like it was okay to go out with Debs as I was, for she knew it was all going on but didn't bring it up unless I did. I don't want to talk about how I really feel; giving it energy by sharing. I can contain it if I just offload here, pen to paper, letting my pen meander along scratching out my pensive thoughts, expunging them from my body; detoxifying.*

The musicians were fabulous the other night but my body just wouldn't move to it but Debs and Tamara were dancing freely; beautifully, majestically and it made me realise how this is affecting me.

I would have been right there, normally; feeling the energy buzzing around my blood. If not letting the music take my mind and body away, I might have been compelled to do a little comedy dancing. I just didn't feel up to any of it; my feet glued to the floor; my mind adhesively stuck on what I had seen earlier that day online. It was unshakeable. It would have been a really entertaining night but I left just feeling so deflated and like I am rubbish company, and wondered if I would ever feel the same lightness again. Such conflicting emotions. It feels like my light has gone out, this week.

Spookily, when I wrote that last bit, I nudged the table and the lamp just fell off the table and crashed, making a huge noise and I understand the saying 'shot out of my skin'. Jumpy does not explain it. I think he is close by, ready to attack, all the time. This isn't right.
END OF DIARY ENTRY.

At work one Friday in 2012, I was rummaging around for something in my bag and had to empty in and then noticed that my front door keys were not in my bag. I searched the car. I had to retrace my steps and go home. I don't remember the drive home. I was so anxious. I parked exactly where I had drove away from that morning and I scrutinised the lane back to the cottage, and even recruited the village groundsman who was working in the churchyard. I stopped by the post office.

They had been handed in but they didn't know who had handed them in, they said. Nor could they remember what he had looked like but it wasn't a villager and it was definitely a tall, dark-haired male. *'Never seen him before,'* they said. Oh my goodness. Nooooo! 'I wish I hadn't, either', I thought and was very aware that I was shaking and it was noticed. *'I haven't had my B vitamins this morning and rushing around, worried about my keys....'* And a stifled laugh filled with nerves... 'Ridiculous*,'* I said to myself.

And I left the post office, passing the redundant telephone box and looked at it wondering if it had been a fugitive's hideout that morning. For the criminal that was committing crimes on me from wherever he wanted to around the globe and always running. No deterrents to stop him. I searched my mind for scenes from the morning.

The scenario went through my mind: seeing myself as we left the cottage and veered around the corner. Had I looked across to the telephone box? No, I doubt it. We had passed the bus shelter. There was a figure in there sat down, hood up. I hadn't thought at the time. We would have been rushing. Always rushing. Never too busy to not say hello, though. Most people pottering around the village say some sort of greeting.

I imagined that I had dropped them anytime at that point, as I would have been scrabbling with bags. Always, lots of bags-laptop, lunch bag, school bag, PE bag...laden down....and he was close by, watching as they dropped....his lucky day.

He picked them up and waited to see our car drive out of site and then had come into the house and looked around and did goodness knows what. Someone must have seen him. We all look out for each other. Oh goodness me. Or, had he copied them? Had he had time to make an impression of them? Of course, of course. But, it was taking a chance, wasn't it? He knew that I was married to a strapping man. Unless he knew that he was away for certain, somehow.

I entered our home timorously and was immediately spooked by a regular loud noise and then realised it was my breathing. I was terrified. *'Come out. I am not scared of you!'* I screamed. My voice surprised me. It was loud and primal. I felt like a warrior but also petrified. I stomped around the sitting room, pulling back the curtains and shouting, *'I am stronger than you!'*. I felt full of rage and it was surprising me how I felt and my voice didn't sound like mine.

I marched around the kitchen and grabbed a cast iron pan and then on out into the hallway, looking in every recess; every cupboard; through every door; behind the coats; up the stairs….stomping, breathing heavily, pushing the bedroom door open and looking under the bed and looking behind me, ready to strike, walking around and onto the landing and another room and so on and eventually, I felt calmer. He wasn't there.

What was I thinking? I went back upstairs and back into the bedroom and checked the set of drawers. They were all open. I don't know whether this was just paranoia but I do know that my life was compromised because of Furran and it made me feel sick and depressed, thinking about how I could not control his actions over my everyday life and how my every day was affected in some form.

We needed new locks now and quickly. I drove to work, crying and as my mind started to go down a depressing, melancholic thought route, that mechanism that I had taught myself, clicked in and brought me back to 'Think positively and brightly. You are nearly at work. Snap out of it, Linz. You will not be defeated. He is not going to win. He will not have any more power over you.'

I arrived at work, took a deep breath, collected myself and walked through the doors, smiling and laughed, rolling my eyes indicating what a klutz I was and commented that they had been handed in to the post office.

I told Steve about my mislaying my keys but nothing about my anxiety about it or the fact that I felt Furran could have actually been in our house. I didn't want to convey how scared I was all of the time. He had enough to cope with but it must have been on his mind, continuously too and our safety was obviously never far from his mind.

That weekend when he came home, he changed and reinforced the locks on the cottage and put a locking door at the bottom of the stairs. We ordered secondary glazing and fitted all windows with locks. It felt more secure but the reality was that I did not feel thoroughly safe anywhere now and after that incident, it was even harder to get to sleep.

The thoughts on my mind when I went to bed were wondering whether he would actually succeed in breaking in one day and take it further. And whether the night that I didn't wonder what was on the internet about me the next day, would be that succeeding night. When thoughts were no more.

CHAPTER THIRTY TWO
The level of fear

Seven years of anxiety and fear was taking its toll. Close friends started to enquire more if I was okay and why I wasn't accepting invitations. They wondered why I was so tired at times. Of course, I couldn't explain. I didn't want to. It was easier to just put it down to motherhood and being on my own so much. Sleep was a commodity and that didn't help. If I heard a noise in bed, I would lie rigid, feeling fearful and convinced that he had broken into our home. Rex and I slept in the same room. I did not want him out of my sight.

I would lie, waiting for any further noises and sometimes, I would go and investigate but mostly, I lay with my heart pounding, planning how I would protect him and how I would fight anyone off. I still had my rolling pin at the side of the bed that I would be clutching as I lay there (by the way, it was brought to my attention that a rolling pin might not have been the greatest defence weapon. But this thing was as large and as heavy as a baseball bat. It is without handles and is 26 inches of solid oak).

It would pack a good defence. If I could swing it when under duress, that is. I had many dreams that I wanted to run but I was stuck. Or wanted to scream and nothing came out. Or tried to move my arms and they would be leaden. Hell, some of my dreams had my eyes stuck in one position. Fear could render all faculties, I worried.

Sometimes, I couldn't hear any other noises but the pounding of my heart and my heavy breathing, which sounded like someone else's and eventually, I would sleep. Then I would wake, feeling defenceless and mortified. I wanted to wake up and grab the day like I used to but thoughts on my mind going to sleep and the first, when waking up were, 'I wonder what crudities were attached to my name and out on the global media platform today for the whole world to see?'.

Giving the illusion of full control whilst focusing on what I could control, felt exhausting though. It certainly felt harder being at home alone with our child and I certainly would have felt safer if Steve was home every night.

The same year in 2012, I had the nerve to tap my name into the internet again and a new website had been made: www.valentinesdayinthenewforest.com. For goodness sake! It was over 7 years ago! The fourth and final date. It contained more fabricated rubbish and the heading: 'I ended it with him on Valentine's Day in the New Forest', implied that I had said that and in a boastful way too, which is just something I would not do or say. It is not in my nature.

But where had he got that from? This was not a quote of mine. There were several quotes and I did recognise some from emails that I had sent to Ames. I had only written words to her about ending the relationship but not words that sounded like I was gloating. It was puzzling me and frightening me. I was still continually changing my email passwords but that didn't matter if he had gathered so much in that first hacking session.

*　　　　*　　　　*　　　　*

The first day of pre-school in September 2012, was for 2 hours only. Great for Rex for interaction with other children and to get into the mode of school. Primary school started full-time as soon as he turned 4 years old. Too soon for me. Too far away for comfort. Sure, we had chosen it because it was safe, confined, secure, with many staff but I didn't know what was on Furran's agenda. One hundred and twenty minutes not in my sight was one hundred and twenty minutes too long.

Of course, nobody knew that I needed Rex watched over. Like a hawk. Furran's obsession with feeding his vengeance kept me on tenterhooks. Conveying my fears would have had Rex being treated differently, thus affected by Furran's actions.

He had to have as normal a time as possible. I had to take a leap of faith and so, I dropped him off, in a dithery fashion and wobbled away.

And sat in the car, with the building in sight, composing cheerful notes, messages of love and funny little riddles to send to Steve to make him laugh. No cause for concern. No need to know.

I want to repeat that: I watched the pre-school building for two hours, twice a week, for weeks…for…goodness…sake!

When my secret was over, I laughed with other mums, '*I'm so over-protective and pathetic, aren't I?*'. Looking back, they must have thought that I was nuts. I didn't notice the raised eyebrows and shocked faces at the time.

They were probably frozen in disbelief.

Insecurity and a constant state of alert kept me on my toes…and kept me paranoid!

CHAPTER THIRTY THREE
Gratitude journal

Perseverance in searching for help online at every opportunity, thankfully never left me. I would find help eventually. I wrote to American criminal lawyers that sounded like they could possibly help, or perhaps put me in touch with a comrade in England but didn't get a response. I wrote to a private investigator that bore the same surname as me, with the pitiful, pathetic hope that he might feel some kind of connection with me and get in touch. No response.

I could not find anyone online in the UK that seemed to deal with what I was going through. Everyone just told me to go to the police. And the police are still saying after 8 years, 'What do you want me to do?'. It was beyond frustrating.

It is just my nature to question and try and find answers, so I would often wonder what the lessons were concerning Saul Furran entering my life. I know that I gravitated to the best in people and often overlooked any negatives. I always love to wear my rose-tinted spectacles! I thought of how some people are with us for a season, a reason or a lifetime. I just didn't know what category he came under, if he had to come under one at all.

A season suggests a pleasant start to finish and then just disappearance, to me. A lifetime was out. A reason? What was that reason? I didn't need to go through anything to appreciate any thing or any one more than I do. Perhaps I was meant to change his life? He certainly has changed mine but why? Seeking meanings wasn't making him stop, though. Perhaps it would all make sense one day, I decided. That I was to do good things with it and turn it around, maybe?

Now everyone deals with constant stress differently and have different coping mechanisms. I had my coping strategy as a guide but depending on the day was how I dealt with it. So, it varied. I just know that you need something and not one size fits all. What I found incredibly helpful and accessible and involving very little effort with very powerful effects was a gratitude journal.

I started doing daily gratitude rituals, which included lighting a candle to give it a ceremonial feel. I would send a wish whilst watching the flame. I would give thanks for the best things in my life and the people that I treasure and for their good health and safety. For the roof over our heads, clean water, good food and a job. I had so much goodness around me and that felt powerful.

These little rituals kept me feeling emotionally balanced and in my Gratitude Journal I wrote every other day about moments, things around me, memories and people that I was grateful for. Such as:

'Grateful for friends and fun memories. Maria reminded me of a laugh out loud day when we had pitched ourselves happily on the beach in Southern New Jersey and then realised that we were the wrong clientele for that beach, were too frozen to move, too overdressed and ended up getting kicked off for giggling so much'.
My dear Maria. We heard each other speaking in a bar in America (she's British, too) and gravitated towards each other and ending up laughing our socks off. We have lost a lot of socks through the years.

'For seeing Nichola, who is a sister to me'. (my Brother's girlfriend through my teens). We kept in touch. She - demure, feminine and pretty. Me - cheeky, walked like my Dad and from the photographs, doing everything I can to make myself look as unattractive as possible. *'As we have grown, I have appreciated her kindness, her warmth, friendship and presence more and more'.*
'Getting a really funny letter in the post from my cousin Karen'. I have received many from her since I was small. Every

one, treasured. Every one, I still have. And they still make me laugh out loud. It's in her DNA to be entertaining, inventive and hilarious. I often say that she should have her own online channel. '*Grateful for my thoughtful, warm, brilliant, trusted cousins*'.

'*For memories of holidays. I found an old photograph today. Faded and overexposed. From the 70s. Taken on an old Instant - and I was there in an instant. We had all just walked around The Great Orme in Wales. Mama, Dad, my brothers and I. We are all smiling, squinting in the sunshine apart from Dad, who was mid-speech. I could smell the suntan lotion and the leather and bergamot from his cologne. The taste of the ice cream was in my mouth, as the warmth from the sun and being in my family cocooned me in that moment.*

Childhood was love, nurture and fun and squabbles with my precious Brothers. Mama, looking stylish, as always with her big, beguiling smile. Memories took me further. I thought of Dad coming home from work, picking me up and twirling me around. Nan, dancing me up the hall. Uncle Art, Aunty Bea, Aunty Maggie and Aunty Pauline…so much warmth and fun. My smile is going to stretch off my face in a minute. All of these things were the big things that shaped me. Love much, laugh lots and look for the joys. Be kind, help people, don't be so serious, eat well, be honest, respect people, work hard and earn a break. Free fun - use your imagination and have adventures, travel as much as you can and get something out of every day. The sun always shined. Never, ever taken for granted. I am lucky for being born into my family'.

The people throughout my life meant the world to me and each and everyone were no doubt mentioned in my journal. Thoughts of them distracted me, as I felt pure happiness in those moments. It would lead me down memory lane and I would get lost there for a while. It wasn't just memories, though, as I said. I posted on there about being grateful for our village community and morning cups of freshly ground coffee.

On one page of the Gratitude journal, I simply wrote:

'*I am grateful for waking up*'.

It is only when something is threatened can you sometimes imagine what it will be like without it.

Waking up every morning was something that I wasn't taking for granted.

CHAPTER THIRTY FOUR
Focus on the good things in life

Seeking solace where I could was also imperative for my mental state. I would sit and meditate and visit happy places in my mind and there, I would go to deserted beaches with the softest sand and the water was warm and clear. Or a dusty library room that I am not sure whether it is a memory or imagination. It is book-filled, so it makes me instantly calm.

Being outdoors, travelling and changes of environment were saviours, too. Being amongst nature or a different culture with different smells, food, colours, landscapes and languages gave respite. Also a different perspective. I am incredibly lucky that I have been and felt able to travel lots to many different countries.

As I said before, Mama always instinctively knew what I needed and she was always up for an adventure, anywhere. The change of scenery was good for us both. In many ways for us, not being in one place at any one time felt safer, some times. Precious time together, too and Mama is amazing company. Distraction, when I couldn't change things, were a crucial part of the coping strategy, as was one day at a time.

There wasn't any good in focusing on things I could not get help with changing. I felt grateful for the area where we lived and being able to nip to the coast and feel the sea breeze and watch the waves. A ferocious need to keep feeling like I was living well was something I could totally keep control of.

And through it all, my sense of humour didn't escape; the burden lifting companion that never left my side/our side. The ability to still laugh out loud and seek out fun and silliness daily, despite the draining horror was a healing force. I am so grateful that it didn't disappear. Goodness. Despite my times acknowledging feeling fed up and isolated from real help, the dark clouds dissipated when something invoked comedy. The most important things in life were bigger than acts of silly vengeance.

There was a lot to smile about by focusing on the best bits in my life. I always think that if you can smile, it is transforming, all around. When you smile and someone smiles back, it is a joyous, far-reaching, contagious feeling with longevity. Smiles lift your heart up and you can see genuine ones in the eyes of others. The power of a smile is transformative and powerful. I certainly wasn't taking them for granted.

Many times, being inside the cottage felt like the safest place to be for us, despite the invasion. Throwing myself into nurturing our home was good therapy. Painting and changing rooms and colour schemes made me feel that I wasn't stagnant. That as quick as a room transforms by paint, so life can be the same way, too. It could all change tomorrow, I would dream.

Messages spun out to the Universe while I painted as I listened to upbeat dramas on the radio and funny quiz shows. Desert Island Discs. Music stations. I would sing out, chant, meditate and loose myself in lyrics. Chorus lines adapted to transport me to the time when it was over. 'It's all going to be magnificent'. Different genres turned up to max, blasting through the cottage. Negative energies exorcised, pumping up the power. Endless artists and endless music, soothing my soul. Love and peace swirling around us and protecting us and one day, this would be all over. I had a lot to be grateful for.

The gleeful thoughts that I had were not going to change. Small things brought me pleasure and there were huge pleasures with a child in our lives.

Nobody was going to take any more of my control away. Sticks and stones may break my bones but names will never hurt me.

Days like these were rejuvenating. Days like these gave me more determination to live as well as we could. Looking forward to the day that it would end. Visualising walking free with a skip in my step again. Those were the days when I felt strong. Nothing would stifle my spirit. Imperative to coping strategies.

Then there would be days when I felt so dejected and dulled with the burden of it all, I would find myself crying in the bath.

CHAPTER THIRTY FIVE
'Someday baby, it's gonna be alright'

I wasn't sure when Saul Furran was stalking me physically but as I have alluded, I saw him frequently. Whether it was really him or just a figment of my sleep-deprived, tormented mental state, I won't know. His conduct comprising of 8 years made me feel watched and fearful all the time. Being on the move felt safer. Sometimes.

I would leave the house in a ridiculously high state of alert. I would look left. I looked right. I locked the door. Two locks. Checked they were locked. Look to the left and to the right again. Did I lock the back door? Open the door again. Lock the door behind me. Through the house. Yes, it is locked. Back out again. To the end of the road. Looking over my shoulder. Who is that over there? Walking to the car. Looking around. Did the incense stick burn out? Did I unplug the iron? Did I lock the front door? Back out of the car and towards the house, I would go.

I recall being at the kitchen sink one night in 2013, washing a glass and looking at my reflection in the window above the sink and seeing the toll of nervous strain on my face and wondered if I would have looked this aged if I had never let Saul Furran into my life?

I wondered what would have happened if I hadn't signed up on that dating site. If I had never responded to that strange man, where would I be now? What if I had responded to the chap that wanted to do a compatibility test before we continued writing? Or the doctor? Would I be travelling extensively?

If I had taken a different path, would I be stood here in the cottage that I share with Steve? Would I appreciate his solid character, his decency, goodness and his rationale quite so much? Without doubt, we would have met somewhere and Rex was so meant to be. I couldn't even contemplate for that to be an option. Would I be as present as I am with Rex? Mental thoughts demanded, *'What happened to you, Furran, to make you do what you are doing?'* I couldn't stand that I was trying to find an excuse for him and that he was in my thoughts, so much.

Beyond my reflection, I could see the bush directly to the left of the window in the garden and at the corner of my eye, there was a quick movement outside.

A mass of white noise flourished my head as I saw his face and I dropped the glass, screaming.

It was real!

It felt real!

I will not ever know whether it really was, to be honest. I won't ever know whether this was my mind playing tricks on me or whether Furran really was in the back garden because I was too petrified to investigate.

Regardless, it felt as real as real could be.

I dropped low to the floor and crawled along through the hallway and upstairs to be by Rex's side. I lay with my body pounding with adrenalin and fear, the whole night, wishing both the landline and mobile phone were not downstairs - and too scared to fall asleep.

Like I mentioned, the up days ran alongside the down days but only visible and felt by me (I think), since I was trying to do a good job of showing up, as I had promised myself. It was sometimes so hard to feel inspired and not be disappointed and resentful, when I had felt ambitious and excited about what I had intended to achieve, only for that to be taken from me, all of those years ago.

People expecting me to be lighthearted though, was a good thing. It pulled me out of slipping down in public. I focused on the creative side of the work in my role at work, on the marketing and advertising side, as much as I could. After filling the websites with information, images, calls to action and technical specs, I was fixated on optimising them in order to watch them climb Google and overtake competitors, as I have mentioned. It's what website content creators do all the time without thinking now, I know.

All the while, I was still wondering if I could somehow saturate the internet with positive things about me and push the horrible things down. Umpteen websites and counting were a lot to compete with, though. I didn't know that it was actually almost double that. Especially as all of them used every variation of my name to the maximum.

Furran had done a good job on search engine optimisation to maximise the harassment on me. It was too much to contemplate. I wrote to various IT companies and asked them if they could offer any scope or ideas on what to do. I didn't hear back.

*   *   *   *

Around this time, Ian died and news about my sister-in-law's terminal illness came through. Too devastating to express. The day that I found out, I received an email from an unknown email address.

'*Someday, baby - It's gonna be alright. Someday, maybe, but baby, not tonight. There's a gleam in your eyes, That's for some other guy not for me now. He'll be kissing the lips that I just get to kiss in my dreams now*'.

Lyrics from Neil Diamond. Saul Furran had grown up with Neil Diamond, too. It was obviously him but I wasn't going to reply back. His pathetic behaviour in comparison to uncontrollable life's tragedies really angered me. It was now entering into the 9th year of dealing with his vindictive, deranged acts and alongside the devastating news that I had heard of illness and death of close people to my life, I felt so bitter towards Furran.

He had his health (I presumed) and he was choosing to spend his days violently attacking me on the largest platform in the world but from hundreds of miles away. Placed and com-

142

pared alongside two people that had illnesses inflicted on their precious lives, bravely facing every day emphasised his cowardice.

Surprisingly enough, I didn't have any inclination to report the email to the police. It would be like carrying water to the sea. Absolutely pointless. The situation and lack of resources of them not knowing what to do, even after all these years, was ridiculous and the frustration I felt was insurmountable.

It would be logged with the knowledge that it wouldn't come to anything despite recording it down; without the scope for help. Surely I wasn't the only one going through this and yet, it seemed that I was. It felt so isolating. I didn't have the time to spare wasting it on pointless exercises. I had to be efficient with my energy. Much better to do something more productive with a positive outcome instead. So, I painted a wall and watched it dry.

And Ian's funeral came. He had chosen Debs and I and four other women to be pallbearers. We were to wear his favourite colour: hot pink. A 'celebration of life day' but taken too young. We all wanted more of a special, highly regarded and unique man. Inside and outside, the church and its grounds packed with mourners. Collective hearts heavy. I see him now. I hear him. Thoroughly wicked and thoroughly decent. So blessed to know him. He had such an appreciation for people; for fine things; for fun.

Funerals. Sombre and reflective. I missed my Nan and my Dad terribly but I carried them in my heart, so they were with me every day. Lucky to have had 13 and 30 years respectively with them. Some people don't get 13 seconds of a great Nan or Dad, let alone those amount of years. I could hear their voices in my head all the time, humming a tune...pointing out the humour in things. Guiding me.

Times like funerals make you take stock of your own life, don't they? Feeling lucky and blessed, I wanted to hold everyone tighter that was in mine.

Apart from one.

CHAPTER THIRTY SIX
'All I want for Christmas'

Not long after in October 2013, Steve went away on HMS Illustrious in the Oman. He was due to be home for Christmas and the ship would be turning around in November heading home. Then, disaster struck in the Philippines. Typhoon Haiyan had caused ineffable disaster on the island and the ship was deployed to help give humanitarian aid via the Sea King helicopters. Steve called. He wouldn't be home for Christmas, as they would be there for a while and as it took 6 weeks for the ship to sail home, it would be a January homecoming at the earliest.

I had asked Rex previously what he wanted for Christmas. He had just started Primary School at 4 years old. All he wanted for Christmas was his Daddy home. I remember driving him to school, tears running down my face, as I kept explaining that Daddy couldn't get home because he was doing a tremendous thing and helping deliver blankets, tools and water to the people in Philippines but we would celebrate him being home after Christmas. He insisted that that was all he wanted for Christmas. It was heartbreaking.

I had previously bought 4 tickets for Santa's steam train excursion across the Mendip hills in Somerset and had decided that I would give Steve's ticket away and just Mama, Rex and I would go. The disaster was all over the news and Rex would scan the papers looking for Daddy and he would ask to watch the news on the TV, avidly, to see if he could see him.

It was so heart-rending. I was so proud of our country's assistance with such a disaster but I couldn't help yearning for Steve to be home for his son's sake.

Days away from Christmas, I got a call from Steve whilst at work. He had a plane ticket. They had done all they could and they were given a ticket to get home for Christmas. It was beyond elating!

I called Mama and we agreed to keep the surprise for Rex and she came to babysit when I went to pick him up at an airbase. I went ahead of Steve on arriving home and announced to Rex, who was cuddling with Grandma at the time, that Father Christmas had heard him and look who he had sent home.

In walked Steve and our darling boy gasped and rushed to him, '*Daddy*!'. Tears of complete elation.

I cry every time that I recall this.

Rex may always believe in the powers of Father Christmas!

We went on Santa's Express train and when Santa came up to Rex in the carriage, Rex just looked at him and said, '*Thank you for bringing my Daddy home!*'. I was filming for the reaction of the sight of Santa and didn't expect this. We all cried. The film is shaky, due to my being choked up.

Santa asked in a strong Somerset accent, '*What did you say, my Love?*'

And I told Santa, with a choked up voice, that Rex was thanking him for bringing Daddy home for Christmas.

Pure. Joy.

This was affirmation to me that despite all the odds against, a positive ending is possible at a moment's notice and to never give up hope.

Such extreme joys were experienced but they were always dulled by the continuum of Furran's vengeful, crass productions on the web and the terrorising calling cards to remind me that he was close by…watching…waiting.

CHAPTER THIRTY SEVEN
A nasty piece

For my Birthday in 2014, we were going to see our friends Jo and Steve in Wales, straight from work.

I had made the huge mistake of checking Google, as it was becoming a common theme to receive Birthday surprises from Furran (9 years and counting). The tormenting curiosity of not knowing what to expect somehow overrode the desperate need to not ruin the weekend.

So, I tapped my last name only into the search engine.

There it was in full glory: a new creation from Saul Furran.

My chest slammed between two clamps, as I sat rooted to the chair. The prickly feeling of heat all over me as rolls of nausea accompanied the anchor that had just dropped in my stomach. Boom, boom, boom. My pulse was audible to all, surely? I looked around the office. I wasn't alone.

Urging my chin to stop wobbling and my jaw to stay shut, I begged the tears not to drop, as the clamp on my chest got tighter.

A picture of my face took up a third of a large laptop screen.

Not quite satisfied with numerous offensive websites about me, he had bought an advertisement banner. You didn't need to click on the ad in order to see the large photograph of me, at the top of Google. (I haven't seen advertisements with images at the top of Google since).

The link was large enough to see:

Check out: www.aboutus.org/anastylyingpieceofwork.-com.

You know when you have seen in a film where a painted statement is on the home or shop window? An accusatory statement screaming abuse in red paint, 3 feet tall, in order for everyone driving by to see? You gasp and think how horrible that must feel and wonder if it is true.

You see the victim discovering it and running up the road crying or back inside, closing the curtains?

I felt like that victim with nowhere to run to and the derogatory words were splashed all over our home, on my forehead and on an even larger scale. Worldwide size. Like the world was watching and it didn't matter if I closed the curtains. It was inside our home and inside my mind; everywhere I looked and available to all.

I couldn't run away from it. I couldn't scrub it off. Even if I could, it had happened and it had been seen.

Waves of nausea accompanied me as I wrote to the ad agency and implored them to take it down. The whole while, my fingers were shaking so much that I could barely type. I rambled on about the perpetrator being under investigation by the police.

They listened. They took it down. Phew. They listened. 'Breathe, Linz. Breathe'.

'We have taken it down', they said, *'but we only sell the space and cannot monitor how it is being used'*.

As I breathed the longest sigh of relief seeing the advertisement banner gone, I realised that www.lindseygoldrick.com seemed to have disappeared, too. The others were still there, though.

Still shaking, I did a search of the domain name.

lindseygoldrick.com was up for sale! I bet it was an oversight of Saul Furran's, missing payment or something. It was hard to believe. At last! It was the very first one and he had been running it for over 9 years.

I could not register my domain name (my name) quickly enough. I wouldn't do anything with it, nor could I at that point but finally, my name as a domain name was mine!

I was buoyed up by these two events, this day. An online company had heard me and took the advert down and I now owned my domain name. The intense angst that I had felt earlier in the day was alleviating and I was rather pleased that I had ventured online and sorted things out, after all.

'Happy Birthday to me!

One more check online before going home to start our weekend'.

Bad idea!

The anchor was back in my stomach and the clamp tightened.

The banner was back! Boom, boom, boom. My pulse was back, too.

On the first page of Google, further down at the bottom.

It had been seen, it had been scrubbed off and it was back up again. Tarnished. Victimised. Violated.

All were understatements.

The loss of autonomy over my life and reputation didn't seem recoverable. It was nine years and yet, he was finding new ways of being creative in his campaign of cruelty.

Buoyed up by great news alongside more bad news was familiar on Birthdays but I truly felt strung up.

As I drove home after work, adrenalin in overdrive, I contemplated the bittersweet Birthdays. Usually spent with loved ones and always with a new violent creation from Furran.

I was beyond sick of his determined, unforgivable, public acts of cruelty and I wished with all my might that karma caught up with him.

For now though, I would have to compartmentalise them, after sending another complaint to the search engines. I would have to divert my thoughts to the special people that were preparing for our visit. His acts were not going to depict how we were going to spend our time as a family. I was adamant about that.

Steve was home, the car was packed up, Rex was picked up from school and off we went to Wales. Not a word about the incidences of my day.

As we waited to cross the Severn bridge, I looked out to the water and back to Steve. I felt leadened. I took a deep breath, 'It won't always be like this, it won't always be like this'.

Turning to Rex, 'Want to play 'Guess what the next driver's name is and what they do for a living', Darling?' And he laughed out loud and we were off. We were in stitches of laughter in no time.

The moments of enjoying being with my boys and being with our friends could quite well have been replaced with my wallowing all weekend, not wanting to leave the house. But I had always vowed that he would never get the better of me.

We loved being with our friends so much; catching up and sharing stories, the walks up the mountains, the doggies, the chickens, the sheep and the delicious gathering for decadent celebration feasts that Jo prepared.

A common theme in our closest people is kindness. A nurture. A thoughtful heart. Time together: an enveloping of love; a good laugh. A transporting to a beauteous space of time together. A strengthening and a reminder that harmonious, non conflicting connections are what it is all about. No questions. No stresses. The ease of being together.

I appreciated everyone more than they would ever know. The comfort of the people around me and time together were crucial to my coping.

Short breaks were equal to big breaks, with thoroughly good, treasured friends and family, and injected energy to aid perseverance.

Love was the antithesis of the acts of Furran, and it was imperative to my survival.

CHAPTER THIRTY EIGHT
No mental escape

2014 brought lots of interludes of fun, enjoying the gaiety of Rex. Rex knew how much he was cherished and everyone welcomed him, with his bouncy blond curls, his curiosity and his big cheeky smile.

I threw myself into working conscientiously, planning holidays and escapes and all the time within me, I kept holding onto a faith that it would stop. Trusting that it would end. Unnerved about how it would, though. Still, Rex gave purpose and an incentive to stay strong, build great memories and keep up the adventure of a good life.

Boxes of gifts would come to the house when it was a Birthday or Christmas. Each and every one was scrutinised, if I didn't recognise the handwriting and post mark. Cautiously opened in the garden, before they were given out. Anticipating the arrival of more ashes or something nasty posted to us.

I would often think that because Saul Furran wasn't getting the amount of traffic to his site, as he expected, that it wouldn't be satisfying for him. He would proceed to get more creative in his harassment campaign, as he was wont to do, to surprise me continually. The less attention he received about his websites and adverts, I felt it might have irked him but I wasn't going to furnish him with gratification.

I caught the train one day to visit Lisa in 2014. She is my darling friend who I had met in New York, twenty years earlier. Our smiles were magnets, mirrored in each other. A fellow spontaneous adventurer found. It was her kindness, her generosity and her energy that was bigger than anything else, to me. Now, we lived in the UK, within a couple of hours away from each other and our children have grown up together but today was just about us.

My boys were doing their thing. I had two hours stretched out on the train to do nothing but escape. It was an opportunity to just sit, daydream and observe. People were knitting, talking, on their mobile phones, playing games on gadgets, texting, checking social media, working on diaries, spreadsheets, planning, magazines and newspapers were being read. Speeches were being practised, earphones, conference calling, dictating, sleeping, listening to things and eating perfect little sandwiches in foil, and I looked outside to red bricks, terraces, fields turning into suburbia…sheep turning into shops, farmers fields turning into stadiums, small back gardens, satellite dishes, small spaces packed with tables and chairs…and sunshine, clouds…back to the carriage; advertisements on the walls - Find us on Facebook, Follow us on Twitter, Visit us at vistus.com….Find someone like-minded on Guardian's Soulmates. I recoiled and shivered. Never any escape.

Later that day, after a gorgeous day of diversion with Lisa, getting off the return train in the dark, I heard footsteps but the station was quite deserted. I could definitely hear steps and I glanced around and ran as quickly as I could up the stairs across and over the bridge. As I turned the corner, I bumped into someone, screamed and apologised, explaining that I thought someone was following me.

I shook us both up and had nearly knocked her over but she was really quite comforting. She had one hand on my arm, as she looked behind me and out through the bridge window and at the station and said, '*There's nobody around - unless it was that old lady on a zimmer!*'. I laugh, '*I am being ridiculous, I know. I watch too many Thrillers!*' (and I didn't at all throughout the harassment. I had my own real life thriller going on!).

I thanked her and as I walked away, I determined that it must have been paranoia. 'He can't be following me', I was thinking as I ran as fast as I could to the car.

CHAPTER THIRTY NINE
Identity theft

It was late at night, early 2015 and I discovered that some of the websites were now registered with Verisign, so I wrote to them. 'Look at them,' I implored. 'Please shut them down and by doing so, you will stop a criminal act'. I also explained that the police were not trained what to do, so they were my only hope.

I also became aware of a Trust organisation that helped with getting personal information off the internet. They didn't respond. Nominet had been so helpful in the past and although I knew that they only dealt with .uk names, I couldn't keep up with the registration sites that Saul Furran was registering the sites with. It seemed that he was bouncing them around and not sticking with the same ones.

Clutching at straws, I wrote to the same gentleman at Nominet, who had been so helpful in the past. The websites were escalating and there were now three pages on Google all about me.

They referred me to another company: Sub 6, to remove www.valentinesdayinthenewforest.com and www.anastylying-pieceofwork.com. They invariably invoked suspension on the websites, only for them to reappear not long after, as with the others. Furran was defiant. Whilst writing to Enom, another domain registry site that had one of the sites registered with them, I went to the internet to copy the link and found that: www.LinzGoldrick.org had been created.

I realise that with each pleading email that I sent to these registry sites, they will have contacted the owner (Saul Furran) who had control. By giving them all a rundown of how desperate I felt, I was actually letting Furran know. It occurred to me that he was made aware of me requesting the removal of them. I am guessing that this pleased him. I must have sounded manic. I was manic. It wasn't surprising that Enom didn't write back to me.

With marketing being a huge part of my role at work, I explored every appropriate avenue for the company's visibility. So despite my personal inhibitions about social media, all the platforms were explored and by now, there were many. So, when I screamed out one day, I had to quickly make something up, due to the open plan office. I was on Twitter. I had dared to tap in my name.

Boom, boom…my heart swirled, pumped and burned. Two Twitter accounts appeared: Lindseygoldrick@ludibriaventis and Linzigoldrick-Liar@potestsolumun. What? A gold ingot with Anamcara (Celtic word for soulmate) next to my name as profile pictures…links to the nasty website…location listed as Tartarus? Which means the underworld, where the Gods imprison their enemies, in ancient Greece. How pleasant!

Several tweets were encouraging clicks on links to the defamatory websites. Lots of hashtags with my name and disparaging quotes (there's a surprise!). This was just really creepy. So obviously not real - but it felt real enough.

Humiliated, I started my rant to Twitter. '*I am being impersonated on your platform. Here are the links. It is clear that defamation and harassment is involved. Please don't allow this criminal, the account user, to get away with it. He is under police investigation. Tell me what ID you want me to provide and please tell me it is in breach of your terms. They need to be removed immediately. Thank you*'.

I knew that being impersonated wasn't illegal but they couldn't allow it, could they? Impatience got the better of me, due to the historic nature of being ignored. I wrote again, waffling on about how I felt, in that unashamed theme of mine. As if in the hope that somebody with empathy might pull something out of the bag for me, if I laid it all down.

I knew deep down really, that the moderators or hosts of the websites and platforms that I pleaded with in my quest to curtail Saul Furran's campaign of abuse, might not understand or be trained to recognise impersonation or obvious crimes being committed. They may only be guided by a question and answer tick list. Or, they could quite possibly be robots.

I questioned whether any website moderators were humans since responses were so devoid of feeling. Now, I know that empathy, understanding and caring attitudes were probably not on the list of requirements for a platform's hire criteria but I would have thought customer service and problem solving would be high.

So, I became more and more convinced that there were other motives for these platforms. If they didn't remove clearly vengeful, hateful abuse and allowed it, surely they are facilitators; aiders and abettors of abuse online. What for, though? What were their motives?

My emotional pleas were just wasted. Of course, I had hoped for understanding and an investigation and a lot more than a robotic response of a pre-worded request for photographic evidence of myself. I waited a day and prompted them for a reply, only to be told that they had been waiting for a response from me.

This is where I realised that this wasn't going to be easy either and I asked them if they had written to the owner of the Twitter accounts, which was not me. I repeated that the owner of the accounts was the impersonator. Subsequently, on receiving my driving license details, they deleted one of the accounts. Only one!

The other wasn't deleted (and that remained active until a Letter Before Claim was sent to Furran from my legal team).

Explaining the latin on the Twitter accounts that he created: Lindseygoldrick@ludibriaventis: the ludibriaventis refers to Virgil and the 'winds of playthings'. Potestsolumun means: 'There can only be one'. 'Apparently not', I thought. 'There can be any amount on Twitter!'.

154

Faith that someone could do something one day never wavered. I listed everything that was live on the internet in an email: 17 websites and more to follow, at this point and sent it to the police.

I ended it with the statement: *'Surely this is illegal? Do you know of any legal person that can help me? Please tell me what to do to make him stop. I want to talk to someone today, please'.*

After the automated reply from the police about adding the information to the incident number for the officer on the case and they would be in touch, I was reminded that nothing would happen, and that my optimism was really a little too…optimistic!

When you reach out to a force that are meant to protect you and they don't know what to do, don't know how to deal with you or your fears and requests and it is your only chance for help, what are you to do? If only they knew what to do. It wasn't their fault. I knew that. They must have felt frustrated about their lack of knowledge of what to do and guidelines.

To this date, I know that this unfortunately still goes on in many parts of the UK. At least police are not saying to switch off the computer and walk away anymore. As far as I know. Probably since our lives have crossed into the digital world and maybe people can understand it more? I almost deleted this paragraph, by the way, feeling that it was so outdated and that surely nobody would even think of that now, as they used to. But it was just weeks ago, on a radio show that a man came on and said it was easy to not feel affected by online abuse. He said, 'Just don't look at the internet'.

The ubiquity of the world wide web does not allow switching off and walking away. We are all immersed in it, one way or another. If only the internet had its own police and put measures into place that required tighter security. If only obvious abuse could be stopped and disallowed. If only algorithms could be made to detect, if only….and the list goes on.

155

If someone was screaming abuse at me continually day and night without stopping, the police would get involved at some point and take measures to control it. There had to be something that could be done. It was not only dejecting but it started to have an impact on my sense of worth.

I actually started to feel like I was a harasser myself, harassing for help.

CHAPTER FORTY
Put the brakes on, please!

Fear of what he was going to do next made me feel so apprehensive and I felt it continuously. So much so that anything that happened unexpectedly made him the prime suspect. For instance, one morning in 2015, ten years on, our little boy and I went to the car and my stomach flipped. The car door was already open. Danger felt close by and my heart quickened as I imagined the worst.

It felt difficult to find reasonable explanations about how and why. I searched my mind trying to trace back to when we were at the car last. Whether I did actually lock the car. Fear that he was close by watching didn't aid that, very well. I struggled with the clarity of my memory of whether it was my fault. It had happened before and there were a couple of possibilities. One possibility was that my uneasiness was making me forget to do things. Another was that I was in a rush running back to the cottage. There was also the possibility that Saul Furran had done this for more stalking purposes, in order to harass and scare me further.

I may have turned back and had someone check over the car had we not needed to be somewhere but I checked the back seats and popped open the boot of the car to find nothing untoward. My silence had Rex questioning what was wrong. We had been singing silly songs on the way to the car and now, I could hear him asking me if I was okay. I said everything was fine in a way that willed and hoped everything to be fine, rather than fact.

I turned on the ignition and the song Sugar Town by Nancy Sinatra came on.... '*And pretty soon all my troubles will pass....'cause I'm shoo-shoo-shoo, shoo-shoo-shoo, shoo-shoo..*'. It stopped me in my tracks. The last time I had heard that was when I was with Saul Furran and I had made a song and dance about loving it. It was entirely coincidental, surely. The chances of a song coming on the radio are pretty high but a rarely heard song? I looked around, heart beating fast, suspiciously wondering why Radio 4 (not renown for music), the station that was default in the car, was playing music.

It transpired that it was a Women's Music special and Nancy Sinatra was a guest on Radio 4. My mind was not allowing for any rationale because I was in a perpetual mode of fear. I drove at 5mph and kept checking the brakes until we reached the high street. I remembered him telling me that I was under his skin. I remembered the email from my nightmare from the beginning that said he was watching me.

My body just shuddered as I thought about him being in my psyche and I didn't want him in my life, however which way. I would have just accepted that I had been absent minded if he wasn't stalking me. I blasted him mentally and told him to get a life.

Believing there would be some sort of help at some point, I didn't give up looking for it online. I felt sure that I would find someone eventually. Cyberstalking was still not a coined phrase then but still, I wrote to the National Stalking Helpline who directed me to Revenge Porn. They could not really help with online harassment back then, as it was two different worlds but there were connections: Revenge and Stalking.

They wrote very supportive, thoughtful emails back and I cried with appreciation. I was at the point where if I got an automated response, I got excited. Two very thoughtful emails were directed to me, with suggestions of what to do. One stating anger about the police. It was a validation.

Of course, what else was written wasn't really applicable to me: staying safe online was not my issue, I did not have any personal information online that I had freely submitted and it wasn't social media related. I had done everything that had been suggested, except one thing: writing to the German police 'be-

cause they have stricter laws over there'. I was lit up with a new avenue to explore.

As much as I appreciated their response, I didn't like Saul Furran referred to as my 'ex-partner' and promoting him as having been more important to me. A partner is someone that you choose to be a partner in your life. The police had referred to him in the same way and it really bothered me. I know that it was more words to say but I wanted him described as 'someone that you dated briefly' or if fewer words were necessary: 'Psycho' would have done it for me!

Taking their advice, I wrote to several of the German police forces, for their help and didn't get a reply. I forwarded the emails from Revenge Porn and National Stalking Helpline to my local police, hoping they could assist and again, with an emotional plea along the lines of, subject title: Ongoing harassment since early 2005:

Dear A&S Police, I need your help please. I cannot carry on with this. Is there a number that I can ring to speak to someone or have someone come over to see me, please? It is affecting me so much. I have contacted two online support groups and I am sending their responses to you. I need assistance, please. They have suggested that I write to the German police. Even better, could you write to the German police? I think it will be taken more seriously. This guy is frightening me and goodness knows where he will go next with this. If you tap my name into the internet, you will see three pages on Google with all of the offending websites and Twitter, advertisements and goodness knows what else. I have contacted a member of parliament and that proved fruitless. I need to try and stop this from continuing because the man has psychopathic tendencies, I know. I would love to chat with someone about this, please. I understand that you must be very busy and are limited with resources but surely there must be something that can be done. Thank you.

They would hardly come flying out in a squad car over an email, would they but I am not sure why I bothered. I hadn't been strangled or anything yet, after all.

I felt like I was known as a pain at the local police station because although not every time, I did keep going back with the same plea, going over the same thing, adding a bit more.

'What do you want me to do?' suddenly started sounding like, *'What exactly do you want me to do, for Goodness Sake?'*. I couldn't bear that I was constantly asking for help. It went against my nature.

Yes, there wasn't physical bruising but I felt beaten up every second that the abusive content remained online.

CHAPTER FORTY ONE
Fight or flight

Saul Furran was ignited about impersonation because in October 2015 (10 years and 8 months and counting at this point), I received an email from wheretoget.com, which operates a website about fashion, make-up and online shopping. I was informed that I was being 'followed' and that I was 'following' 57 people; celebrities that I had never heard of.

I didn't watch any Reality TV or read any celebrity type magazines, as boring as that sounds. I apparently 'liked' revealing clothes and porn star shoes. I would look ridiculous and not be able to walk in those but even if I did, what was he getting at - again?

I didn't like this objectification of women that he had and I had a flashback to that nighty. Wearing and liking revealing clothes and big shoes shouldn't be used as provoking attack. I wrote to them and begged them to delete it but didn't get a response. I wouldn't have been surprised if they had told him about my pleading.

Other websites where I was following and being followed were created soon after and I know this sounds like a stab in the dark but I would put money on them that Furran was the culprit. Pleading emails in my usual style, telling the website's administrators that Furran is a criminal and they were aiding and abetting by allowing him to use their website as a tool, were ignored. No new story there.

I realise that all of this sounds like a slog but it was. After 10 years. I didn't lose hope but I felt less hopeful. It was my everyday. No help. Not important to anyone. It was always there, like chronic pain. You behave a certain way because that is what people expect of you whilst you are going through a silent hell.

Stress manifested in my body. Eye migraines at work had me bobbing to Mama for reflexology more. Memory disappeared some days and I was feeling a little foggy, cognitively. Hardly surprising but enough for me to worry. It bugged me that I had ailments and I knew the cause. I don't visit the Doctor. I like natural remedies. But I went. A blood result came back with hypothyroidism.

My research about the hypothyroidism led to reports that during periods of increased stress, the immune cells were being bathed in cortisol molecules. Which were essentially telling my immune system to stop fighting. Long term cortisol exposure was inimical to good health and was associated with chronic stress and produced further symptoms, including impaired cognition and decreased thyroid function and so on.

There were so many supported reports about being 'in fight or flight mode' for extended periods. I later visited a thyroid consultant, who agreed that extended stress may have played a part in it but it wasn't scientifically proven.

Damn it! Now his conduct had me on lifelong medication. I was convinced of it. Continuous mental strain can make you ill.

Wondering when, how and if this would ever end, I would not have felt such utter discomfiture if I knew that there was any likelihood of help in the near future. It had been over a decade of ridiculous hope.

It was 2015 now!

CHAPTER FORTY TWO
A tree to bark up

My optimism astounds me sometimes because I cannot believe that I still searched online for support. For instance, I must have been on cloud cuckoo land when I decided to tap in 'Best internet lawyer' to Google one day. 'Why do I like to torture myself?', I was thinking.

I expected the 'no results found' and some suggestion of a good internet programmer or something and I could not believe it!

As I hadn't ever seen before on Google!!!

There was Yair Cohen - Internet Lawyer. Oh my goodness! Woohoo!

Oh my! This was astonishing. He was UK-based. Oh Wow. He looked like he knew the internet and had assisted people that were harassed online. Oh, crikey. Here we go. I emailed him straight away. It was nearly midnight. If I could have got through right then and there, that would have been amazing.

The next day, I set up a consultation with him. I got all sorts of excited, after that. I got ahead of myself and started planning my evidence gathering. I contacted the police for a Subject Access Report. This report details (or should) everything that a body or company have about you in terms of data. It is a legal requirement for any request to be fulfilled. Here, the SAR would include the crime report. It would take up to 40 days to receive, so I had to get organised. I had renewed energy! This was so promising.

Oh wow, oh wow, oh wow!

With the sound of a fanfare of trumpets going off in my head and feeling like a cork ready to burst out of a bottle of champagne, I had found help. I knew it. I knew it. I knew it. I had to tame it. I hadn't spoken with him, yet. It felt like someone was walking towards me to help me take off a heavy load off my back that had been stuck there for years.

My optimism boosted. This could possibly be the start to the end.

For the first time since the start of the Defendants' Campaign against me and almost eleven years of continual searching, being incessantly drained and dejected, I felt that I had found help; that I could see a light at the end of the tunnel.

It was rapturous news to hear Yair say what could be done to make him stop. Another fanfare of trumpets goes off in my mind. Then Leonard Cohen popped in singing, 'Hallelujah'. It was the first time someone understood and had solutions. It was the day I had dreamt of. I had thought increasingly that it was absurdly over-optimistic but I had to keep believing.

The best way to start was to get a harassment injunction, he said. Yay! I wanted to scream but I had to try and really concentrate. An injunction, by the way, is an order to prohibit someone from doing something. So, the injunction would stop him from harassing me and if he continued, he could go to prison because he ignored the injunction. Anyway, I was visualising what it would feel like with an injunction. 'Oh yes, please'. Just talking to him helped me feel relieved. He knew what was needed in order to get him to stop.

'*There would be hundreds of hours of work and this would have to be paid for*', he said. It was incredibly complex. I would have to sue him through the civil courts and the costs could really escalate on top of the initial fees, depending on how the case went. There were fees for the courts and forms and after hearing about all of the cost of the court fees alone, I knew that I was unable to afford the legal action. It could hit 6 figures. Who knew? It wasn't like we could start it and stop when we ran out of money. It was a commitment. All or nothing.

Every single penny we had was spoken for. I tried hard to think about how I could get hold of so much money. I felt slightly deflated after the great hope that I had experienced because this was the only time in 10 years, when I had asked for help, I wasn't met with the retort - 'What do you want me to do?'. Help was available! Wow!

I just couldn't afford that help. It was so bittersweet. I knew that this was the person who could sort it all out and make him stop. The knowledge that there was help was tremendous, though. I had a tree to bark up, now.

The Subject Access Reports came from Sussex. 60 pages. None of my pleading emails were in the reports, though. I was hoping to see them. Luckily, my Sent files on email was still intact. What was most disconcerting was when I requested the evidence that they had put in the vault at my local police station, that was referenced in the crime report: the box, contents, notes and envelopes (that were sent to everyone back in 2005 to alert them to the sites), I was told that they did not have them anymore. They had been disposed of.

Why wasn't I contacted before they did this? I believe that after a while evidence is destroyed but I should have been consulted with first, so that I could have the option of having it returned to me. I could have preserved it and now, it would have been superb evidence, for legal purposes.

Another let down by the police. Hey ho.

CHAPTER FORTY THREE
Whose jurisdiction is the internet?

DIARY ENTRY, NOVEMBER 2015: *Gosh, I feel so stifled and stuck. I just want to be doing my own thing. The police are not ever going to help me. There isn't a criminal law for cyberstalking. It all feels so outdated and I resent the lack of understanding, let alone the lack of help and development, ten years on. I am pondering whether to just go to the media now in order to reach out to get help with legal fees but not only does it feel like begging (I am sort of used to begging now, though…for help) but it's also a Catch 22 situation. For all these years, I have not given him what he wanted and have controlled the visitors to his websites by not talking about them. If I do that now, I am also potentially putting myself in a more vulnerable position because he has my location and places I frequent, as well as all of the other filthy stuff. It is likely to be detrimental. No. I cannot do it at all. For all of our safety's sake, predominantly.*

The glimmer of hope knowing that Yair is there though is certainly uplifting and yet leaves me downtrodden at the same time. Knowing instinctively that he won't stop is driving me to madness. I daren't look at what is on there today but I know that Google's pages are all about me when tapping my name in, depicting me as the complete opposite of who I am. What a battle with a depraved soul. I feel sorry for him, swamping the net with defaming rubbish because we were incompatible. It astounds me. It is unbelievable. Proper websites with click-throughs. He has spent thousands of pounds and minutes on all of this. What else is he going to do?

Someone only has to stare at me or turn around to look at me again and I am thinking that they have seen the sites. People could possibly know about them but they are too afraid to mention them. Everyone does online searches on everyone these days. It is only a matter of time before someone else mentions them.

My mind feels muddled: Lack of sleep, constant anxiety and wondering how, when and if this will all stop. Keep us safe, please and thank you for giving me the strong constitution that all the females in our family have. It's going to be okay. My heart melted yesterday. Rex asked me to kiss his hand when I had lipstick on, so that he could look at it and feel me with him all day at school. He had been careful not to smudge it and still had it on at bedtime. Might have to have a word about washing hands but that was simply adorable and my heart grew another size again. That's a lipstick blotting that I don't mind seeing at all. END OF DIARY ENTRY.

I missed an email in February 2016 and when I saw it, I panicked. The domains that I had bought with my name had gone past renewal date and the deadline for renewal had gone. How had I missed those emails? If you have ever experienced hearing your own heartbeat really loudly, as it pulsates through your body, you will know how I felt. I was shaking, thinking that they would have been bought by a certain person again. I logged on, only to find that two years previously I had attached extra security on my account, which was called 2fa but I couldn't remember those details.

I couldn't see yet whether I still had the option to buy them again. The renewal on www.lindseygoldrick.com was no mean feat. In order to reset the 2fa or have it lifted, I had to prove who I was and I feared that whilst I was trying to prove who I was, he was going to buy the names again at that very moment. Now what that felt like in the moment was if you have ever had to get important, lengthy information via text message in the next 10 seconds on a phone that said it had 2 per cent charge left.

I tried to buy time. I told them that this madman was going to buy them, if not and he used to own them and so on. I was panic stricken but I had to prove who I was in order to buy them. The problem that I had was that I was at work and it was hours before I could get home and give them the security documents that they needed. I wrote them an email to hold the sites for me until later on that day, knowing full well that if they had interest from someone else (Furran) in the meantime, they wouldn't be worried about waiting for me to buy them, even if one of hundreds of moderators at the domain site did get the email from me.

I left work early, in order to do so, because it is all I thought about and it was so important. I got home and in a panic, got the ID details to them and was able to lift the 2fa and retain the domain name. Phew!

At the same time, more online rubbish appeared: twicsy.com/linzigoldrick - a social media app that shares photographs from Twitter. I didn't need some generated app online spreading the word, too. 12 years on and the harassment continued.

Each time, when I found a new possible lead to help online, I would perk up and send an email to them in hope. One day, I found and wrote to a cyber intelligence department to ask for their assistance. I didn't receive a reply. I flashed back, thinking about Yair. He was there and that was a comforting thought. No help for anyone existed before.

I still wondered why the internet search sites wouldn't ban or block all of the sites permanently. I had alerted them to my name as a website being used so many times, so why did they allow more and couldn't they just stop them? Why can the privacy shield be offered so willy nilly, giving the account user power and privacy and not be investigated first? Why were sites facilitating the privacy of criminals? Why couldn't there be some strict regulations of some sorts? Why couldn't I take the URLs to a local criminal court and have them blocked in this country, even if someone that had made them lives anywhere else in the world? Which would give reprieve, even just blocked in the UK.

Why did I have to have lots of money to sue someone to stop them committing a crime against me by using the digital world as a tool, when I knew who it was and where they were?

Why was getting help for harassment (wherever it is being committed), prohibitive to people that didn't have the money to sue? When the criminal act of harassment on the internet should be dealt with by the criminal justice system? Why wasn't anything in place and consistently being used by the police, yet?

The digital world is now immersed into all of our lives as an essential part of our world and harassment is more prevalent as it was on the street. It is unnerving how ungovernable the internet is and that there was scope for more creativity from Furran. And he knew it.

No deterrent.
And nothing deterred him, regardless.
Not the arrest, not the caution, not the warnings.

CHAPTER FORTY FOUR
11 Years later

DIARY ENTRY, APRIL 2016: *I keep researching how to get a large amount of money so that I can get the internet lawyer's help. It can't be crowdfunding because he will get traffic to his sites and I can only imagine that will give him pleasure and give me more anxiety. It has to be discreet. There isn't anyone that I know that has a spare five figure amount of money to initiate what has been proposed and then I would need more thousands to carry it through the courts and how long would it take and will it be successful? Legal fees could carry us into a debt that we would never recover from and we have to keep our home.*

I am in such a pattern of being awake all night and working hard all day, which gives me a sickness in my stomach and a fog in my head, whilst ensuring that our boy has a good, happy, healthy and adventurous life. Also, dealing with the everyday stuff like house maintenance, groceries and appointments and then things that go wrong. Like the pipes bursting the other day and blockages. No big deal but just too much at the minute, with work and school and being on my own with Rex. It would all be fine otherwise.

And the car breaking down several times and things just all getting on top of me and wishing, wishing with all of my might that I didn't have this incessant horror that I can not stop. Was it wrong to start wishing that something would happen to Furran? At least then, the websites would expire in a couple of years and I wouldn't be in fear of our lives all the time. END OF DIARY ENTRY.

I wrote an essay to the police:
'*I have had ongoing contact with you for over 11 years for online and offline harassment, online impersonation, privacy invasions*

and stalking, to say the least and I know that you say that you can't help me until he physically harms me.

I will just interrupt there and point out that having a description of what was going on was a way forward and almost happened overnight and the coined phrases: online harassment, online impersonation, online privacy invasions......were now familiar, used and understood. Help was getting closer. I could feel it.

Back to the essay to the police: *It should all be in my crime reports. I was invited to give another statement last year but I didn't feel well on that day and I didn't see the point because I have been reporting it over and over for all of this time, to no avail. Harassment, as you defined it too, is something that happens twice and causes anxiety. You arrested him for it. Does it matter where it is performed and does it matter what tool is being used?*

It is exhausting going through it over and over again from the beginning. I am on my own with my child all week and my husband is only home at weekends and I work, so time on my own is limited. I am worried and worn out about this and I don't sleep. I am constantly aware of these horrid creations and anyone searching my name will read untruths about me. Or just anything about me, to be honest.

This psychotic person optimises the websites, so they are always prominent on the net. He has more up his sleeve that hasn't appeared yet, but there will be more. I know it. He is never going away and I know that he physically sees me from somewhere because he updates the websites to reflect my life. He is obsessed with trying to bring me down. 4 dates I had with him! I feel vulnerable, scared and violated. How can I stop him forever? Just having them taken down would help. Please help. I worry about all of my family and my son is 6 years old. Soon, he will see these things on the internet about his Mummy because he is already savvy searching things up on Google. Please, please help. This person will go further. Thank you.

This time, the police wrote and said that it was clear that this was affecting me (understatement) and they added it to my notes and someone would be in touch.

I was assigned a female officer and had to start explaining what had happened at the beginning again but with fresh hope and a new face, (and she seemed keen, if a tad perplexed), I don't mind saying that I intended to latch onto her and be insistent. I had had absolutely enough. I got her direct email address. She would collaborate with the Chief Inspectors, she indicated.

'How can you be sure that Saul Furran knows where you live?' she asked.

'Well, he researched extensively to find people's addresses to tell them about the websites and he had only heard their first name, if at all. If he had found them via my email account, then still, no last name or addresses are in there. I am not on Facebook and I don't freely submit details about myself on the internet. If he has bothered to find out where they live and he doesn't live around here, he most certainly knows where I live,' I replied.

She asked, *'Why?'*

'I cannot be certain but I have an inclination that he does. Why just stop at their addresses? My instinct tells me that he is in close proximity sometimes, too.' I said and I proceed to tell her about the *'hand through the letterbox, the smashed window'*…the gates were open now…. *'the websites reflecting that I had got married and when I became a Mum. Then, there is identity theft impersonations, email hacking and…..'* and I trailed off, feeling like I had lost her.

If I heard another *'What do you want me to do?'* I thought I would flip out.

She then asked me what I wanted her to do!

Bubbling up and feeling the tears flood in, I told her, louder than I expected,

'I want him to stop! I want to feel safe! If it wasn't for the people around me and my responsibilities, I feel like I would go crazy.'

Is she still listening? *'I wake up with a sense of dread every morning and it's the last thought on my mind before I go to sleep'*. I am sobbing now, as I babble with unnecessary information, *'I have suffered 11 years of constant fear, dread and isolation, interspersed with love and gratitude for the people in my life,'* Somebody stop me now, please…. *'which kept me alive'*. I gasped at my outward sorry feelings for myself.

She was speechless but I had her attention. *'Perhaps if you could find out where he lived and if he was back in the country?'*

'I can send a request form to border control but it may take a while. Is there anything else you think might help?', she asked.

'Perhaps contact from the police would be taken more seriously? Do you mind writing to Google, Clook and Twitter, to request to block what I told you about?' I asked.

She asked me to write the requests and give her the email addresses and she would send them from her police email address. With a spurt of optimism and something new to go towards possible help, I had them to her within the hour.

Later that week, the police officer confirmed that she had done what I had asked but she hadn't got a reply and it was obvious that there weren't any changes online. An email to the host sites and domain registers from the police weren't taken seriously, either. I felt absolutely stumped.

She kept saying that she didn't know what to do, unless he harmed me. It wasn't her fault. I could see that she genuinely couldn't help and didn't know what to do but wanted to. She had spoken with the Sergeant who spoke with the Inspector who spoke with the Chief. There wasn't anything in place what to do about harassment being committed online and how to support a victim of it. Avon and Somerset Police and Commissioning Crime Officer ascertained this, too.

Harassment online was just the same as harassment offline, if not worse but the problem was that the perpetrator was in another country and he must have had this sense of being invincible because he was committing the crimes from outside the UK.

Being told over and over again that nothing will happen until he hurt me physically just enhanced the stress for me. It played over and over in my mind. I had told and re-told them my story so many times. It was all just so exhausting…and frustrating.

CHAPTER FORTY FIVE
Attacked to my core

It was now 11 years and three months since his sick and twisted violence started and late one night, I lay in bed feeling so very, very tired but not being able to go to sleep. I had so little sleep and with fear and paranoia by my side, striving vigorously for it not to affect me, I felt so unhealthy with a jet lag feeling, as my circadian rhythms were all shot.

The noises in the night were unbearable for my imagination and didn't allow for a restful sleep. The creaks on the stairs were Saul Furran walking up them, the clicks from the fridge was the weapon he was going to use, the wind outside was the brush of his clothes up the stair well walls and when the owl hooted, I fell out of bed!

Dark rings were around my eyes now and I just didn't have the energy for work but I had to keep going. If only I could establish where he was living and where he was now, I might at least feel that we are safe when we come home or leave the house but then, there wouldn't be a safety guarantee with that knowledge. Oh goodness, I wanted this over, so badly.

The police lady ascertained that he didn't live in England or Germany but she couldn't tell me where he lived. She asked me for any evidence from the last six months about what he had been doing. I told her that it was all there on the internet and could be accessed by anybody at anytime and most definitely things had changed on them recently. They were all current and I sent her evidence of one being updated just that month.

I had started taking screenshots of the front page of all of them, as evidence, on a regular basis and she could see what one looked like just two months ago as opposed to what she could see that day. I also forwarded the websites and reiterated that they were constantly maintained and updated, so the evidence was there - all over the internet, refreshed every day! The original website was printed out and given to them, I told her, in 2005 and it was placed in a vault.

I explained *'you can see that there are different ones now and if you look them up, you can see when they were created and last changed, for instance: www.anastylyingpieceofwork.com was last tweaked this August. I keep expecting to see my friends' private information on there one day, too'*…I rambled… *'because he keeps making new ones and the hacking'*. I don't think I paused for breath whilst I was talking to her but when I did pause, I could have dropped to the floor when she suggested I changed my name.

Due to the foreboding feelings and continuous angst that I was experiencing, it was becoming increasingly hard to work and not be cocooned at home. I had to keep a job and I had to keep going for Rex's sake. I worked as hard as I could at work and conscientiously gave my employers the best that I had but it was a struggle.

I felt attacked to my core and some days were harder than others. I needed daytime hours to myself, where I didn't need to concentrate on anything. I felt exhausted mentally and physically sick and clumsy and disorganised. I started to feel like I was in overload and couldn't make decisions or have opinions. Maxed out. Enough to make me worry. I hoped that it was temporary, to not have the words - any words, when words used to be so easily there.

I used to be articulate and I was finding the simplest of sentences a challenge. Had all of what was happening causing impairment? Was it temporary? Yet nobody seemed to notice because I was receiving enough praise for what I did at work for it not to be questioned and I was always quick to laugh and excuse my clumsy or ditsy behaviour away. Being known as being jovial kept me buoyant, for I wasn't about to convince them otherwise.

Regardless, it felt imperative to my sanity and although it was a struggle monetarily, I reduced my hours at work and Steve agreed that we would live frugally to get me through this.

DIARY ENTRY 2016: *What a sad existence that Saul Furran was still obsessively spending money and time on this online vendetta. I noticed that I wasn't feeling ashamed about his conduct anymore. I was starting to feel annoyed at how pathetic he was and how he had no inclination or deterrent to stop. I couldn't bear thinking that I had given him any time at all in the beginning, that a quarter of my life had been taken up with his crimes against me and that he was allowed to get away with it.*

He should be in prison, not swanning around in Europe or wherever, running his business whilst torturing me and quite possibly, without his wife knowing about it. He needed to be found and he needed to be made accountable. He needed to be made an example of because nobody should be subjected to such heinous wrongdoings and certainly not for relationship incompatibility.

Having time to myself, I reflected on how, for 11 years, he had affected me. Not only the affect on me and my life emotionally, physically, socially and financially but my husband and quite possibly the people that knew he hadn't gone away. I would like to think that Rex didn't feel any indirect effects because my focus on him was entirely there all of the time and feeling adamant about him not being affected. But what about all of my people that thought that he had gone away? My behaviour would surely have been different to how it would have been without the harassment, despite my determination for him not to have the power. Surely, right? How would I ever know? Plus, the thousands of hours I have spent trying to find help to no avail which would have gone towards building the business that I intended. No good wallowing but I cannot help feel resentment. I am grateful that I am not the person that he is and he possibly won't ever imagine what I have felt like and feel remorse or empathy but 11

years? I think I may have to do something drastic. The media? With-
out protection? Legal help is needed more than anything. But where
do I get hundreds of thousands of pounds from, to acquire it? I keep
wondering that, I know and praying for help and hoping that some-
how, something will manifest. Got to stay positive. It is the only way.
END OF DIARY ENTRY.

CHAPTER FORTY SIX
The laughing policeman

DIARY ENTRY, JUNE 2016: *Rex is now 7 years old and I actually don't feel the need to hover over him anymore. I can be further away from him without my legs feeling like jelly. This amazing, spirited, highly-energised child that was an absolute gift is keeping me sane and distracted. He gives me purpose and the impetus to stay strong and have faith. His online savviness is perturbing me though. I worry that he will Google me one day and that it will have a lifelong damaging effect on him. I love being a Mum. I love being his Mum. I hope that he can't feel what I am going through. I am doing my absolute best that he won't feel anything other than love and happiness.*

Tonight, I didn't ask the internet to help me. I am sitting in the garden, staring at the moon, thinking of the greatness in the world and space and the universe and reverting to reaching out for something more powerful and greater than the internet for assistance. Goodness though, the internet to me, felt just as large and just as powerful in its presence in everyone's lives continually; immediately. Accessible to all. Nobody was denied.

I have written in my gratitude journal about all the things I am truly thankful for and I continue to feel hope for something to happen to make him stop. A windfall of money to pay civil court fees, would be amazing, so I can crack on with getting my life back. Volts go through my body when I hear people say how amazing the internet is and yes, I absolutely agree. Wouldn't be without it. It's the criminals that use it that spoil it but the good outweighs the bad.

I find it hard to believe that the internet has been around for almost 30 years and there aren't any laws or rules, as to what you can and can't do on there, nobody is talking about it happening to them and no website platform or host will block him from doing so. Nobody can control what he is doing and he knows it. There are no deterrents. He was arrested and he carries on.

It feels surreal. I can hear the heavenly Einaudi music that Rex requested to listen to fall asleep to and tears enter my eyes. Such an absolute blessing to have this wonderful, happy boy in our lives, that reminds me of Dad so much. One that I hope to see grow into an 8 year, 9 year old, 10 year old… He asked me the other day, 'Am I a lot like Grandad Bernie?' And I told him that he was and it was an extraordinary thing to be like his Grandad. I am crying now. I won't ever know what these 7 years of his life would have been like without having the continuous trauma of what Furran was doing. I am doing my absolute best of giving the illusion of control whilst my life feels so out of control but then I am focusing on what I can control, which is a lot, actually. END OF DIARY ENTRY.

11 years and five months later, despite my asking the police to never call me at work, as it was an open office and it would only invoke curiosity and I had not told anyone, the police proceeded to call me at work. My colleague took the call and told me when I came into work. Everybody wanted to know why they were calling me.

I responded quickly, surprisingly, since I was taken by surprise and told them that I was helping with an investigation in our village. I emailed the police, copying the female constable in (and I believe this was the last time I wrote to them) and asked that they deleted my work number and to not call me there, as nobody knew about what was going on. I forwarded screenshots of the latest websites with changes and asked her to *'Please help me and tell me what to do to make this stop; to stop him - wherever he is'.*

It was only a couple of days later, in August of 2016, that I got another call from the police at work. It wasn't a surprise, even though I had asked them not to call me at work. The male constable told me (jovially, I might add) that he had taken over from the female officer (I couldn't help but get a strong stench of chauvinism).

He said that they had tried their best but there was nothing they could do and so, they would be closing the case after 11 years. It was all so matter of fact! I could feel myself bubbling up with tears but had to hold myself together and watch my words, as my colleagues were all in ear shot and I was pretending it was an ongoing investigation regarding a neighbour.

'Nothing they could do? Had he seen the sites? Was he one of those types that thought I deserved it? How could they close the case and not care about even keeping it open? The sites were still there and I had told them about what else he had done. Why was the constable so bloody cheerful?'

I gently pleaded, since I was in earshot, for him to do something...anything... but he reiterated that there was nothing they could do. Containing your emotions for the purpose of your surroundings is really challenging, if it happens to you, right? An eruption that you cannot contain but you have to. I could hear my heart beat so loudly and I was surprised that nobody else could.

I may have been wrong but I felt that because the female officer kept asking me what to do and was at a loss, and my consistent emails asking her to help me somehow, may have had her at a loss too. Which led to this male officer taking over to 'relieve her' of the position.

I was trying to hang on to someone that was clearly trying to help, despite not being able to, and despite my knowing that she was unable to. The fact that she was showing willing was enough for me and this felt like another major let-down. She wasn't able to do something but she was someone that held a drop of hope, since she had been in touch with me regularly and she was in the police. One day, I figured, some miracle might happen where the police would be given a defined code of practice to follow or training in this sort of thing.

Why hadn't she told me herself? Was I becoming intimidating in my quest to get help with something that could have been nipped in the bud in the beginning? Was my grip too strong?

It is unfortunate that I hadn't taken down the male constable's name though because I would really like to have a word with him about why it was possible to just close the case and shut me down when it was ongoing? I would like a strong word with him on how to talk to people that feel desperate for help and that have been continually harassed for over a decade and felt fearful.

I would like to say to him, '*Imagine if it was your daughter? Or, if it was your wife, sister, friend, mother? Anyone that you treasured? Doesn't matter what sex they are. How would you also feel towards a police officer who spoke to her in a voice entirely wiped of human sympathy, telling her that there's nothing that can be done and the case was being closed?*' And throw a few laughs into it whilst you are at it.

This also reiterates the need for police to have training in how to treat people that are being stalked and harassed online. To understand how they are feeling. To take reports seriously. To believe, to be unbiased and to investigate. As well as the need for police to be given some computer technology training and understanding. Being untrained is dangerous for people that go to them for help with online harassment. Simple stuff would go a long way.

In the same week, at one o'clock in the morning, I woke, startled, to banging on the door and it kept on. My heart was pounding. Was it Furran? Was it about Steve? I opened the bedroom window and a male police officer stood there outside. News about Steve! No! I looked for his colleague because there always had to be two when they gave you bad news but what with cutbacks, who knew what the new rules were? My mind was racing and the adrenalin was pumping. He was alone, though and I was sceptical. Anyone could wear a uniform. It was one o'clock in the morning.

I couldn't see his face properly and I realised that I was shaking. '*What is wrong?*' I asked. '*It is the police, Madam. Please can you come to the door?'* and I pelted down the stairs, stumbling a little, thinking that it was quite possibly news about Steve and they were short staffed. All sorts of horrible thoughts were rushing through my head and I didn't want our little boy to wake. I grabbed my rolling pin, checked the spy hole and cautiously opened the door with the chain on. The policeman didn't look old enough to be out so late (which shows my age!). I waited, with dread, for him to speak. Urging him to spit it out much quicker than he was.

He was wanting information relating to the neighbourhood investigation about a recent incident. I stood, disbelieving my ears. It was one o'clock in the morning and it was not to do with Steve. I didn't have any details and said goodnight but it was unbelievable. I went back to bed but not to sleep.

My mind was awake now and I was irritable…. 'Goodness me…. the very people that are meant to help me that never can are now rubbing salt in the wound. First night I have actually slept for what seemed like years for more than three hours….. and I was woken by them for a bloody neighbourhood investigation in the middle of the night. This is not funny'.

If I didn't have a neighbour come over and talk to me the next day to see if I had been woken too, I would have thought it was another bad dream. We agreed that it was quite disturbing to get a police call in the middle of the night and not acceptable, doing their investigations. My neighbour's poor wife had been anxious ever since. They had thought it was bad news, too.

As soon as I thought Steve would be awake, I called him. He answered on the first ring, thank goodness. *'Hi, my Goldstick.'*. Choked with tears and no words for a moment. Relieved to hear his voice. *'Everything okay, Linz?'* And I managed to talk.

He got angry quickly and wanted to call the police as soon as possible, so we hung up. I didn't think I could feel any more anxious but my anxiety levels shot through the roof that night and as I made Rex's lunchbox, Steve called back. He had demanded why the police had freaked us out in the middle of the night and they told him it was because they had such a backlog of work to do that they were told to call on anyone at any time. It was a new routine. Unbelievable but true.

As well as it being incredibly unacceptable for anyone to be woken in the middle of the night to answer police queries, wouldn't it be common sense to know whose door you were knocking on? I worried about elderly people and ones with nervous dispositions (and who wouldn't be with a bang on the door in the wee hours?).

What about the police constable? He was only a young lad and he faced rather a lot of potential negative reactions doing his duties - on his own. Let's face it - if anyone got a knock on the door from a police constable in the middle of the night, their nerves would be on edge.

I dropped Rex at school and I went into work all blurry-eyed and with palpitations. I pondered us moving in with Mama.

CHAPTER FORTY SEVEN
Praise for Pro Bono

Despite feeling lucky and grateful in life, and clutching onto my spirit, I worried that this perpetual state of anxiety was starting to have a deeper melancholic effect on me that I may not be able to shift. A dejectory state of being. Listless.

It was like I was on a flimsy boat and I was managing to stay afloat with all of my strength but I didn't have a life jacket. It might take one more big wave. I checked in with Teen and asked her if I appeared miserable or dampened down. She replied that I was doing a good job of hiding it. 'Still crazy funny and happy smiley, Linz', she said. That is all it took. 'Hang in there. Keep it together'.

On a family front, Steve didn't work too far away now and wouldn't be going for long spells away again, which was more settling.

One moment that I had been dreading for years, almost happened. Rex was Googling family names with his cousin and he had just done his Daddy's and it was inevitable that I was up next. I managed to sweep in and grab the device and suggest playing another game, just in time. My stomach was churning. I was shaking.

They were easily distracted, thank goodness. I rushed to email Yair to ask him what I could do and coincidentally, he had sent me an email to see how I was, that very day. I told him that I was feeling desperate and would do anything to raise the money and did he think that the media would listen or should I try and crowdfund?

It was a complex case and it would involve hundreds and hundreds of hours of work. He referred me to the Pro Bono

Centre, which is a national charity that match-makes volunteer barristers with people that need legal help and cannot afford to pay for it. I knew that I couldn't be too hopeful, as they got hundreds of requests. If I got a barrister, then he might be able to help too, he offered.

Simply put, barristers advocate, defend and represent clients in court or a tribunal and offer specialist advice. A lawyer/solicitor prepares the legal documentation and performs the majority of legal work in a law firm setting. There are exceptions to the rule and case. This is just a brief, for those that don't know and may find Google more helpful. For research, of course!

I applied, providing a brief, a list of the websites, the crime report, challenges, reasons why I needed help and an in-depth financial report, gave the package a big kiss and a wish and sent it on its way.

The truth is that I was too afraid to think that it might go somewhere. It was a vigorous procedure of checking, reviewing and allocating. There wouldn't be a chance for me. So many occasions, I had dreamt, visualised, hoped and prayed. Each email, each phone call, each letter, each appointment, each plea - hundreds over the years, that were made optimistically, that soon became let downs.

I could hardly allow myself to feel vulnerable, wanting it so much, waiting and hanging to hear. Not wanting to pin my hopes on it, I put it far away in my mind. So much so, that I almost missed the email that said that I had passed the first stage and that I had so many days to respond to accept. The email had been sitting in my inbox for a few days! Goodness! If I had not have seen it when I did, I may not be typing this now. I had wanted it so much that I was scared to keep checking my emails. It was at the back of my mind but at the front, if you know what I mean. I had barked up too many trees.

I had passed the initial stage that checks the reason why I need help. They could see that I needed help. Glorious to read. I felt validated when I read that email. They needed to know how much I appreciated this and I also accepted that I had more hoops to jump, so of course I wrote to them and stated this and thanked them for the opportunity. I had a hop, a hope and a spring in my step!

It was going to be hard not to keep checking my emails now, I thought and yes, I checked every single day and it wasn't long before I was told that I had passed the second stage, which looked at the costs involved and the money that we had (or hadn't). It was intense. I had one more stage to pass. I had only a few days to wait for that decision and no, I didn't check my email 12 times a day, at all! It could have been more, actually.

When the email from them popped into my inbox, I closed my eyes and sent the silent prayer of 'please, please, please….say yes' and goosebumps flooded my skin. Then I froze. I stared at the screen for so long. I didn't want to know that I hadn't passed that last stage. It would be too crushing. What if I hadn't passed the final stage? And that is the thought that made me open the email. I was too used to let downs and dashed hopes. 'This would not be anything new', I told myself. 'You are pre-pared. You have had 11 years of "What do you want me to do?". Go for it'. I urged myself, 'Do it. Open. Just click on it and read it quickly'. And I did.

I clicked on it and closed my eyes. I opened one eye and squinted. I shook my head. 'Did that really just say that I had passed? Did it really just say that I had passed that final round?'.

Did it really read that the 'reviewing barrister recom-mended that a volunteer barrister should be found to provide ad-vice as to merits of proceeding with a claim in harassment, in or-der to obtain an injunction?'

'That they would proceed in searching for a barrister to assist me - although not guaranteed?'

'Really? I had just read that correctly, right?'. I went back and read it again and again and again. As I write this, I do not know who the reviewing barrister was and I have not thanked her or him yet. I would dearly love to know who it was that was part of the team that saved me. I almost wrote 'from the brink of despair' but I was beyond the brink!

I called Steve over and over, until he picked up. I never do that.

Then, one incredible day in October 2016, just weeks later, I jumped with exaltation when I opened up my Yahoo email account.

They had written to me to say that they had found a barrister that wanted to help me. I shook my head in disbelief. Really? There was another barrister that saw it and thought that I needed help. It was Gabor Bognar. Who subsequently wrote to me promptly, moments later, introducing himself and suggesting a telephone conference.

The sun shone, champagne corks popped, the orchestra played a crescendo....the piano was played...elated emotions danced around my head...and I closed my eyes, tears dropped down my cheeks and I whispered, 'thank you'.

He asked me to collect all documents that I had relating to the matter, a compilation list of the websites and the URLs and dates of their existence, and send them to him in preparation.

Without delay, I started my task to do so and midst it, I took a seat back and breathed deeply, contemplating that this was actually happening. 11 and a half years later. I know that I bang on about it so much but this moment had been dreamed about for so long, for so many days, so many months, so many years. Dejection and rejection experiences had my expectations quite low.

I knew that nothing could be guaranteed and nothing concrete was happening yet...but this was happening. Gabor actually contemplating my case was a huge, longed for and momentous occasion. It is an unforgettable email because Gabor wrote in a detailed way that was of offering and kindness. Of strength and support.

I will never forget that day. It was of course, a day I had dreamt of. I looked Gabor up on the internet and I now had his face in my mind, too. Thank you, you very kind man, Gabor.

CHAPTER FORTY EIGHT
Would there be light?

I couldn't believe it and couldn't wait to call everyone to tell them the great news. I had to remind some of my friends and family to remember my issue from 2005. Most were shocked that it was still going on 11 years later because they had forgotten about how it started, since I hadn't talked about it. It felt so freeing.

Emailing Yair, thanking him for the advice and stating that I possibly had a barrister, I asked could he please help after all, too?

Monday, the 31st of October, 2016 was the wondrous day when I spoke with Gabor. I was fuelled up with adrenalin and kept checking the phone was hung properly. I got myself a pen and paper. I drank water and wished I hadn't, since I didn't know however long I would be on the phone with Gabor.

My tummy flipped over and over and over. Gabor could be my lifeline. After almost 12 years on a continuous quest of seeking help from wherever I could see fit to seek it. After almost 12 years of puzzled faces, what do you want me to dos and nothing, nothing, nothing. A perpetual yo-yo feeling of hope and despair, hope and despair…no light was ever seen at any tunnel and I just kept travelling along in the darkness, stabbing away, hoping to get lucky….Oh my!

Freedom from almost 12 years of torture rested on this man.

I had to curb it somehow and not jinx it. He wouldn't know how I hung on his every word, how I prayed with all my might that he wouldn't change his mind after talking with me. He talked about his role and the process of the Pro Bono Unit and asked if I had any questions. I asked him what had made him want to help me and he said, *'a few things'* and I could not talk for the tears as he said words to the effect of, *'Because this is an area of law that is new to me and that interests me, the case is very real and you need help!'*.

Before he could ascertain whether he could definitely actually help me, though, he needed more chronological information and any evidence I had. He also wanted to know what I wanted to achieve so that he could understand in both a legal and practical sense. Of course, my main concern was to make Saul Furran stop but my mind was wandering already at this point about how to assist others further down the line, so that my experience wasn't in vain.

Steve had taken leave that day and kept glancing over to me and I was willing him to not distract me with his glances whilst I was on the phone with Gabor. He had my full attention. Every single thing he said and asked me, I heard. I was tempering waves of emotion. I could hardly believe the call was happening and I was in discussion with a barrister that might possibly be able to help end this. Tears dropped from my very sore eyes when he said he wanted to help me on Pro Bono. My eyes were stinging from the cleansing tears. I had to concentrate on the words I was hearing because I had the distraction of fireworks popping all around from my imagination.

Whether or not he could help, I would find out in due course. Oh no! Please, don't go away. He needed to review all that we talked about and all that I submitted to him, after our conference to see if he was the right person to help me. 'You are the right person, you are the right person'. I made a silent prayer that Gabor would be able to help me and tears of hope released from my eyes, as I thanked him and followed Steve out to the garden.

I sat on the grass, quite numbed with disbelief of the possibility of actually getting help and that the websites may possibly go away. I couldn't imagine a life without the oppression, the websites and the feelings of fear. Steve reached out and hugged me and I sobbed, '*I hope Gabor can help. I don't want him to go away*'.

This was a significant breakthrough. It all depended on whether he felt that he could help me and that he was the right barrister to do so. What if he saw a hurdle and he couldn't help me, after all? I felt sick to my stomach that it might not happen.

I lost my appetite until we spoke again.

CHAPTER FORTY NINE
My faith in humanity, restored

November 2016. I almost dropped the phone when Gabor called. I was shaking with anticipation. So much relied on what he was going to say. For the short interim that I waited for his review, I had let my mind go to imagining the peace and the contentment that was a possibility, there on the horizon. The light was getting brighter. I could see it. Then, suppressing those thoughts just in case Gabor went away and couldn't help. My heart couldn't take a rejection when it was so close and had seemed so amenable.

I could hear my Dad's voice in my head. It was always good to draw him in to make me feel calm…a few words of wisdom… and then from memory, as he always mixed humour with serious issues, lightening things up to rest my worrisome mind, I could hear him humming a theme tune purposely not very well.

The phone rang precisely at the moment that Gabor said he would call. The promptness was appreciated, beyond belief. There was a trust there, already. I could rely on him. I wanted to rely on him. Oh, goodness, please tell me good news, Gabor.

And he did. Gabor wasn't going anywhere. He came back to tell me that yes, he thought he could help me. And I think he understood my '*Thank you*' that was more of a howl of happiness and appreciation.

The intense feelings of absolute elation are embedded in my soul. It was through the roof. Even today, I am choked by the appreciation for Gabor's assistance. At last! 11 years and 9 months since the torturing conduct of Furran had began. Somebody else was listening to me, like Yair had and that somebody was going to help me and then because of that, Yair could possibly help, too! Tears of joy were streaming down my face, as he talked.

The feeling of isolation that I had for so long was not something I would feel again. It took a while for that to truly sink in. In fact, now that I address it, I didn't fully believe that it was happening and kept fearing that something would occur that would cause it to be abandoned. I had that feeling a lot throughout the litigation. A whole new set of emotions and feelings, that included an 'uncertain possible excitement' with stomach flips and being afraid that something would go wrong and spoil something so amazing. The news was too good to believe after over a decade of striving to find help, searching for anyone to do something and quite possibly every spare moment alone, scouring the internet for some sort of lead to get support.

Subsequently, we had to make an application for assistance to The Pro Bono Unit for each stage of the process that Gabor was providing. The first was to provide advice on the merits of proceeding with a Harassment claim in order to get an injunction. Then, the Pro Bono Unit were approached to review for further assistance to provide advising on the drafting of the pre-action correspondence concerning a civil claim in harassment and then, again for drafting the claim form and particulars of claim and so on.

So, as you can imagine, it was a case of doing lots of praying that they would permit each stage when Gabor submitted the requests, over the duration of the trial. Gabor was going to act as my barrister throughout. I felt like the luckiest person in the world when Gabor said that he would take on my complex case on Pro Bono.

We began collating the evidence for the case. Piecing together the history of the whole experience and gathering facts. Yair emailed with the brilliant news that he would act as my Lawyer, now that I had a barrister in place. It would be on a No Win No Fee arrangement and he was available in January. I had this amazing legal team. Wow. Gabor believed in my being successful and wanted to help me on Pro Bono and Yair did, too. He wouldn't have agreed if he didn't think that I would win. My faith in humanity restored. A momentous time.

Ames had the early incriminating evidence of emails that I had sent to her. About meeting him online, offline, the first website and the onset of his threats. This was such crucial, important evidence. I needed to tell her of my amazing news, too, so I called her. But first I had to recap. Which was the oddest thing for us, since we knew what each other did most days. It felt difficult to explain, when we wrote about the nitty gritty of our lives daily, that I had chosen not to talk about something so immense in my life.

With conviction, I made the right decision, for sanity's sake. Focusing on the aspects of life that I could control. Protection - to stop others worrying. And to stop me worrying about others worrying about me and distraction. Pure respite. Details unrelated, including comedic moments were great therapy. With everyone.

My interest in their lives and sharing their great tales were magical. If I did not have those moments of pure reprieve, I would certainly not feel as balanced as I do today. Recharged immensely by this relief. Ames, of course, had presumed he had gone away.

It was also a relief to tell everyone, knowing that everyone would root for me, in the following months. Quite possibly years. Going through the process of litigation to sort it all out. I couldn't wait to now share all the details and be cheered on.

And she wrote: '*Only you know what is best for you and you shouldn't apologise or try and justify why you did what you did. My only concern was that you were burdened with it for so long. I know that if you felt like sharing it would help, then you would have. I don't question why you did what you did. I just wish that you didn't have to do it alone and I am so glad that you finally have help. There's an end in sight. There's a solution around the corner. That's what's important. And kudos to you for all the effort that you put into it alone. That bastard. I want him castrated*'.

Gabor stated that we would work on the Letter Before Claim together, to be sent as soon as possible. So, through November and December, every spare minute was collating evidence. There was a lot of stuff because I had been bombarding everyone for so long.

Most of it was in my Sent file, still. Which for a moment, as I went to access it, I had a thought of 'What if it is empty?'. I knew that there was good evidence that was irretrievable. Like on the old Yahoo email address I had used, for instance. Over the time, through lack of use, Yahoo deleted it. I wrote to them to ask if there was any way that evidence from almost 12 years ago, could be retrieved, of course. No leaf unturned.

I still wondered why the Subject Access Report from the police didn't include my emails. Disappointed also that all the evidence were not returned to me before destroyed. The 52 page website printout, box of ashes and notes sent to everyone would have been handy now. I read through it. There were two female police constables that had tried to do their job of helping me. It hadn't got very far, despite their efforts. It looked like it was just abandoned.

I felt sorry about how let down I was by the government as a rule, not equipping the police with a sufficient guide/code. Which only happen when there is a need for them, I knew and my experience spoke volumes about that.

It was niggling, also that in the report, they kept referring to him as an 'ex-partner' throughout, which made me want to spit (and I am not one for spitting!). I objected to him called an ex-partner, as you know. I kept telling them that a partner was someone that you chose to share your life with. Not someone that you had less than a handful of dates with.

What transpired was that I could have sued the police, too. For negligence. It had to be done within three months and my last contact with them was in fact, 5 months. I had no idea that they were being negligent. I was led to believe that there was nothing that they could do. It hit me like a ton of bricks how incredibly let down by the police, I had been. Thank goodness help was happening now.

CHAPTER FIFTY
Evidence gathering

I had also, on Gabor's advice, paid for an account with DomainTools. From there, we could see the owner and history of each of the websites. Along with the activity and proof of Furran and his company, owning and maintaining them. We could see what dates they were tweaked and optimised. This is when I found out that a lot of the websites were actually bought in January 2005! Despite meeting me and emailing pleasantries to me until we ended in February 2005. My ending it, had not caused him to be unhinged. He already was.

Because it was preconceived, I wondered what else. So many things were unfolding, as evidence was gathered. It was daunting. It was revealing and sometimes surprising and I thought I couldn't be surprised anymore. Yet, not surprised at the same time. For instance, meta tags in the back end of the websites, like 'sexual fantasies' which would lead anyone seeking such, to be led to his sites. Not just anyone searching my name. So, he wanted me to rank under sex searches. We could see that he had updated some that year. He had registered some until 2020, which was four years from this point. Saul Furran did not have any intention to give up.

Gabor's chronological report that he had compiled from the evidence had me shaking my head in disbelief. Seeing what had occurred and when, in black and white, hit home. Emails to Ames helped that didn't include the details but were good memory jogs of time. I had forgotten about those early bits. As I dug around in my memory, once unplugged, the dialogue and the rest flowed. Unearthing and delving into the scenes felt like I was uncovering somebody else's nightmare.

Tapping into the history, feeling shock and violation for the victim. Experiencing anger, as though I hadn't allowed myself to truly feel it, at all, at the time. I couldn't believe how long it had gone on for. Some of it was very uncomfortable to look at and I had waves of embarrassment. How had I not gone insane but also wondered if I had and nobody had mentioned it? Deleting so much evidence at the beginning didn't make it go away, did it? Well, I learned from that. I regretted it. The police destroying evidence without consulting me was another bugbear. Still, there was enough.

It was humbling how much time Gabor gave to my case. It was a massive undertaking, I am sure. His precious time of weekends and nights, given to help me. Evident on emails sent to me, conference calls arranged, availability to explain outcomes. Emails through the night when I was actually asleep. Sleep. I was sleeping for the first time in years.

As I slept, Gabor worked on my case and there was so much comfort in that. When so long I had sought help in the wee hours or worried about what might happen if I slept. I was being looked after in a way that had surpassed any help imagined. His investment. His expertise. Assisting me! My resolve, strengthened. His generosity, immense. It could be 2 years or more. I was on the path of freedom and no longer was harassment walking beside me.

Suddenly, I was talking about it all emphatically to everyone, and thought at one point, I might stop strangers to tell them. I certainly wanted to scream from the rooftops. The sheer thought of not having anything hanging over me or jumping out from the internet was quite simply exciting.

When Gabor sent me the Letter Before Claim draft for me to read, I was sitting at the kitchen table at home. Although this letter would bring no certainty of outcome, tears flowed as it gave me the feeling of vindication. He was being called to accountability. I allowed myself tears of pleasure. He had been caught up with. I gulped tears of relief, again.

Gabor had composed 58 meticulous paragraphs to support my claim, summing up the turn of events of Furran's conduct over 11 and a half years. It was astonishing. I was lifted to great heights. Such indelible support, such elevation and an unsurmountable sense of relief, already. I couldn't wait for it to be sent and it was going to him and his company. It was me against 2 defendants.

The letter began stating the claim that I was making against Saul Furran and his consulting company, for civil harassment, breach of confidence and the tort of misuse of private information and possibly additional causes of action.

Then the background facts of what supported the claim. So to explain in a clearer way:

To reiterate: Harassment is an act when someone's behaviour causes anxiety and distress and is committed twice or more on a person. It is a criminal offence and civil wrongdoing.

There would be no argument that he was committing Harassment throughout with all of the creation, publication and maintenance of the websites and Google adverts. The content that was published on them, including the images were privacy invasions, so they were Breach of Privacy.

Telling the world extremely private information about myself would be covered by Misuse of Private Information because of the loss of my right to control my private info. Also the mental distress that I suffered because of it all. Much of what he did was entwined with Breach of Privacy, too.

Impersonation - on its own is not illegal, per se, but the acts that were involved and how and where he impersonated me, in general, amounts to Harassment. For instance, signing up for the Twitter account (to commit the impersonation) would come under Breach of Privacy. The owning of domain names and the email hacking and copying and removing files was Breach of Privacy. Communicating with my friends and family about the websites, the signing up and maintenance of all internet services in my name and the repeated phone calls. All without my authorisation, of course. That would be all Breach.

Are you still with me?

I couldn't prove that he was involved in the other close proximity events, of course. Everything that we laid claim to, had to have evidence to back it up. Which Gabor detailed. From the history of meeting in 2004, what happened when, the dates the websites were registered, the email address that he used to register them, which was: lindseygoldrickisaliar@yahoo.com at his UK address or Paris address, under his company name or under a privacy shield and all proving that they were all current.

I have listed the full list of websites that I found after litigation here but there were 10 websites and the impersonations for the evidence bundle, at this time. It includes how long they were up on the net for. Some of them weren't even going to expire until two years after the Letter Before Claim was sent, as they had been re-registered. There may have been more.

The list of online creations:

2005 - 2012 lindseygoldrick.com was the one he told me about in January 2005. The one that he didn't delete, as promised. He registered this website anonymously but forgot between the 23rd September 2005 and the 23rd March 2007 and registered it to his Mum and Dad's address, which he also used as his business address, in Sussex. On several dates between 24th March 2007 and the 17th January 2012, the email that he registered it with was: lindsey-goldrickisaliar@yahoo.com
2005 - 2016 LindseyGoldrick.com
2005 - 2011 lindseygoldrick.net
2005 - 2009 lindseygoldrick.info
2005 - 2014 linzigoldrick.info
2005 - 2017 LinzIGoldrick.com
2005 - LinziGoldrick.com
2005 -2017 - linzigoldrick.com Again, there were various dates when he had added a privacy shield but for three years, it was registered to his business address, the email as above and

another, which was the email he had used to communicate with me in the very early days.

2005-2010 Linzigoldrick.org
2005 - Linzigoldrick.co.uk
2005 - lindseygoldrick.co.uk
2005 - 2010 Myanamcara.com
2005 - 2009 soyouthinkyouknowlinzigoldrick.co.uk
2005 - 2009 yesweknowyouknowlindsey.com
2006 - 2009 YesWeKnowYouKnowLindsey.com
2008 - 2018 Anastlyingpieceofwork/lindseygoldrick.-
com was updated during the litigation process, just after we received his Witness Statement admitting everything. It expired two and a half months after the court day. He registered it to his usual address and email address for the first year and went under a privacy shield after that.

2008 - 2016 anastylyingpieceofwork.com
2009 - 2017 linzIgoldrick.com
2010 - 2016 linzigoldrick.org
2010 - Nastypieceofwork.com
2010 - nastypieceofwork.com
2010 - MyAnamCara.com
2012 - Google Ad Banner with the link to: anastylying-
pieceofwork.com. I noticed it in 2014 but as Furran said in his statement that he had been paying for it for long before, I ascertained that it was indeed made two years previously.

2012 - 2016 valentinesdayinthenewforest.com
2012 - 2020 Valentinesdayinthenewforest.com. This was another that Furran re-registered during litigation, using his business email address.
2015 - LinzGoldrick.org
2015 - Twitter accounts: LinziGoldrick-Liar@potest-
solumun, Linzigoldrick@ludibriaventis. One remained active during litigation.

Notes: The websites were registered to Saul Furran and Furran Consulting at various addresses, in the UK, Saudi Arabia, Paris and Germany and the email he used was my name, too. He sometimes registered under a privacy shield when registering them again (but wasn't consistent) and this is how we ascertained that he was the owner of the sites, using DomainTools, when gathering evidence.

There were other websites with my name under every permutation attached to names that only meant something to him or were derogatory statements but I couldn't remember them all. Most of what was listed in the letter were what we obtained proof of. There were registrations at Mum sites, social media platforms, the box of ashes, the anonymous phone calls, some of the threatening emails (but seven were enough) to my yahoo account and work account and so on, and many things that we didn't have concrete evidence of.

The letter finished with a recapping on the laws that I was relying on to state my claim, the remedies that I was seeking and then requesting an acknowledgement receipt.

It was sent to Saul Furran, his company and to Clook, the hosting site, on the 21st December, 2016, via email and also, by post. I thought about Saul Furran's Christmas and that this would give it a slight edge. I thought about the 12 Christmases that I had had, filled with fear, dread and a heavy burden because of what he had been doing to me. I wondered if he felt anything about finally being caught up with and I think his response told me rather a lot and further on, so much more.

There was a quick response from clook.net who confirmed that the websites registered with them were in breach of their rules and they had removed them permanently. Oh, how I had longed to read those words years and years ago. Removed! Breach of rules! Finally! A website had rules.

So, with the accustomed churning in my stomach that always accompanied entering my name into a search engine, I tapped my name into Google, as quickly as possible. I could not wait to see 'no results'.

The thrill of seeing significantly less of the websites was liberating. There was still a few there but this was what I had dreamed of. Progress. Website removal. I couldn't wait until they were all off and then I could breathe. I felt that I was gasping on a large intake of breath until the internet was completely clear of my name in an ugly way. Then, I could breathe until the next stage.

Myself and the police had been ignored but they sat up and listened to a legal letter. This was instant and it felt incredible. I also felt like that reiterated that the police's involvement didn't really have any impact with online companies, at this time. Especially with multi-jurisdictions and overseas registered service providers. Many sites were non-UK based. Unless it was a UK residing perpetrator and hard evidence was found and they were taken to the criminal court. And control was actually taken off people that laugh at arrests and cautions. Along with a consistent use of applicable laws across the forces. Sorry to harp on. Just being sued or threatened with closure made sites sit up to attention because action would most definitely happen. Nobody wants to lose traffic or revenue.

Being hit in the pocket often makes people stop and take action.

Money talks. Sometimes.

CHAPTER FIFTY ONE
Vigorous denial

Now, Steve had said to me that he thought that I may be suppressing anger, since I hadn't shown any over the years. As you know, I had my coping strategy and that had helped pull me through but there had been segments of feeling angry, when his behaviour was forced on me at poignant times of life and death. So, I didn't think I had any in me. Until the point of the beginning of the litigation; when Saul Furran responded to Gabor's letter.

Which was via email a couple of days later. From an email from his company, that he had used to actually register some websites with.

Saul Furran wrote, asking what his company had to do with it and that he vigorously denied it, anyway. That was it.

This was not going to be easy and just the audacity of the man had me feeling combative.

Then we received a letter from Furran's first appointed Solicitors:

The response to a 58 paragraph carefully detailed letter from Gabor was skimmed over. He denied accessing my email account and stated that the initial website was a gift and that those websites were not live anymore (*I screamed out loud at each sentence, as you can imagine and here, I yelped that those particular websites were not live anymore because Gabor had made them go away and that they would still be up there, if not for him*).

He wrote that he was angry because I took my time returning his gifts and he was right to be upset (*I don't scream at this one because I am flabbergasted by this blatant suggestion that this would in any way justify the magnitude of violent behaviour spanning 12 years. Not returning a gift - which you could question who the gift was actually for, if you thought further on that and I had ac-*

tually worn a see through nighty? If it was a gift for me: I am more of a cotton wee willy winky type, actually).

It continued that everything he wrote was true and no emails were doctored and everything was deleted now. He also wrote that he had accepted that the relationship was over in early March 2005. *(I am speechless here. No words).*

He also said that he didn't want any contact with me whatsoever. *(That was a wish that I had 12 years ago, Furran. I hadn't wanted the stalking, either. That was a way of staying in contact wasn't it? A way of making sure that you stayed in my life, surely? I would have loved no contact since February 2005. Truly.)*

He strangely added that he didn't want to be friends. *(Again, a puerile, childish tone underlying. It took me back to the very bizarre, twisted, long email again. He had mentioned in there that his Mum and Dad were disappointed in me. Now, if I had been with Furran for years and lived with him and was close to his family, too, I could accept that this sentence was plausible. Yes, the parents of someone that you shared a life with, may have thoughts and feelings about you not wanting to be with their child anymore, despite not knowing the true reasons but… how little time did we have together? And here, didn't want to be friends? It was quite disturbing).*

And asked that I don't contact him *(I haven't contacted you since that last email back in early 2005, Furran. To ask you to stop harassing me. This wasn't simply a method of contacting you, Furran. This was a letter to let you know that legal action against you for your criminal behaviour was in progress. Not any other ulterior motive. His interpretation of receiving a legal letter where I was being represented, didn't seem rational. It had me concerned that he was thinking that I was sparking up direct contact with him again).*

He denied the anonymous phone calls *(of course he did)* and that 2 of the 10 websites were not registered to him *(well, that makes everything okay and obviously makes a big difference, right? There was only 8 websites that were registered to him)*. He also refuted that I had any claim for damages and that he was going to vigorously contest everything.

That was it! A one page knee-jerk rather immature response, vigorously contesting everything. Gabor's letter was so meticulous and stated evidence to be relied on. Furran had failed to put forward a valid defence and denied that I had any valid claim for damages against him. He was not taking responsibility and he wasn't sorry for what he did and it reeked of revenge.

I looked up his solicitors and noticed that they specialised in mental health issues. I concurred with Steve that I might not get the result that I wanted because now he will be excused. It was clear that anyone in a regular state of mind would not do any such conduct, so he had been wise to choose them.

He wasn't healthy mentally but as long as he doesn't re-register, deletes everything and doesn't do it again, I thought, that is the aim. If he wants to claim that he is ill then maybe he can get help, too and that would be reassuring. As long as I got a guarantee that he couldn't come near me or do any more harm by way of an injunction, it would give me some peace of mind. I did wonder if I was one of many targets and if I would ever find that out.

My mind fast forwarded to the courts. I didn't know how this was going to pan out but the thought of seeing him again, made me feel nauseous. Also, the court situation in my mind was based on a version of a TV Drama and the internet wasn't providing me with any answers, either. It was all rather daunting. If he was contesting that he had any responsibility or because of mental illness, then I envisaged the witness box and giving evidence. It was making me feel sick, the possibility of being cross-examined, despite nothing to hide.

I imagined the impassioned barrister pacing back and forth, his cloak swishing around, dishing out highly emotive and confrontational questions and looking pensive, '*Do you, Lindsey Goldrick Dean admit to sending poetry to Saul Furran?*'. Whilst the Judge strikes his gavel down, in a dramatic finale.

In the grand scheme of things, what had I done, other than communicate creatively via email and meet willingly over a 6 month period? It manifested in my dreams because I had a vivid dream one night that he was sent to prison and he wrote to me from there and told me that he would find me and kill me when he got out.

The Letter Before Claim had been so cleverly crafted that the response of course, gave an indication of how to angle the case. So, Furran denied everything. But he didn't deny civil harassment, breach of confidence and the tort of misuse of private information, which were the three litigating things that covered what he had done. This meant that we could go to court and ask for a non-disclosure (to access confidential information legally, where needed).

In the meantime, I would leave no stone unturned as I worked hard to find every single piece of evidence to prove all of his harassing conduct for 12 years at that point. I hoped that nothing escaped my mind, since it was a long time. I do recall having a recoiling feeling that I may not have known the extent of it, since many times I couldn't investigate too deeply. It was beyond enough to know what I could see that I couldn't remove.

One website would have felt haranguing, not saturated results, as I clicked next page, next page…

CHAPTER FIFTY TWO
The snipping of shackles

Entering 2017, I hadn't had such a feeling of optimistic anticipation and prosperity for a new year since 2005, despite my wishes and deals with the Universe. There was concrete evidence that change was afoot.

The fact that Yair was working on a No Win No Fee and Gabor was working under the auspice of Pro Bono and having such confidence in me winning gave the case more weaponry because it clearly stated that they expected me to win. The fact that they both believed in this, of course, had me buoyant and fortified and seeing that freedom in sight. Oh, it was so very exciting, imagining my life without these feelings of persecution.

I had to keep remembering that anything could happen though. What if he simply disappeared? What if he did actually go into hiding and start creating more or even get more ideas about how to torture me? My expectations needed to be managed. I was pinning my hopes on it all stopping forever but who really knew but him, what he had up his sleeve?

Oh but this was a whole different emotional battle, I could see. Hope was most definitely cemented and stronger. Suspense, thinking about the 'what if's'. But a brevity and lightness came with the freedom to be able to share the story, the process of sorting it out legally and also, that there wasn't anything for anyone to see online now, out of curiosity. Had they still been up, I would have kept shtum.

When advised that I needed compensation and reimbursement for fees incurred, it threw me, really. It was the last thing on my mind, if at all. I wasn't motivated by a financial reward, at all.

I really want it to be clear that it was not about the money!

It was about getting my life back!

My main focus was about making him stop and gaining my life back.

No amount of money could help me do that. Control over my life was more important than any amount of pennies and I had to have the last say. I had to control the end. Compensation would be an admittance…responsibility…a public acknowledgement.

I thought about errors in print and public notices of apology where information was published wrongly from previous publications. Tiny notices saying… 'In the so and so dated publication, we stated that blah, blah and it was actually blah blah and we apologise for any upset'. I wanted something like this but big scale. The largest notice possible in public! So that it would eradicate any misconceptions about me, un-tarnish my name and counteract damage as much as possible.

What was available to me going through the civil court in order to do that made financial restitution part of that process but it was not my concern. At all. It really was no motivation in the quest to make him stop and get full control of my life again. How could it be? I wanted to be free and for him to be penalised enough to make him stop. Which helped me understand the civil court process more and it was so very different than criminal court, with it's black and white punishment process.

I couldn't quantify what I had lost psychologically or emotionally anyway and UK's civil laws wouldn't cover me for emotional hurt. I wanted to just ensure that he didn't do anything else against me in the future but as Yair said, most people do just want to get on with their lives but financial ruin would make him stop and give a clear message to the public.

An amount would be calculated from loss of earnings. I pondered how many people's money would get swallowed, seeking therapy after mental abuse because money was no comfort. My mind was on the legally binding mechanism that would be set in place in order to secure a long term solution that was discussed.

The terms: 'Legally binding' and 'Long term' had me dancing in my mind. I really cannot emphasise what those words did to me.

I had to stay focused what would have a long term effect on me too, though. It was all about control. Autonomy. I could not be controlled any longer. Now that it was possibly going to happen, I could almost feel the shackles being snipped, one by one.

It had concerned my legal team as well that Saul Furran had an opportunity to make amends following the receipt of the letter of claim but chose not to offer an apology, compensation or a promise to refrain from harassing me in the future. His assertion that I was not entitled to any form of compensation (and here, compensation to me was a public acknowledgement) and that he didn't apologise meant that he wasn't acknowledging any wrongdoings.

I thought then that this was going to take a while but I felt so safe for the first time in a long time. It felt like I was being wrapped up and told that everything was going to be okay after this. We just had to be prepared for a long litigation process. His reaction to the Letter Before Claim was a denial. We needed to decide whether to write to him again or file a claim against him to ensure that he didn't use delay tactics as a way of continuing to harass me.

It really didn't take much thinking about what to do and Gabor and Yair advised that filing a claim against him would force him to face his actions and finally acknowledge his wrongdoings. It was inevitable that the case would come to the attention of the court sooner or later by way of resolving the claim or by way of asking the court to approve a consent order between us.

The consent order's terms would state that he had harassed me and he would have to agree that he had and would refrain from repeating similar conduct. Given his response so far about denial, my legal team felt that he wouldn't agree to what will be stated in the consent order either.

So, the next step was that Gabor proceeded to draft the particulars of the claim, which was a more detailed letter than the

Letter Before Claim. It included the nature of the claim, remedies sought, a statement of value, evidence relied on, chronological turn of events, laws relied on to support the claim and so on. Yair and the legal team prepared the court bundle, the list of exhibits and the witness statements. It was all so meticulously prepared. After each meeting, I just felt elevated.

Once everything was prepared, we would be filing the claim with the High Court of Justice in London. Wow! What a building. This seemed surreal. I would be entering this stunning Victorian Gothic building that I had only ever seen from the outside. It had always stood for power, this building. It was significant. It was perfect for me, for the symbolism. For closure. It meant something to me.

I had always wondered what the building looked like inside and little did I know that all I had to do was get stalked for 13 years for my dreams to be fulfilled!

CHAPTER FIFTY THREE
Preparing for trial

Standing in the witness box, though? It came back to me again. What if I am cross-examined and they lay into me and I cry? What if they think that Furran is entitled to freedom of speech? What if the judge thinks that I deserved it and led him on? Shall I wear my glasses so that I can see him in detail or leave them off, so he will be blurry?

My stomach was flipping with anticipation, daily and I needed something to centre me. Aunty Maggie reminded me about meditation and talked me through one, using visualisation. I would totally recommend this as a method of balancing yourself. Deep breathing. Dispelling negative. Rest. Relax.

I visualised a good outcome, 'seeing' myself stepping into power - walking, head up, into a space where eyes were on me. When I spoke, it was clear and it was lucid and strong. I was that powerful person sitting and standing confidently. Totally in control. Powerful stuff. It was most definitely a fantastic practice to have.

Each day, I felt the benefits and my stomach flipped less and less. The unknown is exactly that and preparation seemed impossible but I figured that preparing for being in the public making a statement would not go amiss. Since, wasn't I planning to talk publicly about this experience?

It was noted that Saul Furran's Solicitors had only mentioned that they were acting for Saul Furran and not Furran Consulting, and thus, it was flagged. In February 2017, Yair received an email from Saul Furran at Furran Consulting Ltd, similar to one that Gabor had received at Christmas and it contested that Furran Consulting had anything to do with the allegations, which again, were largely denied. As well as a reiteration that any action would be defended vigorously. Of course, the denial of responsibility email was sent from an email address that had been used on various dates for the registration of www.valentines-dayinthenewforest.com.

He wasn't very good at covering up his tracks, consistently. It was all haphazard. Sometimes, he remembered to be anonymous and then other times, he must have dismissed any thoughts about ever being caught.

We searched for a photograph online of Saul Furran and I wish I had thought of it before he had got his Letter Before Claim because he had worked quickly on removing all evidence of himself. He hadn't posted a clear one on his Soulmates profile and I did not own one. I hadn't taken a photograph of him, either. Gabor had found him on LinkedIn and he had posted a picture of John Wayne as his profile picture and the summary: A Gentleman, A Scholar and An Acrobat. He could now add Psychopath to that list, I figured.

He listed himself as being Director of Furran Consulting Ltd for 17 years at that time. I pondered how his business and his career had prospered for 12 of those years and how he had poisoned mine and robbed me of a quarter of my life and how it had shaped differently. When I had so regretfully shared my dreams with what turned out to be a madman, there wasn't even one thought that he would obliterate that dream. No thought on earth that he would own my name, for goodness sake and that he would commit such violence on me. How the hell had I felt sorry for him?

My Witness Statement took a few drafts and it was interesting, that on every rewrite, I was unlocking the feelings that I had experienced. My first draft had the word 'fear' in it 7 times, the second had the word 'fear' in it 20 times and in my third one, I had written it 34 times. Fear is not a word I could use legally, for that would have taken us down a different legal route, so I had to find alternate words but I most definitely had felt fearful for all of those years and had locked them away.

How does one prove fear? You cannot prove emotions, can you? I also wrote 'harassed' a lot but that was a legal term and I wasn't allowed to use that, either. It was up to the judge and jury to decide that I was harassed. I was prompted to think about how many hours I had laid in a state of anxiety and what emotions had I felt? Could I quantify these feelings in a more concise way? I wrote to Ames about my witness statement.

DIARY ENTRY, 2017: *It's been part of my life for so long and it isn't like I buried my head but now I have help and I am unravelling, there are lots of revealing things unfolding. I cannot believe that it is now 12 years and 3 months since he began his tirade of terror. His unrelenting revenge, his every which way that he tried, his ugliness, his denial and lack of responsibility. He has worked so hard in trying to exploit me. I want that person to learn a lesson, more and more as the time goes by but I am not sure that he has the ability to learn anything and it is rather alarming, since I do not know how this is going to swing.*

He was incredibly creative and thought about all ways that he could affect my life, detrimentally. One thing I am so thankful for is that his troll gang recruitment ploy failed miserably. I didn't have anyone else, as far as I know, join him. Fingers crossed that I haven't jinxed that and some goodness awful something doesn't pop out of nowhere on a site.

I am grateful for my strength to get through it but now it is coming to an end and acknowledgement, I feel a stirring up of something not so pleasant and not sure what it is, when I think about him and what he has done. I guess that I am facing my emotions and this is healing time. It is not in my nature to feel angry. I don't want it in my life. Steve told me to be aware that I may have suppressed it and that I may need some professional therapy but I truly feel that I have had my therapy throughout, as I mentioned, that helped me shift my focus and this experience is being expunged by my writing about it. With each chapter, it gets deeper and I get lighter.

I had actually thought that Steve may need help, too. He has told me that there was so much more 'new' news for him to absorb since I have been gathering evidence; things that I didn't share with

213

him to protect him, whilst he was away. He told me that he was having trouble with some of the things he was finding out but didn't want to discuss it, yet. This leaves me with an uneasy feeling, not knowing what his thoughts are, what mine are - and what is on Furran's mind. I will be so glad of the day that comes when I am not wondering what is going through Furran's mind. I wonder what it will be like to not think about him at all? END OF DIARY ENTRY.

June 2017 - Ames's reply about the statement: '*You are so close to being done with the Witness Statement! It's both scary and exciting, right? That it could have some closure sometime soon? I am not even sure how you wrap your brain around that. I so wish I could have been there for you. Will it be for more than one day? Have they prepared you for what it is that is going to happen? What kinds of questions they'll ask you? I am worried that they will attack your character and imply that you led him on. You are ready for that, right?*

I haven't seen you in more than a decade but I can see your face when they are making you uncomfortable and it hurts my heart. You need to keep reminding yourself that you did nothing wrong and convey that with confidence. You did nothing wrong. He's the psycho that has put you through this for 12 years. He's to blame and he needs to pay. Sorry for that - I just get so angry thinking about that prick!'.

CHAPTER FIFTY FOUR
Too much evidence

Furran didn't admit any responsibility of what he had done to his first lawyer and their letter pertained to such. He denied it to us all. Until he couldn't deny it any longer because we had too much evidence but then, Saul Furran showed incorrigible behaviour because in April 2017, he registered two websites again for another three years until 2020, which was absolutely alarming.

This was during the litigation process, which, for me, volumised his irrationality and disregard for accountability!! Anxiety levels rose again because although I felt safe and buoyant with my legal team, who could ever know what he was going to do? Being vigilant hadn't really left me at that point. I hadn't become too complacent. It was not over yet.

A collective gasp occurred when I told everyone. I was keeping everyone updated about the process and this really weirded me out. It gave the case more clout, of course and surely he would know that but he obviously felt invincible, still and this was a confirmation to me that he might not be finished, regardless of the outcome of the trial entails. It was rather concerning.

Ames wrote, *'It's been a little less than a week since I heard that news and I haven't heard from you since and that is unusual. Are you okay? Should I be worried? Just send me a note that your stalker hasn't abducted you and I will be all set. Just a one liner? Or a text?'*

My dear Ames's concerned words just ascertained how much I would have worried her and anyone else over a long scope of time, if they would have known about this madman's conduct.

It was summer 2017 and I was at work one day. It was during the litigation process and my phone rang twice and I missed the calls. I called back and it just rang and rang until it said, 'The person that you are calling is not available. Please leave a message after the tone' and I hung up. It wasn't typical of a sales or scam call. An online search of the number revealed that it was a personal Vodafone mobile number registered in Germany. Too much of a coincidence.

I called Yair. I have had a great rapport with him, since that first phone call. He wasn't able to help me then and he was now. It meant the world. I was in amazing hands. Although knowing that I was his client and this was business, I felt like he was a trusted friend that wanted the best for me.

We talked about tracing the number if it happened again. Oh, my sweeping mixture of excited and apprehensive emotions. And I kept thinking that something might happen that would compromise the case. That Furran would abscond again. Or conjure up a creative way online to surprise me again.

I worried that my legal team would be pulled away from me, despite knowing that they were committed to me. Up and down. Mostly up. Then, I was feeling an anticipation about court and the possibility of the judge being incredibly old fashioned. Again, I had those thoughts about saying that I had led him on or that Furran was entitled to freedom of speech. 'Was it possible?', I asked Gabor and he said that anything was possible. Nothing could ever be guaranteed, right?

Mama was offered a friend's villa in the Canary Islands, all very last minute. She invited us. I was packed before she could finish her sentence. So, Mama, her friend, Rex and I had a smashing respite. A huge dose of fun. On the flight home, left to my own thoughts, I felt a release and just burst out crying. I had just had this fabulous respite and it occurred to me that it wasn't quite over.

Yet, I could not believe that almost a year had gone and we were at this stage, when I was beginning to think it wouldn't ever stop. Astonishing to get my head around some days. I could not wait to not have this hanging over me. Still, anything could happen. Almost there but not quite. I couldn't imagine what it would feel like, my every day, without this. I could not imagine what a holiday would feel like without it. So lucky to think that there was an end in sight. It filled my head with such excitement that I thought I would burst.

If I hadn't found Yair, and Gabor hadn't picked up my case out of the great goodness of wanting to help, where would I be and how would I be now? The litigation had started 10 months before and that would have been 10 more months of feeling desperate, if it hadn't. They saved my sanity, I know it.

When we got home, I found out that my case had been filed in the courts and the bundles of evidence and particulars of claim had been sent to the crazy man's lawyers. I had taken to calling him crazy man and I hadn't called him anything through all of those years. Filiz, who was working on my case with Yair, had sent me a picture of the bundle - 3 huge box files!

I also heard from Gabor that Furran had applied for his company to be struck off the Companies House register. Being struck off can happen for many reasons but Steve thought that it was so that his wife wouldn't find out about it because she was listed as a partner in the company and it would be hard to hide. So, a letter was sent to Companies House to protest against his application because of the court case (subsequently, his application to strike his company off the register was suspended for the duration of the trial).

I was feeling buoyant and lucky. So, I tapped my name into the internet and nothing! Nothing! No results for Lindsey Goldrick, Linzi Goldrick, valentinesdayinthe…, anamcara…… yesweknow……and so on. Wow! So much had happened in a week. I was rejuvenated and there wasn't just a spring in my step, I was positively bouncing down the street.

CHAPTER FIFTY FIVE
Gang of bullies

His lawyer wrote, asking why he had received the bundles, including the incredible amount of evidence, and Yair wrote and told him that it was courtesy, as another bundle had been sent to Furran's UK address. He then summarised the particulars of claim for them and what we were suing Furran for.

Within half an hour, they wrote and said that they were not going to represent him. I surmised about their decision why. Perhaps that they had realised that they were dealing with a deceptive character and would be difficult to deal with but most likely, they would not judge, would they? And rather just think that it was a complex and too big a case. I just worried that he would disappear if everyone thought this and then what would happen?

It cast within me an urgent need for tighter security again and extra vigilance, worried what he might do if he couldn't find anyone to defend him. I didn't think he would venture closer to me physically but how could I be sure? He wasn't acknowledging responsibility, I reminded myself. So, I subsequently started seeing him in the phone box near our home and in the bus shelter again. They weren't him but in my mind, first glance, they were. Everyone lurking in corners or dark places, was Furran.

DIARY ENTRY, 2017: *I have been pondering about his poor parents. They were innocent in all of this. I presumed, of course but I felt sorry for them. How flummoxed they must feel about this bundle of criminal activity evidence against their son, delivered from a law firm. I doubt that he would ask them to open it but would he return to the UK and open it? What if he goes into hiding? What if he doesn't turn up to court? Will he be arrested when he does enter the*

UK again? Would this go on for years? He has shown he doesn't care by re-registering those websites? He has denied it all.

I am feeling a little anxious about it again now. What if, even with this help, there isn't an end in sight, after all? Why am I even worrying about how it will be in court, when he may just disappear? What if he kills himself? It is close to Rex's Birthday now and boxes are appearing. I keep thinking that another one from him will arrive. Am I being melodramatic? He knows when he was born, for goodness sake. Because of him, I will never know, at this point in least, what it would have been like to bring up Rex; play, chase, love and see him with so much love in my heart, what that would have felt like without the continuous impact of what he was doing. How dreadful it made me feel. But then I reason that Rex is having an even better life because I am adamant about him and us not being affected, so he has so much attention and so many trips and adventures.

Furran isn't a regular thinker, though. He is capable of all sorts. I am guessing and speculating and coming up with theories and actions that he may or may not do and it is no good, I know. I just want this over now. What if they turn it on me in court and scrutinise my behaviour? How do I describe my optimism about a blossoming romance and then after too many issues, it was clear that we were not meant to be? Just like that, I decided. Just how it was. Don't all budding romances start as a leap of faith? END OF DIARY ENTRY.

I wrote to Ames about my feelings about that and she reassuringly, as always, wrote back:

'I think it is good that you are thinking about it a lot. You need to be prepared. You need to know that this is not going to be easy. And you have to be in the right head space to take this on. Just be yourself. And be strong. You have been wronged. We all make questionable decisions throughout our lives. You were in a vulnerable state at the time - recently divorced and feeling the need to be adored since your marriage lacked that and you dated a dolt. We have all dated people that we look back on and cringe about. That doesn't make you wrong. It makes you human. And if anyone pulls the card of question-

ing this, I would ask the lawyer that is grilling you, if he has ever dated someone that he wishes he hadn't. Even if he hasn't, the jurors will certainly go through their own mental check list of the dating mistakes they've made'.

In August, 2017, we received a letter from a new Solicitor that he had appointed and it had me relieved. He wasn't going to disappear and he was taking it seriously, after all. He was getting legal assistance. Phew! Subsequently, the letters came back and forth between us. By now, Saul Furran had to accept that there was too much evidence against him (1,025 pages of exhibits, including the Crime Report, Titled: 'Violence Against Person. Offence: Harassment. Full Course of Conduct) to deny anything.

What was becoming apparent though, was that the Defendant's Counsel letters were contributing to the harassing nature of the whole affair and they caused me even greater anxiety. The tone of the letters made me feel bullied. You don't tell someone that has been harassed for 12 years that they should be *'grateful'*.

And when I received the one that read: *'You can appreciate our client's desire for anonymity'*, I fell on the floor! More on those later but I want to note that Furran had found his comrades. Not via the internet as he had sought hard to do but by his lawyers, advising him how to defend against his victim and how to try to intimidate her. A perfect match. Bullies with bullies.

September 2017 and we were enjoying a visit from JoJo from the States, along with her darling Mum Pam from Nottingham, which was a fantastic, welcome reprieve, for my days were wrapped up in the anxiety of not knowing how the case would unfold. Of course, it was so liberating just to talk openly about any developments but I was still on tenterhooks. I wasn't home and dry yet.

I wish I had kept Teen's clever and funny, stress-relieving texts to me throughout the process. I was so worried that my road to freedom and the litigation would be usurped by something that I deleted anything that may be incriminating. Gabor's words of '*Anything could happen*', reverberated around my mind. I could not take anything for granted.

Anyway, we were about to go Lyme Regis for the day, with Mama. We often go. It holds a special place in many of our hearts. It had been my Dad's favourite place, it is where Steve and I had one of our first dates and also where we had got married. It is where he was now on a woodwork course. He had asked us to visit him. I just needed a quick check on the teamwork programme first, which delayed us by a good hour. I read it out loud to the girls.

I read that Yair had spoken to Furran's lawyers. Furran would agree to an undertaking in line with an injunction. Also, an undertaking to delivery up all materials. If I didn't accept his offer and it isn't settled promptly, they would try to claim that the conduct was historic and that we refused ADR (alternate dispute resolution). They were querying if a success fee is available.

His lawyers had suggested a quarter of what my legal team had put together in a statement, to include damages and costs. Yair had advised them that it will be rejected and advised me that I should accept no less than 75% of the claim amount in order to avoid going to trial.

Again, money didn't incite anything for me, since I wanted him to stop, first. Then, I wanted a public acknowledgement and I wanted for him to be made an example of. I wanted people to know what he had done and I wanted it to be a deterrent for anyone else. I wanted to stop others from being harassed in such a way. I wanted him to suffer and so, as Steve said, if it meant hitting in the pocket, that may get him to stop.

No amount of money could erase what he had done. Nothing could compensate for the mental anxiety that he invoked on me. Any amount of money couldn't compensate for my health. How my career had been stumped. How a quashed ambition affected me. My feelings of safety. He had hijacked my life.

221

Nothing could give me that time back and take away those memories and the rest but offering me a quarter of what my legal team had decided, largely based on a lack of earnings for 12 years of fear, terror, a life and career hijack, was another big kick in the face.

'It is worse than offering me nothing', I stated to the girls, and I caught them up to date, venting along the way.

I didn't want anything, I wanted to scream. I wanted Furran to pay in other ways. Feel remorse. Feel sorry. Furran and his Counsel disgusted me. I thought back to his LinkedIn Pink Panther description: A gentleman, a scholar and an acrobat (bilious taste again) and then the picture of a cowboy.

I wrote to my legal team as soon as possible:

'I wondered about a few things:

An undertaking in line with an injunction - Does this mean that it is a promise that it would be 'like' an injunction but not an official injunction? I would like the protection of a court injunction, if this is the case.

What does 'undertaking to delivery up' mean, please?

What classes as historic conduct, please? He was tweaking around 2 websites just this Springtime. I need to know that none of them or anything like them will reappear and my guess is that unless he is ordered to stop legally with all of the ramifications of that order, he will continue. Whatever he has done historically, is having a very current impact on me and will continue to do so.

I am willing to go to trial, if it means that I need to in order to achieve the above. I am presuming that the trial may be long and drawn out and that I will be cross-examined and perhaps ruthlessly, but I am also aware of your time and costs. Please would you advise. Thank you'.

I had gotten all worked up and kept reminding myself that anything could happen. It was moving. I was grateful for that.

My pensive mood shifted by the time we had got in the car to head to Lyme with the buoyancy of accumulative positive thoughts from the girls and a wisecrack from JoJo.

We were going to have a splendid day!

CHAPTER FIFTY SIX
I really was finally angry

DIARY ENTRY, SUMMER 2017: *I have been stifling my anger for so long and now I had an outlet and there's no stopping me. I was finally angry about it. I have channelled my fear and my frustration into finally giving him the anger that he deserved. I was now allowed to let go of all of those emotions that I had suppressed to get through. They were coming out at a good time.*

I so desperately wanted to know then why it will most likely settle out of court, if I didn't agree to any amount of money that would warrant 12 years of abuse. If he is pleading guilty, there was nothing to discuss in court though. I wanted the judge in the robe, slamming down the gavel which would symbolise that it was final (obviously, all of my courtroom experience was based on TV Dramas - nothing like the real thing!).

I want it splashed all over the media and for it to be a warning to others. I want to know why I cannot have a trial. It now feels like I cannot have vindication if it settles out of court. I want to feel in control and I would like to make it public. So that nobody again should ever have to go through anything like this.

Then there would be meaning to what I have been through.

We need the court for shaping future cases and providing reference. I don't want to make a quiet agreement. I want everyone to know what he did and that I stood up to him and won in the end. Awareness is not going to happen if I stay quiet about this. If the media are interested in this case, then I help others and it may encourage others to think twice and that people can be found, even across the world, even when they think they are hiding their identity. Strong message, regardless. I need to do good with this and he needs to be made an example of. Im in control now, surely?

Trial has been talked about since the beginning and I didn't think there was an option, unless money was agreed instead of a trial but I don't want money but if the crazy man is admitting to it all, what is there to argue about in court? I want to set a precedent in law. That would be my vindication and I would feel like the last quarter of my life was not in vain.

It looks like, at this point, that the civil courts encourage you to settle out of court. Would it go against me, if I didn't? I need the court to get the injunction and to ensure that he won't do this again. How could I ever be sure of what someone like him would be capable of or not do it again? It will not be reassuring if I don't have an injunction, though and he can hide away and no-one need know what he has done. His lawyer may be feeling that money would be attractive to me since I have a Pro Bono barrister and a No Win No Fee solicitor. I really don't want any money. He needs to pay in different ways to be stopped from doing any more or to anyone else and it needs to be a deterrent.

Online abusers think they are safe behind the internet with a hidden address, wherever they are, with their nasty bullying, childish vengeance and their sad lives. My getting my life back and not allowing my mistreatment over the years by all of the people in authority and the lack of regulation on the internet can not go wasted. No human being should ever have to go through what I went through. There has to be a STRONG message that comes out of this. END OF DIARY ENTRY.

The letters went back and forth and our letter to him gave him a clear instruction that money was not of interest to me and they responded by asking for an extension for 28 days. Why did I have to be so reasonable and allow him this? Why should he be allowed so much extra time? It was another month. I wanted it to be steered to court as soon as possible and being reasonable to him is nothing I would ever want to be.

Why would the court see this as a negative that I did not want a monetary settlement out of court in order to save the courts time? There wasn't another case like it and nothing to compare it to. So what if he is poor, as his lawyers told us. He found plenty of money to make and host 25 plus websites and online banner advertisements.

I bet he didn't have to reduce his hours at work through fear and nervous tension and being constantly in the fight or flight mode. Or find it a hard slog to earn money after being up all night long trying to close someone down and stop them from doing something so life-changing and so far reaching across the world wide web, that was escalating and ruining his life? I bet his last thoughts at night were not dread about what the next day may bring with a pounding heart and fear for his family's safety?

I fell down the stairs when I was pregnant and nearly lost my baby because I thought he was in the house, for goodness sake! Why did I have to consider anything about his state of affairs at all? Yes, I knew that I could be done for being seen as unreasonable but I really, really wouldn't ever feel that charitable towards him, funnily enough. Now, that's reasonable!

With those thoughts playing on my mind when I went to bed, I had a nightmare: We were in the courtroom and Furran's lawyer was a huge man and his shirt was bursting at the buttons. He was sweeping around the court room, urging people to join in with jeering with his smarmy remarks that he was throwing at me.

Furran was handcuffed and told that he was going to prison and he shouted to me that he would find me afterwards and do what he had intended to do for all of those years; that he would find me and kill me and his face twisted as he laughed out loud. I woke, screaming and Rex was by my side, asking if Mummy was okay. I held this dear, exquisite little soul so tight and cursed the day that I hit 'submit' to Soulmates and blasted my silly, romantic self. There was no reprieve when dreaming anymore.

The nightmare stayed with me, day in and day out. I couldn't wait for this to be over but I felt afraid of how it would end, despite knowing that I had the most fantastic legal team. I just felt that this wouldn't ever be over for Furran.

CHAPTER FIFTY SEVEN
The threat of looking 'Unreasonable'

It was a week later that a letter came from his lawyers and he had made me an offer of money to settle, along with a threat that if I didn't take the money (and they sent a form to sign to accept it), then I would look unreasonable.

I know that I mentioned it before and I knew that this was a term for a court case but some terms just had me hopping. Unreasonable? Because there is nothing unreasonable about the way he has treated me for the last 12 years, is there? It's unconscionable that the term unreasonable would ever be a term applied to me.

I wrote to Ames:
'He should be treated like the criminal that he is, Ames.
Having to sue him through the civil courts is my only option, as he wasn't treated in the criminal courts and the civil courts are designed to settle out of court. The Part 36 rules try to make you sort it out before you go to court. If he'd have contested it, he wouldn't have made an offer and it would have gone straight to court. If I appear less than reasonable because I don't accept the offer, it could go against me. He hasn't contested and so it doesn't go to trial. I have had a legal team that have spent a gazillion hours over this and I have spent a gazillion hours searching for evidence and reliving every little detail just to agree to an amount of money and an agreement that the defendant can 'voluntarily' stay away from me? And hand stuff to me that he created about me that has been digital and public for 12 years? That is it? It cannot stay so hush hush. I feel worked up'.

Saul Furran did not deserve such an easy sentence and I truly thought that he would not learn a lesson by such a quiet and easy resolve, if one such as him could learn a lesson, that is. But it would give a strong message to the world and certainly do me good long term, if he admitted and apologised to me publicly. Where was the deterrent, other than if he did anything again? He was living his private life with his career and his wife in Germany or Switzerland, I believe. Nobody would ever find out. His name wasn't unusual. He could slip away. It was calculated. It was deliberate. It was intentional hurt and so public and so damaging and unending.

Why could he, after committing crimes, walk away, quietly, scot-free? I wondered how his lawyers, knowing that they were defending a person that had so obviously done wrong for 12 years without intention to stop, could join him by way of writing aggressive letters to me. I wondered why they felt they needed to put another layer of bullying and intimidation in the bag and actually be okay with that. It was downright unnecessary.

Ames wrote back: '*You need him to be outed. The story needs to be in the paper. He needs to be shamed for the rest of his life as the weirdo stalker who wouldn't let go of a woman he dated for 3 seconds. And though I know you know this, you could have slept your way through the States and England and it still wouldn't justify what he has done to you! Your relationship history has nothing to do with this. Nun or whore (none of which you are, clearly! Ha!), he is 100% in the wrong and you need to get the justice you deserve by being wronged. Stay angry. You have put so much time and energy into this that you didn't have to do if it weren't for that bastard*'.

I was confused. My legal team explained that there was a case where someone was accused and he took the blame and offered money. The Claimant wanted vindication and asked for a Joint Statement in Open Court, which would mean that it goes down in legal history. The court awarded it but both parties had to pay the legal costs, which was thousands. I was told that the court may suggest I get more than the offer or less.

So, the dilemma was - do I risk it? Or accept the offer and write about it to make an example out of him and to make changes going forward, so that others will benefit?

228

I felt disgruntled about having to accept an offer of money and not getting time in court and bringing it to justice and making an example of him. I would look unreasonable if I don't accept? So, what was it all about because it wasn't ever about money to me? I was all sorts of upset because I didn't like this money talk and offers and all of that because it was about control. That is what I wanted from this. To feel that I was in full control of my life again and that he doesn't get to have the last say. He gets to carry on with his life and his wife may never know and nobody will learn from this. I felt so upset with the system.

Yes, I know he was bobbing in and out of the country and that was hard to monitor but there had to be a way. If they had been able to help, then he would have been tried at the criminal court and been punished. A long time ago. Money would not have been part of it. Now there was a chance that I may incur costs. It is so wrong. I had been blessed with a legal team to help me sort it out this way and the hours that they had put in, had to be worth it. I know that they would get satisfaction from helping me but I had to maximise the results, right?

So, we declined his offer and made him an offer which was significantly less than what he had offered me and too good to refuse for him but I wanted it proclaimed in public what this man had done to me because what he did was very public. I wanted to say out loud and clear, at the top of my voice, how he had impacted a quarter of my life so dramatically, for so long and people would hear it. It was necessary.

I had to turn it into something good to bring about change. I would never move on without that public acknowledgement. I didn't want anyone to go through a day of what I went through without support, help and understanding from authorities and change happens when people speak out. It started here. For me. For others.

CHAPTER FIFTY EIGHT
An unexpected response

So, that public announcement, the Joint Statement in Open Court was attached to my offer as a condition. Upon acceptance of a settlement offer in a libel, slander, malicious falsehood and/or misuse of private information claim, I was able to apply for permission to the court for approval, to make a statement in open court because I was not only bringing a claim against Saul Furran for civil harassment and breach of confidence, but also the tort of misuse of private information.

If it wasn't going to trial, at least I would have my public recognition of how my rights had been infringed by public disclosures on the internet. The apology from him to me would be compensation and the Judge agreed that I was entitled to a public commitment. It was not to punish him. It was for closure. This was the most important part of the settlement for me. It mattered so much!

This had to be approved by a High Court Judge, of course. Not everybody could have one but this would satisfy the public vindication, as what he did was very public for 13 years and with a Joint Statement which would have been mutually worded, we were offering Saul Furran the chance to acknowledge his wrongdoing and publicly apologise to me.

We also promised that we would not seek Aggravated Damages for the particular bad behaviour, which was: The reply from his company email address, the one that he used to register one of the sites, to deny all of the claim against him and also, in spring 2017, during litigation, he renewed two of the domains.

It was too good to turn down really because I was being 'reasonable' and wanting to settle out of court because it created cost consequences which are quite rule-based. Now, cost consequences with Part 36 Offers - if I even began to explain them, are complicated and I would definitely lose you if I tried (if you have made it to here). To simplify, it would make his life difficult if he didn't accept.

Now, when a letter was sent, a date was given for the other side to respond by and that date lingered in my mind, never needing to write it down, despite the busyness of life. So, the date rolled by and they were not always on time but this time they were.

His lawyers wrote back and declined the offer and said that, wait for this….I fell on the floor…because along with the initial denial, the renewal of new website registrations during litigation…the lawyers stated that their client, Furran………

does not want to be found on the internet!

Astonishing to see that in print. I am going to repeat it, for dramatic purposes:

HE DOES NOT WANT TO BE FOUND ON THE INTERNET!

'Neither did I, Furran. Neither did I! You also knew that I was so adamant about privacy. You loved devoting your time to putting me on there in a slanderous way. Ensuring maximum exposure by search engine optimising those sites. It was a determined exercise'. I was flabbergasted. I was angry. His legal team must be delusional too - for actually typing it up.

He does not want to be found on the internet!

So, because he wasn't going to agree to a Joint Statement, which would be found on the internet, we were now preparing for court again. He cannot have it is his way. He cannot and will not have complete control of this.

By declining the opportunity of making a Joint Statement, of course he wouldn't be looked upon favourably. If he had agreed, he was admitting to it publicly. He wanted neither but of course, I didn't want him to have the last say about this. It felt extremely important to me to be publicly apologised to and for him to admit what he has done publicly.

So I applied and was approved by a High Court Judge beforehand to make a statement by myself: a Unilateral Statement. Of course, when it was clear that I was permitted to make such a public statement (and his lawyers fought hard to convince me otherwise) about what he had done and it was going ahead, he realised that this would be out in the public and of course, he didn't want it to be. I was in control.

So, then realising that he would look worse and that the High Court Judge had ruled that I was entitled to one, he retracted and wanted to make a Joint Statement after all, but it was too late at this point. He had his chance to make a Joint Statement, which would have been mutually agreed.

Then, it was so unbelievable to me that they wanted to approve my statement beforehand with the view to make changes. It was my Statement.

Again though, after discussing it with my legal team, because he wasn't a rational person, he could very well fight it to the end and the letter exchange costs money, so from here, extra costs could occur, as I had refused the offer. The judge may offer less. I could incur all costs onwards.

It would also save time, to settle on the words out of court's time, which of course was encouraged, as you could imagine the hours ticking by whilst words were being agreed. So, we agreed that Furran could approve my statement beforehand. It gave me a really bitter taste though, I will admit but that is when it hit me:

No amount of words on a statement would ever be justice.

No words in black and white could really depict what had happened.

We could go back and forth forever but my mental health was more important. I couldn't be stuck here wanting the wording to be perfect. It never would be enough.

I had to settle as soon as possible, so that I could use it as a tool to move on and heal, as soon as possible. Nothing would ever provide me with the justice for what he did to me but what I did afterwards, was what I needed to move on, mentally. The courts were not a magic wand. It was part of the process, just as was the anger that I was experiencing.

I had to get through it in order to do greater good and to help me move. It is what I did with it afterwards that would bring me peace. It wasn't to do with him. There was no him making an impression on my life in a negative way anymore. He had to deal with the consequences of what he did and although I don't think he believes that he was wrong and is sorry (I couldn't change that ever), I believe in the greater realm of karma. I would heal. He wouldn't. I was more important.

That is why at this stage, I adapted my mind. I trusted my legal team and they were doing the best that they could for me and it could quite easily have gone a different way. I could print the truth and whatever I liked, going forward.

Focus on what I can control.

What I am in control of is my future.

CHAPTER FIFTY NINE
Statement in Open Court

I have included the original Unilateral Statement in Open Court (USOC). Due to the defendants' requests for removal of so much detail, it was reduced considerably and what was read out was a concise version of the below. There are more details below the Statement, which is around five pages away.

USOC: *From about March 2005 until the start of these proceedings in August 2017, the Defendants engaged in a course of conduct against the Claimant which amounted to civil harassment, the tort of misuse of private information and breach of confidence.*

Throughout this period, Defendants' unlawful conduct was carried out primarily by means of designing, registering, creating, publishing, owning, maintaining, updating, administering and controlling at least 10 websites ('Offensive websites'), some of which were named after the Claimant and all of which contained materials about or relating to the Claimant, including a mixture of offensive, private and/or confidential information. Neither Defendant sought the Claimant's consent to any of this activity, nor would she have given her consent had it been sought.

To refer to the First Defendant's position on these matters in the present proceedings, his Witness Statement dated 11 October 2017 stated at Paragraph 36: "Although I did not think of it in that way at the time, with hindsight I accept that a lot of my conduct following the break-up of my relationship with the Claimant could be characterised as harassment."

Also, according to paragraph 37 "[…] appreciate that the publication of some of this material may have constituted a breach of confidence and/or misuse of her private information, although I did not have any appreciation of the law in that area at the time. I can see that it looks unreasonable, and indeed, spiteful of me, to have pub-

lished his material in that way, and that I should have known that it would upset the Claimant".

Further, the First Defendant's Witness Statement stated at Paragraph 38: "In respect of some of the Offensive Websites, I used the Second Defendant - Furran Consulting Ltd to register and / or purchase the domains."

Between at least March 2005 and June 2005, on a number of occasions the First Defendant emailed, telephoned, and/or sent post to the Claimant, despite her repeated requests to him to stop communicating with her.

During the same period, the First Defendant also used similar methods of communication to make contact with members of the Claimant's family, as well as several of her friends and acquaintances to bring the Offensive Websites to their attention.

According to his Witness Statement, paragraph 39: "I also accept that, on a handful of occasions, I contacted third parties whom the Claimant knew and directed them to the Offensive Websites."

The Claimant complained to the police on several occasions about what she then perceived as a campaign against her by the First Defendant. After one of these reports by the Claimant, on 15 September 2005, the police arrested the First Defendant for harassment of the Claimant and gave him an adult caution.

As his Witness Statement stated at paragraph 56:"It is correct that in September 2005, I was arrested on suspicion of harassing the Claimant. [...] I admitted everything that I had done, and expressed my regret. I was given a caution."

But this still did not convince the Defendants to cease their campaign against the Claimant. From October 2005 to December 2005, the Defendants created further Offensive Websites.

In addition, according to Saul Furran's Witness Statement, paragraph 62: "[...] at some point in this period (between December 2005 and August 2007; I do not recall when, I deliberately 'search engine optimised' the Offensive Websites to try and ensure that they ranked prominently on a search of Lindsey's name."

In about November 2007, the police again made plans to arrest the First Defendant, but found that he was living outside the

235

UK much of the time and eventually sent him an email stating that, unless he removed the Offensive Websites, he would be arrested.

Yet, the Defendants' campaign against the Claimant continued. In September 2008 and February 2012, the Defendants created additional Offensive Websites.

As Saul Furran's Witness Statement - paragraph 63: "[…] I became aware that Lindsey, the Claimant was taking steps to have the websites removed from the Web. I appreciate that I should have left her to do this, or better still, removed them all myself. Instead, I accept that on 17 September 2008, I registered a further domain […]."

And according to his Witness Statement, paragraph 66: "I accept that on 2 February 2012, I created a further domain […]. I admit that I did this because I knew that Lindsey was taking steps to have the others removed or blocked by Google. This was the last of the Offensive Websites which I created."

In about 2014, the Defendants bought a Google banner advertisement which included a photograph of the Claimant and a link to one of the Offensive Websites.

As Saul Furran's Witness Statement stated, paragraph 67: "It is true that I created a Google advertisement (which Lindsey describes as a banner) for one of the Offensive Websites. I cannot remember when this was."

In 2015, the First Defendant created two user accounts on Twitter , the social media website, using the Claimant's name. To each account, the Defendant posted messages containing the Claimant's photograph and a link to one of the Offensive Websites.

According to his Witness Statement, paragraph 68: "It is also true that, at some point in 2014 or 2015, I created two Twitter accounts in Lindsey's name. These both contained between one and three Tweets that I wrote with quotes from the Offensive Websites […]".

As of December 2016, when counsel for the Claimant wrote a letter before claim on her behalf to the Defendants, at least two of the Offensive Websites and one of the Offensive Twitter Accounts remained online and available on the internet to the general public. A copy of the Letter Before Claim was received by a third party which was providing hosting services to the Defendants for the two Offensive Websites in question. The Third Party then reviewed the content of these Offensive Websites, found them to be in breach of its terms of business and took them offline. Sometime thereafter, the remaining Offensive Twitter account was removed, but the Claimant has no knowledge of how this came about.

Despite the Letter Before Claim, the Defendants' Campaign against the Claimant did not end. In March 2017, the registration of a domain name previously used by the Defendants to publish one of the Offensive Websites was updated by the First Defendant and / or the Second Defendant, with the result that the expiration date of that domain name was extended to February 2020. In May 2017, the registration of another domain name previously used by the Defendants to publish an Offensive Website was updated by the First Defendant and / or the Second Defendant, so that the expiration date of the domain name in question was extended to September 2018.

The Defendants' campaign against the Claimant has caused her enormous anxiety, mental distress and embarrassment. It has adversely affected the Claimant's health, her relationships and damaged her professional career.

The First Defendant, on behalf of himself and the Second Defendant, has now apologised to the Claimant for their unlawful conduct (on his Witness Statement below - the obligatory legal bit that he did not write)…"I wish to apologise to the Claimant for the matters that have given rise to this claim……[…]…..I very much regret this and have given my assurances to the Claimant that there will be no repetition of the conduct complained of […]."

The Defendants have agreed to pay damages to the Claimant and also to pay her legal costs. Further, the Defendants have agreed to a number of undertakings akin to equitable remedies, including:

1.   Not to pursue any conduct which amounts to harassment of the Claimant, or to a misuse of private information about or relating to the Claimant, or to a breach of confidence against the Claimant.

2. Not to publish on the internet any information about or relating to the Claimant, whether on a website operated by any of the Defendants or otherwise.

3. Not to impersonate the Claimant, whether by opening accounts in her name on websites operated by third parties or otherwise.

4. Not to access or otherwise interfere with any computing equipment, communications equipment or software used by the Claimant.

5. Not to communicate with the Claimant by telephone, by email, or by any other form or electronic or non-electronic communication.

6. To deliver up to the Claimant any documents in their possession, in any electronic or physical format, which are about or relate to the Claimant.

7. To transfer to the Claimant the ownership and control of any domain name, presently registered to the Defendants, which includes or refers to the Claimant's name and which has been used by the Defendants for the publication for an Offensive Website.

My Lord / Lady, for the record, the statement I have read is made unilaterally by the Claimant. The Defendants declined an offer by the Claimant to settle this litigation in a manner which would have included a joint statement in open court. The Defendants refused to agree to any such joint statement.

So, here is what Furran requested to change on my Statement out of court:

He asked me to take out the fact that he had a Police caution and with hesitation, we agreed, eventually. Only because I wanted to get this over and done with. It is an important fact in the case, though. If I broke the law through lack of knowledge, I would still be breaking the law. Ignorance is no defence. A caution should be a deterrent. He went against the Justice System. It is an important, integral aspect of the case because he was warned and he carried on. His Course of Conduct continued in the same vein despite that important police cautioning. Continuing on emphasises his resolve in pursuing his intent of harassment.

They insisted that the caution was spent but it wasn't because it was for the same crime that he committed, which he took no notice of. Still, in order to lessen court time, I agreed to keep it out of my Unilateral Statement, so there wouldn't be anything to contest. This was an extremely significant compromise from me because it was a highly aggravating feature in the case.

They complained about the length of the statement but we didn't change that, because such a statement is an expression of freedom and I was entitled to that since there wasn't a limit on words as a rule.

He didn't like that I referred to the websites as 'offensive' and I think I coughed and spluttered quite a bit over that one. Offensive was actually a very toned down word for the way they made me feel and what they were but of course, I am going to keep expletives to the minimum. Because he didn't like that they were referred to as offensive suggested so much to me, also. It suggested that he wasn't agreeing that they were offensive, of course and that is exactly what they were: Offensive (among other things).

He didn't want it read out in court that he had declined an offer made by me to settle the litigation in a manner that included the Joint Statement in Open Court.

I read that out to everyone that wanted to hear and the general consensus was: Wtf? Apart from those that don't swear! He didn't want anyone to know that he was admitting to 13 years of violence towards me and he didn't want to apologise for it, either. That is the truth. That is the cloth of the man.

They didn't like our Statement at all. They even, (can you believe this?) sent a total rewording of my Statement; one that 'they approved of'.

He had missed his chance and now wanted a total wholesale rewording in what I was saying in my Unilateral Statement in Open Court. He didn't want to make a Joint Statement but he wanted a say in mine! The nerve of it all. It made my blood boil.

The fight for control was made even worse by this legal gang. Furran and his counsel. Absolutely appalling. Although, I was willing to negotiate (begrudgingly and with a bitter taste in my mouth) and make some changes because they may have contested it in court (and again his lawyers reminded me, by way of a threatening letter, that if I was seen as unagreeable to settle out of court, I might incur costs), and that the Judge might (or might not) agree to their changes and at this stage, I really wanted to save time.

I look back at this, and I remember thinking that 'surely the court wouldn't lean on his side. Surely the court wouldn't contest my words. Surely this and surely that. The truth is, as stated: 'Anything could happen. No guarantee'. You cannot predict what is going to be ruled and it was always better to err on the side of caution. At this point, it was clear to me that it would be a huge compromise but I still felt I had to control it as much as I could.

His witness statement that he wrote just made me feel sick when I read it for the first time. I would go so far as saying that it was astonishing. It was so completely incredulous to me. We are three years on since I received it and I respond sarcastically here now but at the time I was hopping up and down and turning purple; so emphatically flabbergasted was I.

Subjecting me to all that he did was trivialised by him with 78 paragraphs that screamed of self pity and a plea for understanding (which only deepened the worry for me that he thought this was explainable, which accentuated his irrationality and that perhaps he believed that anyone might say, 'Oh that makes sense. She was besotted with him for a few months and then ended it and that's why he sabotaged her life and harassed her for 13 years').

It is beyond ridiculous. It is pathetic. It is so astounding that I was gobsmacked and I don't think I talked for a whole day when I read it…and that is saying something.

240

CHAPTER SIXTY
His Witness Statement

His Witness Statement read that he believes he is the victim and that he didn't believe that it was unlawful (which to me, emphasises the disregard for the police arrest and caution). He only admitted to what there was concrete evidence of, which was enough. It starts out with the obligatory apology. The first 9 paragraphs, we get a biography about his achievements in life and what he does and doesn't like, i.e. He didn't like his Maths and Physics course at university.

Then, he moves onto the journalism course and writing for a newspaper and then setting up his own business - technical writing in the UK and overseas and how under the terms of his visa, he had to leave Saudi Arabia once a month. He used that requirement as an opportunity to try and see a different foreign country each time, and explore the world, *'which was a wonderful experience'*, he wrote.

Isn't that lovely to know? It warmed my cockles. Of course I was moderating my feelings with humour, when I wanted to combust. I was simply irritated that he was painting a nice little picture in order to somehow seek favour and that he would even consider that he could possibly be excused. As well as blatantly pointing out that he had been having a *'wonderful experience'*. It also clarified that he was incapable of empathy.

Paragraph 10 started out like a piece from a travel review site and I think it ended up in his statement by mistake: *'Riyadh is a strict and conservative Muslim city, and fraternising or flirting with women outside of marriage is strictly prohibited. Alcohol consumption is also illegal, and unlike some Arab states, exceptions are not generally made for ex-pats (or they were not whilst I was there). For those reasons, a lot of my time away from work was spent alone in my flat in the Faisaliah Apartments. When I told people on my travels that I was living and working in Riyadh, their response was always along the lines of 'oh no, poor you'. Many of the other ex-pats there used to fly to Bahrain or Dubai, which were (relatively speaking) a lot more liberal, every weekend to have a 'blow out'. I tried this, but after a couple of occasions, it did not appeal to me'.*

Then it moves onto how he only wanted someone to write to when he joined the Guardian's Soulmates. What was wrong with penfriend.com or ionlywanttowritetosomeone.com? Why would you join an online dating site if all you want to do is write to them? Irrelevant.

Anyway, backtrack to his statement and how he dated someone and then he was free for a bit and then, I contacted him (which I don't recall but that is neither here or there) and *'most women lost interest'* when they learnt where he was *'but not Lindsey, who was 3 years younger than me'* (what the heck has that got to do with anything?

It reads like a novel) and when he came home to visit his dying Uncle in Cleethorpes, he squeezed in a date with me in Oxford (perhaps that is because Oxford is only 170 miles away from Cleethorpes - just a skip and a hop and yet I recalled a visit solely to meet me. Funny how stories change, isn't it? And each person's different perspectives of events. Anyway, where was I? Back to the 'Let's feel sorry for Saul Furran' novel. I have to show you paragraph 15:

'From that very first date, Lindsey seemed very keen on me, to the extent that I was somewhat overwhelmed. I had to fly back to Riyadh a few days later, but thereafter we were in almost constant communication. I quickly got the impression that Lindsey was in love with, perhaps even besotted with me. I stress that I do not say this now to embarrass Lindsey or rake up the past, but simply to try and put some context, events that would happen later'.

There isn't any embarrassment…just astonishment. This is the reason why he did what he did? It was because I was besotted with him and then I wasn't! He was the victim? I was so besotted with him that I ended it? It had nothing to do with his

242

ugly behaviour at all. Rake up the past? Raking up the past is what I have had to do in order to give a chronological run down of your vicious conduct since you started this campaign 12 plus years ago, Furran. That is what I call raking up the past. Was he serious?

Then, he talks about having no internet connection at home (so he used work's time and their equipment to create everything about me) and reminded us all that *'this was 13 years ago'*. He talks about when we met again and gets dates wrong and all that but 'it was 13 years ago'.

He writes about knowing that I wanted to have my own writing business and that he thought I would enjoy reading his cuttings file that contained a few local football match reports in, so he left it with me, even though it was *'the most important thing that he owned'*.

He didn't come back for Christmas and felt that I was judging him harshly for not being with his family (whilst Mama and I were packing for The Maldives). He talks about going to an Embassy 'do' and how he had told me that he had met a girl there and that I appeared upset by this (this word 'upset' that is flung around is really bugging me. It isn't even appropriate here. It is a too strong word here and yet, a too weak one in others. His journalism course paid off, I see).

He then moves onto the New Forest, where I said it had to be the end (I had sinusitis, he was cruel) and he says that I was quite different (could have been the sinusitis and the pounding head, yes?). And *'Lindsey wasn't clingy or needy, as usual and actually quite distant and I was taken aback by this and I asked her if she wanted to break up with me.*

Lindsey was quite a social animal, at that time, whereas I did not drink at all, owing to living in Riyadh. I told her that if she wanted someone local to go out dancing at weekends with, then she should but it was definitely not over!'.

There are a handful of comments here from me:

1. I hadn't been called clingy or needy before, as I had always been known as independent, free and confident but it was his delusion, I decided and reading through, I knew that there would be more.

2. Social animal is something I used to be, pre 2005. You are absolutely right!

3. Dancing is not reserved for just the weekends.

4. It most definitely was over!

5. If I was clingy and needy, do you think I would have chosen to date someone that lived in another country for most of the time, that I would see on a splattering of occasions? It is just that I am sure that if I felt needy, it would be a prerequisite for someone to be more local, maybe. I could be wrong.

Then he talks about the setting up of: lindseygoldrick.com and lindseygoldrick.net and initially putting odes on there to me as a gift. He wrote that he thought I would appreciate them and despite my saying that I didn't and implored him to '*get them down immediately*', he registered another one and another and another.

He was wondering why I wasn't emailing or calling and it left him feeling isolated in a foreign country (but let's remember that he had to leave soon as part of the visa requirements), where it was scary for foreigners (but he chose to be there and it wasn't military or aid work). He would lie in foetal positions in his apartment with knots in his stomach, he wrote and then when he was able to get up, he would take the highly dangerous walk in the middle of the night to where he works (to use the internet and work on the websites and send threatening emails to me).

He states that he was aware that these websites might be causing me great anxiety and that it could be considered harassment and so he proceeded to make more. He justifies all of his conduct by suggesting that I led him on. He stated that I quickly fell in love with him and that I was so besotted with him and it was overwhelming and that when I ended it, it made him angry and he wanted his cuttings file back and the (pervy, weird) nighty and underwear (?).

'*I also accept that, on a handful of occasions, I contacted third parties whom Lindsey knew and directed them to the 'Offensive Websites'. I never had to do any extensive research or snooping around to find the contact details of these people. Nevertheless, it was clearly unacceptable behaviour which, again, I accept would have likely caused Lindsey some upset*'.

You know how I feel about 'upset' but the rest of this paragraph? How can he deny extensive research finding them all? I was not on Facebook, which only started the year before and it didn't do it for me, so I closed my account before I met Furran (and Twitter didn't exist until 2006) and nor did he ever meet anyone that is close to me, know their last names or addresses? How did he find my ex-husband's private email address and he had a different last name? How did he find Debs's landline number, when he didn't know her last name? No, no extensive research or snooping around, hacking or stalking was necessary, was it?

He states that he was aware that I was taking steps to having the websites removed, so it encouraged him to make another in 2008. And after giving himself a little break from creating more websites and just tweaking the ones that he was continually registering, until 2012, he decided to make a couple more: valentinesdayinthenewforest.com and co.uk. Bearing in mind that all of them stayed live and the advertisement was in between those times. He also accepts that he changed some wording on the websites in 2016, to reflect my age and keep it updated. Yet he claims, with unreflecting audacity, that back in 2008, he had stopped thinking about me because he had a wife.

(I cannot express how many times I had hoped that genuinely that would have happened. He had a wife but he was still thinking about me).

He talks about closing his Company down long before the litigation but it had just been filed when we contacted Companies House to put it on hold until after the litigation. He claims that he is the victim. He keeps saying how silly everything must sound and that he could see how I would feel upset (there's that word again!) And 'with hindsight, my conduct could be characterised as harassment' and because he was highly emotional about it and irrational (but only some of the 13 years), he decided to send me the box but didn't mean to cause alarm and there was nothing sinister about it (just the ashes and the lipstick blotting and the threat!).

'As per the foregoing, I did not understand that the relationship was truly over until Lindsey's email to me in early March 2005. I believe this email to be her email of 6 March 2005, produced at page 553 of her exhibits. Even if I was mistaken (and clearly, I was not thinking particularly rationally at the time), none of my actions or communications with Lindsey prior to that date were designed to cause her any alarm or distress, nor did I believe they could'.

But the next 13 years were!!!

'It is true that, upon receiving Lindsey's email of 6 March 2005, I replied (on 7 March 2005), 'I knew you'd find some excuse to keep the lingerie. Send it back or I shall be forced to drive down there and pick it up myself. And we wouldn't want that would we, knowing how 'private' you are!....' Reading this now, I appreciate that it sounds both ridiculous (in terms of demanding the return of the underwear) and threatening (in terms of the threat to drive to her mother's house). I do not deny that Lindsey may have been alarmed or distressed by that email, but it was sent in immediate response to her own email saying that she wanted to sever all ties with me'.

'Although I appreciate now that Lindsey was quite within her rights to go to the police, at that time I became very angry about it. I felt (however irrational it may seem) that she should have talked to me about things, rather than go to the police (as I saw it then) telling them lies'.

'Astonishing though it may now seem, it is correct that in the months following my arrest and caution, I registered three more domains, lindseygoldrick.org, yesweknowyouknowlindsey.com and lind-

246

seygoldrick.info. I suppose I felt unable to let the matter rest, feeling that this would give her the last 'word', even though (in my mind at least), she had lied to the police'.

He states that he realised that I was attempting to shut the websites down and that although he was in a happy relationship, he created another 'offensive website' and admitted to search engine optimising all of them, so that they would rank prominently when anyone searched my name.

To further maximise coverage on the biggest media platform to sabotage my life he decided to pay a lot of money for an advertisement banner to go at the top of Google with my photograph and a direction to ANastylyingpieceofwork.com and *'Lindsey said it was August 2014 but I think it was earlier'* (it was on the web for longer than I knew about. This was either a curve ball to evoke trust in the rest of what he said or it was blatant detachment) and then he said, 'but really, my life had moved on!'. Really?

Things stayed as they were for a while, just 25 websites in total and an advertisement until he admits to feeling creative again in 2012 and made valentinesdayinthenewforest.com, which was all about that brief time from 7 years ago at that point but he was *'happy'* and he had *'moved on'* and so *'decided to set up two Twitter accounts in Lindsey's name and attach ANastylyingpieceofwork.com to them'* and made amendments to reflect her current age on the websites, a few years later.

Receiving my barrister's Letter Before Claim, he says, worried and surprised him, so he asked the first lawyer that he appointed (that dropped him after receiving the large amount of evidence) to take a circumspect approach (there wasn't any circumspect approach to what you did for so long and so brutally, though, was there? You were not unwilling to take risks there, huh?).

But he accepts the majority of the claim (too much evidence). He goes on to say that his Brother had begged him to *'let it go'* and that he understands why I remain worried about the possibility of him repeating the conduct (was I alone in thinking that he really was extremely disconnected and unremorseful?) but he didn't want to lose his wife.

They must have made a deal that if he does it again, she is leaving!

I hope to goodness, that he doesn't lose his wife - Ever!

How will he react if she leaves him at anytime in the future?

CHAPTER SIXTY ONE
His Confession

The Witness Statement was a confession and I could have taken it to the police and said, '*This is what I am talking about!*', but as I was to find out later anyway, the police would not have treated the situation any differently, at whatever time it had been presented.

His Witness Statement had me riled. I could imagine him sitting there, compiling the words as to how to sound like a rational person that was just doing the thing that anyone wronged would have done after 4 dates. And that he was the victim in all of this. The audacity at the attempt! The belief that anyone would understand him.

I admit that there were parts of me that had thought that it was possible that it may be stated he was entitled to free speech, after feeling 'led on' when the litigation was underway, despite that being so wrong. So much of it aggravated me, though. This mad man hadn't known me, had presumed things about me, had made assumptions and was delirious enough to say that I was besotted with him.

The psycho had splashed all over the internet that I '*like being buggered in a gangbang situation!*', for goodness sake. How dare he talk about wonderful experiences and feeling happy and 'moved on' when I felt NONE OF THOSE FEELINGS REGARDING HIS CONDUCT AGAINST ME SINCE 2005.

How dare he attempt at appearing regular, normal (whatever that is), rational, when he was one big messed up psychopath. I cannot believe that I have not gone crazy. This is someone seriously screwed up and I have just endured all those years of feeling unsafe and worried and fearful and he is responding to my statement with things like, '*I can see how she would get upset at another 5 defamatory websites!*'. That despicable man. Truly. He is abhorrent.

Of course, Steve went through each and every letter with me, helping me make decisions and his responses matched mine. I sent it to Teen and Ames and asked them if they could almost feel sorry for him if they didn't know me.

Teen's reply was, '*Never in a million years!*' And the rest was unprintable. And funny.

Ames: '*I have just spent an hour going through the old emails from when you met the madman. His witness statement made me feel angry and I hadn't remembered you being smitten or besotted. But, apparently you were?? You mentioned this guy now and again over several months, then nothing. We must have talked about it in Slovenia. You mentioned the website and the creepiness that followed. But I have an issue with his statement. It's like he is trying to justify his behaviour. Like it was normal because of the way you felt about each other for 3 seconds. It pisses me off. The apology is there but it doesn't sound like he feels like what he did was wrong*'.

Of course, the good news about his statement was that Furran admitted to it, even though not to the hacking, and that if it goes to court then I was pretty sure that the court would think he was liable. We now had a statement to help with the wording of our joint statement now; one that wouldn't be contested because it would basically say what he has admitted to.

DIARY ENTRY, 4AM WINTER 2017:

I woke up thinking about how delicate we have to be and how precise and how this wasn't just a regular court. This is the biggest, highest court in England, that only deal with complex and special cases. I feel so blessed and lucky. I have to pay it forward when all is done. I have an amazing legal team. I didn't ever envisage this, after being told for so long that there isn't anything that could be done. Hallelujah.

His lawyer's bullyboy tactic letters and Furran's pathetic Witness Statement are giving me even more of a fire to get maximum

benefits out of this. I know that Furran's Lawyers are working for
him but the letters that they write on his behalf are written in such a
way that they strengthen the feelings of being harassed and bullied
because they are considerably condescending, manipulative and
threatening to me. It is completely unnecessary and especially because
I hadn't done anything wrong. I know everyone deserves legal defence
but I don't want him to have anyone 'defending' his actions in such a
way that they seemed like a team of harassers. It reminds me of how
he had sought similar on the internet. A gang of bullies. He doesn't
deserve being 'defended', even though he was going to be paying out so
much money for this defence. This is how I feel.

As if I could be persuaded by money? He should go to prison
for what he did and not be able to carry on with his life, as per usual.
It seems like he has wanted me to be forced to think about him as
much as he has thought about me with his obsession. It is a 'If I can't
have her then I am not going to let her kick me out of her life' sort of
thing. There are a million moments in one day, let alone 12 and a half
years and each and every one of those were underpinned with the far-
reaching effects of his horrendously tormenting harassment.

I am not vindictive in the slightest but at this point, his
lawyer was part of his gang and that gang was making me feel infuri-
ated. Saul Furran deserved no consideration and his legal team need
lessons in how to word letters and deal with someone that has been
tyrannised by a criminal, their client - the Defendant- for over a
decade. END OF DIARY ENTRY.

I am including some of the quotes taken directly from
his lawyer's letters and I include my remarks about them because
they maddened me and it feels cathartic to do so. Yes, I recognise
legal jargon used regularly and as a standard but they were not
thought about and it left me feeling really bothersome.

'It may provide your client with some comfort for us to
indicate, on an open basis, and without prejudice to the issues of lia-
bility and damages, that our clients are prepared to submit to an order
in.....' -

Let's look at the meaning of the word 'comfort' in the dictionary. It means: 'A physically relaxed state without any pain or other unpleasant feelings'.

I think that 13 years is a seemingly large amount of time to be subjected to abuse and wrath - publicly - globally, at ground zero, 24 hours a day without break. Choice of words is really important. It can make all the difference. You can change people's thoughts, emotions and reactions with them. The fact that they had used 'comfort' made me feel anything but. I would go so far as saying that it made me feel the opposite. As far as I was concerned, anything associated with Furran will never equal comfort.

I stress: What 'comfort' could come at any time, dealing with discussing the liability and damages that he was 'prepared' (which insinuates he is doing me a favour) to submit to, when he really should have been dealt with at criminal court? Yes, again… it may be excused as regular solicitor/lawyer jargon and yes, what words should one use but I am merely pointing out my interpretation, when feeling hopping mad about the subject matter.

His lawyers: *'In the event that your client will not agree to an extension, then regrettably, we will be forced to make a contested application, and the additional costs, including of any hearing, will naturally be sought by your client'.* -

Always threatening when they knew that it was a tall ask!

Lawyers: *'This letter made clear that, at that time, our client had not even had sight of your client's evidence'.*

This was in response to a letter from us responding to their 'extended' time extension. We responded with: *'Whilst we accept that this case involves some complexity, this was most definitely caused by your clients. Both of your clients presumably know very well when and how they committed the conduct…and how they sought to conceal such conduct'.*

His lawyers: *'As our clients have previously indicated in open correspondence, they are willing to submit to injunctive orders in terms broadly the same as those sought by your client'.*

Me: Broadly agreeing is not the same as agreeing. What are you not going to agree / comply with? No clear definition.

Lawyers: *'The 'sticking point' appears to be our client's desire to resolve these proceedings confidentially and your client's desire for a Joint statement in open court'.*

Me: It certainly is a sticking point. I am not going to change my mind. This statement would provide me with a public admittance and apology because what he had done was very public. A High Court Judge decided that I was entitled to this.

His lawyers: *'In response to the Joint Statement in Open Court, he also accepts that your client would have been upset as a result of those publications'.*

Me: Upset? A continual mental attack campaign that would be still continuing after 13 years? 'Upset' is what I feel when I can't start the car and I am running late. 'Upset' is what I feel when I stub my toe. Traumatised would be more apt.

His lawyers: *'Furthermore, Mr Furran has since served a witness statement which makes an open, public apology, and admissions, and explains his actions'.*

Me: How is it a public apology, if the only people involved in the case were the only people seeing the witness statement? How 'public' was that? His WS did not read like an apology to me and the 'apology' paragraph at the beginning was just obligatory legal jargon.

I have saved the best until last:

253

His lawyers: '*Indeed, it appears to us that a statement in open court is only likely to harm both our individual clients' reputations in the longer term. Your client presumably, does not wish for the most prominent results upon a Google search of her name to be press articles concerning her harassment*'.

Me: Of course, what was previously there that their clients had created and maintained for 12 years at that point, was really good for my reputation, wasn't it?.

This letter was jaw dropping! Anything was better than anastylyingpieceofwork/lindseygoldrick.com, lindseygoldrick-.net, soyouthinkyouknowlindseygoldrick.com............and so on, for three pages on Google!

As for not harming the defendants' reputations - that really wasn't on any priority list of mine. I couldn't give a rat's arse about Saul Furran's reputation. He had tried his best to sabotage mine for over a quarter of my life. It was not for his lawyers to form any views about what my best interests are. I had nothing to be ashamed or embarrassed about by having been publicly harassed by their client, who had also shared private material and information and outrageous untruths about me for 11 plus years to a global audience of people who used the internet.

Let's not forget the terrorising at ground zero; in my home. 24 hours a day. This particular letter riled me. I wanted it to go to trial at that point, so that I could look them all in the eye and tell those bullies exactly what I thought of them because you know what else his lawyer's statement of perplexity about surely not wanting my name to be attached to harassment under a Google search translates as?

That I should want to keep quiet about it because I should be ashamed of being a victim of harassment!

That is exactly what it implied. Nothing else. It was so clear. Appalling.

The tone of their letters were consistent in their reinforcement of bullying and harassment.

CHAPTER SIXTY TWO
An offer with an unbelievable caveat

Subsequently, he obviously didn't like the idea of a statement being read out in the High Court and for it to be ultimately in the media and he made me an offer of £3k more, along with the words, *'we believe that this is a very generous offer and we have advised our client that the amount would be considerably more than the court would award'* and the next paragraph:

'With the caveat that you, Ms. Goldrick Dean, will not speak about it with anyone, nor anybody that knew about it and to instruct Cohen Davis to not publish any promotional material about it - or we will seek damages from you'.

Yes, he would sue me.

AN OFFER WITH A CONFIDENTIALITY CAVEAT! Silence money.

So, I would not be able to talk about it with anyone. Really?

They thought that I could be controlled further by offering me just over half of what my legal team had put together on the statement. Surely, they had got the message that I would not be swayed by money. This ignited me, even more. Not even if he had offered me one million pounds would I be silenced. I was fuming with the bullying, controlling coward.

This gives the message that someone can do something really bad and then, the Civil court process allows you to throw money at it and it goes away. Of course, others have been bullied into it because there is a risk of bankruptcy. If you are not a millionaire, you risk losing everything - as I was warned, before I turned the silence money down.

Civil law is designed for people to settle out of court: If you don't accept the defendant's offer, then you could be liable for their costs (when it is because of them that you are there, in the first place). If the courts offered me less than what he had offered me and I had turned it down, then I was liable for not only my costs, but his too. If it reached the Supreme Courts, then we had the risk of losing everything we owned. We risked bankruptcy because of what he did to me.

It feels horrible when you are presented with the knowledge that if you refuse an offer that came with a confidential caveat that stopped you from telling anyone that someone performed criminal acts on you, that any legal work costs thereafter, may be your responsibility to cover. Not the responsibility of the person that put you in that position. Obviously, it is there for a reason but I couldn't stand to think that silence money could have such a weight.

It was a huge risk also because we couldn't predict what Saul Furran would do. He was not a rational person. He was arrested and was warned and carried on for another decade. When he was called to task with it with Gabor's Letter Before Claim, he lied about it. He was a man that ignored the caution, the arrest; the police, lied to us and carried on updating and maintaining the ones that were still registered, during the litigation. He had the conduct of an irrational person and his lawyer may not be able to help him be rational and he might pursue it to the bitter end to try and clear his name.

There was a risk that it would be a very long fight at this stage because he did not want it to be out in the public. Steve and I talked about it and decided that we would take the risk. It was huge but I was not going to be silenced, controlled or bullied after 12 years of oppression and I had to take it further. It was always about vindication to me and hopefully helping others and it not happening in vain.

I wrote to Ames: '*He has offered me £3k more, Ames. With the caveat of keeping silent about it! And, they believe that it is a very generous offer. Seriously? They think that I would be swayed by £3k more and not be able to talk about it or I will get sued? Do you know how much I want to combust, right now? Firstly, it's not about money and they are still not getting that message but they think it is worth a try, since I am getting pro bono help. Secondly - to be threatened with being sued if I talked about it, if I accepted the money?? I want justice, as you know and no amount of money would sway me nor compensate for the sleepless nights and panic I have endured. I am sick of hearing that he doesn't want anyone to know what he so violently and purposefully did, relentlessly for 12 years. He needs a taste of his own medicine. I am not vengeful but he really needs to know what it feels like when you wake in the morning and your name is slashed all over the internet in a derogatory way. Even if this does come out online, nothing about him will be untrue that is written. I have had lies and highly offensive publications written about me by him and he has ruined my reputation, career and confidence for a quarter of my life. I won't get that back and he did that to me. Every day, my stomach turned over, wondering what had been written, who had seen it and how I could get him to stop and get them down. They multiplied. It has really plagued me, Ames. I have not wanted to give him power but unless I can help others, the last 12 years were in vain. No amount of money will stop that. A precedent would help people. Who the frigging hell does he think he is? I am sobbing. It makes me feel sick. I am so grateful that we are here and it is moving and I thank goodness for my legal help every minute. Goodness knows what I would have done without my family and friends over the years. You have all kept me sane. That madman has to pay and people have to know what he is capable of and also, it is a clear message to all.'*

Ames' reply: *'You want my feedback? Here it is: I am steaming! Fuck him and fuck his money. You wanted confidentiality for 12 fucking years and didn't get it. Fuck him! Fuck his wishes. Fuck his lawyers. Assfuck! The sanctimonious prick. Like a few extra grand is going to make a difference. Hush money. They're saying it's more than the court would award because seemingly, they want you to shut the hell up about it. Tell them to multiply it by 10 and you still wouldn't take it unless maybe it wasn't confidential!'*

Yair wrote to me: '*It seems that Furran's desire to have the matter resolved with little or no publicity is paramount to everything else. For the record, he will be considered the most notorious UK internet troll ever, so I understand your wish to make sure that he is never allowed to do this again to anyone else. If I was advising him, I would probably tell him that, provided that you (Lindsey) insist on a public hearing, at least in relation to the quantum, which in a way is worst for him. Any public hearing will give you an opportunity to expose him publicly for what he is, whether the purpose of the hearing is to make a joint statement in open court or whether the purpose of it is to simply determine how much he should pay in damages. It makes no real difference, as far as his exposure is concerned, how the public hearing comes out.*

Either way, his conduct is susceptible to public scrutiny. So, he can either go through a public hearing in relation to damages where his conduct will be heavily scrutinised in court, possibly with the media sitting in the public gallery, having spent huge amounts of money trying to bring the amount of damages he has to pay you down to double what he offered or so, or he can just accept your offer, make a joint statement in open court, with at least some of the information pertaining to his conduct being kept away from the public. He needs to realise that he is far better off accepting your offer of settlement than giving it to a public hearing over damages. For a deeper analysis of his recent offers and suggestions, it will be helpful, as always to hear from Gabor'.

I was asked if there was any amount of money that would buy confidentiality because Furran was so fixed on that to settle. Of course, there wasn't, I said.

If I accept his money and confidentiality offer, then he wins and he continues to control and I will never have peace in my heart. I want to risk not accepting any amount.

If I end up out of pocket, then I will crowdfund publicly. I am adamant about not signing a silence agreement. Even if the money was attractive to me, how could I ever control what others may say? Ever?

He could then sue me for what he did to me for 12 years? I couldn't get it out of my head.

CHAPTER SIXTY THREE
Risking bankruptcy

DIARY ENTRY: *I have been thinking hard about what I want from this and what will make me satisfied forever. When I look back at how it all ended, what do I want that to look like because if it doesn't go in my favour, I will be troubled by that forever. I need to heal and move forward, not stay stuck and controlled by the unfavourable outcome, too. I don't actually want it to be fair to Furran because he should be penalised for what he has done and would still be doing, if not for my amazing legal team.*

It doesn't make sense for others not to benefit. I want to help others through this. Of course, I won't have control over what the court decides. My heart says I have to fight it and stick with my convictions. My head says that I don't want us homeless. Mama and Debs both expressed their worry about me being out of pocket and that very often good people end up broke and not getting justice. I had a fleeting moment of visions of us struggling to keep a roof over our heads, whilst trying to pay the court fees.

I cannot believe that his actions over a long period of time that were premeditated and relentless has put us in a precarious situation. We could lose everything. The three of us seriously impacted by his repugnant acts of revenge. It was astounding that this was a possibility. Steve reminded me that if I have to pay the damages plus his fees because of what he has done, then the media would love it. I thought about how it was important to me to get my message across that you cannot buy your way out of committing crimes against someone always, and you cannot go on a long, pre-meditated splurge of internet trolling and get away with it by offering money and asking for confidentiality.

At least, I will be controlling that - and he won't. At least I can talk about being sued. Good would come out of it if I stuck to my principles and in so many ways, and that most importantly, I could sleep at night, knowing that I fought for it.

If I take the money and sign the confidentiality agreement (which is most definitely not what I want, even if it was for a million pounds), I will feel like I have lost and he has controlled it further and he gets to breathe deeply and my breath is still laboured. I think I deserve the deep breathing - not him. He deserves to sweat and wonder about how it is all going to end up.

Or, I may sweat and wonder if I have damages to pay for court but at least it will help me sleep at night. I have been silenced for 12 years. Accepting would have me never, ever feeling settled and he would have won, still have control and nobody gains from this but him and he doesn't deserve that ease. I want to come out on top and be released from this oppression. I want to then turn it around to assist even just one person by making changes. There's no reason for this, unless I can make an example of it.

I have cried on and off for most of this weekend, feeling depleted and whacked out. Almost there. I feel like I have a virus. My body is releasing. I haven't been so sick on and off ever. Steve wants me to get a sick note and just rest but that isn't something that I do. I can work through it, can't I? As always. Not long now. END OF DIARY ENTRY.

As I had chosen a course of action that was financially risky, it was suggested that I got a second opinion from a barrister that dealt with confidentiality, about whether I should pursue a claim for a Joint Statement, as I was ultimately exposing myself right now to the possibility of bankruptcy. This is where Gervase de Wilde joined the legal team, who also offered his assistance on a Pro Bono basis. I felt incredibly galvanised by this amazing legal team and they all believed in the success of me winning the case. It felt so powerful.

It was a precarious time in the litigation. Anything was possible. Having him participate in a public acknowledgement of what he had done was most important to me but if he didn't want to publicly apologise, I couldn't force it. I would do it alone but it had to be done in order for me to feel vindicated. It wasn't a punishment, like I have already mentioned. It was because his crimes were so public. I needed the acknowledgement that he was caught and made to stop. It would be unfortunate if he didn't apologise but that would only look terrible on his behalf. Gervase subsequently didn't take long at all providing a comprehensive analysis.

It was hard though, to comprehend that we were now looking at the possibility of homelessness and losing everything because of a brief period of time with a madman and his preposterous, criminal behaviour. Our boy may be affected, after all. I felt enraged. I was so overwhelmed with the unfair system and I couldn't not talk about it now because it may be of media interest and I wasn't going to shy away from spreading awareness with the hope for change.

It almost verged on a confession, as I began to tell people. Finally being able to talk openly because it was almost over had me nervous, excited and overwhelmed with pent up frustration all at the same time because there was a major possibility that we would have to sacrifice our home in order to get justice. It was so hard to get my head around that this was actually happening. Finally getting help but jeopardising our home.

It was like a question mark was dangling in front of me on a pendulum. Which way would it swing? Neither way looked like freedom at this point. And as it swung from left to right, one day passed into another and on each day, I told someone new and told my story over and over again. So much so, I couldn't believe it was me that it had happened to.

The amount of incidents that I was talking about was incredible. So much to digest. So much to say. Telling my story was met with shock and disbelief. One, that it happened. Two, that I hadn't ever showed distress. Three, that nothing was done by anyone. Four, that we faced bankruptcy. 'But..' people quizzed. 'You are always cheerful.' 'I don't know how you are not

262

crazy or angry'. I had worked hard, with gusto, so my employers and colleagues were dumbfounded.

It was so confusing for some people. *'Why don't you just settle and be done with it?'*

'Because that means he controlled the outcome, too and I will never be free from him. You cannot throw money at every thing to make it go away. I need closure to move on. It is worth the risk, so that I have the power. I am more determined than ever to make this public.'

Apart from feeling that they had wished they had known, so that they could have supported me more, nobody would have guessed. And I am glad for that. I hid it well. It would have been a restless, disordered state of affairs if I had re-leased all of what went on on a daily basis. Because now that I was able to talk, it was like a dam had burst.

People knowing about it, talking about it - to me and not to me, worrying about me, asking me about it, thinking about it, concerned about it.......all of it, would have caused me great anxiety over the years, if they knew.

The anxiety of other people's anxiety and concern would have been quadrupled in me. It all made sense - to protect others and to try and keep a grip on what my life with everyone would have been like organically. I knew that it was a suppressed ver-sion of my life but it excluded (somewhat) the reality of the hor-rendous privacy attack and fear.

It could have been so different and to this day, I am grateful for my decision, especially since nothing could be done. It would have been quite different if there had been help and un-derstanding at the beginning and of course, I didn't anticipate 13 years. I controlled it as much as I could and got respite as much as I could. It is imperative to how I coped, drawing on the connec-tions and time with my loved ones, without their need to worry. I drew on love. Pity would have weakened me.

It was so huge and the extra burden on other people, just by knowing and caring about me, was too massive for me to

cope with. I know that I did the right thing at the right time because of the lack of resources to make him stop. Things are different now and I would advise anyone to speak out from the start
because there is so much understanding now, and that makes a
world of difference.

Nobody should suffer silently, without help.

CHAPTER SIXTY FOUR
Preparing to go public

I wrote to Ames about standing up for myself, setting a precedent and giving hope to others and the risk involved.

She replied: '*I will keep this brief so that you know I am here and thinking about it but the bottom line is, that you need to stand up for what you want and need for this to go to public. Period. And I can't help but think that the Universe has your back. Karma goes a long way and you have a bounty of it. You need to feel settled and like this has a finite end to it and if you accepted that offer, you never would. You deserve for this to go your way. So, it will. I honestly believe that is a scare tactic and that it won't go to court. They are going to think that this threat is going to have you back down. Once he sees that you won't, this asshole will realise he can't win. He has to do what you're asking. The alternative is serious media coverage if it goes to court which will be more damning for him in the end. Stand your ground. You're doing the right thing. Don't worry about the potential ramifications because right now, you can't control them. I wish I could help you.*'

Our dear family friend called me and said that he was worried that I will lose everything and that the British Judiciary is for the rich and many innocent people end up with nothing, trying to get justice. It is true. Just because I am right, it doesn't mean that I won't end up paying his costs (because I refused settlement and carried on to the High Courts) and it doesn't mean I will get my precedent. Plus, it could be a long process.

Steve called next and said that he was proud of me for sticking with my principles and he was right by my side. We were going to take the risk because he wanted me to get closure.

A letter from his lawyers came, in response to try and stop me from having the public Joint Statement in Open Court, which would expose him.

1. Our client believes that he is not liable to your client in relation to misuse of private information and breach of confidence.

2. This is not a claim where publicity is required to remedy reputational harm or to vindicate your client - Ms. Goldrick Dean's rights.

I expressed how I felt about this letter via email to my legal team.

The reply to Furran and his lawyers was conveyed powerfully and exactly by Gabor, in a comprehensive and legal way, stating full particulars, referencing laws and paragraphs and court of appeal decisions to rely on to support my position. I will explain it as simply as I can:

We disagreed with the two points that they had made and pointed out that the two points actually justified the reasons why I wanted a Joint Statement. We also pointed out that Joint Statements were not limited to defamation cases and that they were in fact available in relation to claims for misuse of private or confidential information and so, we were relying on the tort of misuse of information and breach of confidence as causes to apply for a Statement out of Court.

Gabor wrote that when they claimed from previous letters that a Statement in Open Court would *'harm both of our clients in the longer term'* and then again in another: *'Our client's personal reasons for wanting to avoid publicity around this litigation are obvious'* and then reiterating that it *'wouldn't be in Ms. Goldrick Dean's interest either'*, points were made:

A). As to our clients best interests, she regards your comments as inappropriate and offensive. It is not for you or your clients to form a view of our client's best interests. Our client has nothing to be ashamed of or embarrassed about by reason of having been publicly harassed by your clients and by having had her private information and material disclosed by your clients, each during a period exceeding 11 years and before and to a global audience of internet users. Nor does she have anything to be ashamed of or embarrassed about in now seeking a legal remedy for the wrongs she has suffered due to your clients' conduct.

B). Your clients stated desire to avoid publicity around this dispute is not a legally relevant interest. Naturally our client has no intention to harm, nor an intent in harming your client's respective reputation. If any publicity relating to this litigation does have the consequence of causing reputational harm to your clients, that will be merely a result of their own unlawful conduct which is the subject matter of our client's claim. Your clients have only themselves to blame for having engaged in such wrongful conduct.

We note your client's position concerning a Joint Statement out of Court. It amounts to a blank refusal. In our letter dated 8th November, we invited your clients to propose amendments to the draft Joint Statement out of Court, which formed part of our client's settlement offer. Your clients have chosen not to try and negotiate any alternative wording for a Joint Statement out of Court, despite our client's expressed flexibility in that regard.

We also note the contents of your letter concerning a potential Unilateral Statement in Open Court by our client. You wrote 'Our client reserves the right to object to such an application'. We wish to make four points in this regard:

First, your foregoing statement appears to refer only to the first defendant, Mr. Saul Furran. Please indicate at the earliest opportunity what position is taken by the second defendant, Furran Consulting Ltd. about a potential Unilateral Statement in Open Court by our client.

Second, we refer to the telephone conversation between Mr. X of your firm and Mr. Cohen, where we addressed the reasons why our client wants your clients to publicly accept responsibility for their unlawful conduct, preferably by way of a JSOC (Joint Statement). During the same conversation, we conveyed to you the immense distress your clients' continued refusal to do so has been causing our client. We consider her request for a JSOC, which as we explained would allow our client to put a closure on the matter and move on with her life to be reasonable in the circumstances of this case.

Third, during the same telephone conversation, we also explained that our client would not be willing to enter into any agreement with your clients which would impose any restrictions on her human right to freedom of expression. As we explained, our client feels that she has been unable to respond effectively to your clients' unlawful conduct over a period exceeding 11 years and that she is unwilling to accept any constraint on her ability to lawfully discuss your clients' conduct with whomever she wants, if indeed she ever wants to do so.

Fourth, our client considers your clients' persistent unwillingness to publicly acknowledge their wrongdoings toward her to be inconsistent with parts of Mr. Furran's witness statement dated 11th October. Considering the nature of her claim, she also considers that refusal to be unreasonable.

We respectfully disagree with your clients' intentions marked 1 and 2 for the reasons set above.

Finally, we reject your client's suggestion that our client's proposal of a JSOC, as part of her 36 offer dated 26th October could constitute an abuse of process.

It was a triumph. I loved that response. Perfect. I shared it with a few people and words of cheers were sent back. The support brought out another few tears of appreciation. Ames's response was:

'I just cheered out loud! He just bitch-slapped them, lawyer-style. This is exactly what needed to be said and I love it. Oh, but I can't wait to hear what they come back with. What's the timeframe? I'm so pleased. That was kind of in your face, you bloody idiots kind of letter. Yay! Can't wait to hear what's next'.

What came next?

This, from Furran's Counsel:

'Our individual client has provided a 21 page Witness Statement in these proceedings in which he has given a full and frank account of his behaviour dating back 13 years. At para 37, he admits he published private information about your client and goes to say that he appreciates that publication may have constituted both a breach of your client's confidence and a misuse of her private informa-

tion. He also accepts that your client would have been upset'. (Pause here just to make a note of that word again: UPSET? It makes my face screw up). *'We have advised that these claims are statute-barred (no longer enforceable) because the original publication dates back over a decade and it's something of a moot point whether your client should still have the right to pursue such claims 10 or 20 years later'.*

Pause for interjection from me: (But they were still up and live for 13 years since they were created! Plus, up and live websites meant constantly refreshing web pages which meant, fresh and new, every single day.

There was every opportunity to un-publish them but by leaving them on the internet? It really was a ridiculous argument. I couldn't believe that they were arguing about the first publication that he created that was part of the harassment claim and was the onset of his conduct and it would have continued and was still, 12 years later.

That original offensive website was constantly re-freshed, updated, maintained for at least 9 years, running along-side others, until he did totally fresh ones. It was only a few years ago that it expired and I believe that it was through his own ad-min oversight. He did not renew the original - www.lindsey-goldrick.com quickly enough because I got there, first. It came up for sale when he had missed the re-registering of it and I grabbed it.

The rest of them that would have been still running to that day had Gabor and Yair not taken them down, were varia-tions of the original. Also, let's not forget that he re-registered two websites during this litigation. Some wouldn't expire, I re-peat myself, until 2020.

I am not sure that his lawyers had any clout in the claim related to old publications. Didn't make sense. Furran's conduct started with five websites with all the permutations of my name and ended with 25 plus websites and all of the other publications and harassing conduct.

Let's also remember that if a website is on the internet, it is constantly new not old, unless you take them down. We could also argue there, that they will always be on the internet in archives, even then, because of the nature of internet indexing. Argue that I didn't have a claim for harassment?

I cannot stress how much, even knowing that his lawyers were just doing what they had been hired to do and doing their best on behalf of their client, they incensed the hell out of me. It is the nature of the beast, I know and they were hardly going to send letters of support about me, were they but they went overboard. I just found his legal team stating unnecessary facts and adding threats and insults emphasised my feelings of being bullied and attacked more. They repulsed me.

'I have had enough of being harassed, Bullyboys. I have been subjected to such horrendous abuse on the internet and have had my life hijacked by your client and I won't take anymore from you, either,' I wish I could have screamed this to his lawyers directly. I was angry.

To get more bullying from the perpetrator's lawyer just seemed to tip it over the edge somewhat and create a nasty taste. I was beyond thrilled for the sight of the end of the harassment campaign and that I was going to feel vindicated, though. And help create change, set a precedent and do good with it all because it would have been in vain, otherwise. And I get unnecessary words thrown at me via his legal team. They were representing a criminal, all the evidence of very public harassment was there, their client has admitted to it and they continued to try and weaken and intimidate. It only encouraged me to stand up to the bullies. It felt like a war.

Anyway, back to their letter - *'Our clients have accepted responsibility, apologised publicly (by way of an open witness statement)'*.

ME: *'Please explain, how public a statement is, if only two legal offices can see it? This is not a public apology. The lack of want-*

ing to publicly apologise makes it even more obvious that he doesn't want to apologise, in fact'.

Back to the letter again - *'Their refusal to enter into a Joint Statement is not intended to diminish that apology much less to exacerbate the distress your client has suffered'*. Really? Really?

'We are reserving the rights to the Statement in Open Court, not necessarily to seek to object'.

Another thing I found with their letters was there were a lot of ambiguous words. Nothing was direct. That meant that I could make several interpretations. This lack of directness was irritating me.

They continued: *'Our failure to our client as plural was a typographical oversight and one we thought was transparent. As we've pointed out previously, our corporate client played no active role in these events'*. (I interject with: Just the small matter that Furran Consultants Ltd was registered as owner of a few of the abusive websites about, that's all).

They noted my refusal of the Calderbank offers. (Note: The two types of offers I was made were called Calderbank and Part 36, by the way. Calderbank allows creativity and flexibility and a court can't refer to them - unless for costs at the end. Part 36 is rule-based and is up for grabs for the duration with a certainty for how costs will be treated at the end. If you are interested, Google is more enlightening than I am!).

They also pointed out that there were two earlier offers they had made and that the reason why the case had not been settled was my insistence on the Joint Statement (that would be quite correct, Defendant's Counsel, because this is not about money. And since it wasn't going to trial, I had to have the public apology because being portrayed in an all encompassing crude and cruel way on the largest media platform that ever existed, that anyone, anywhere in the world could access that crushed a quarter of my life and my voice, a public apology wasn't much to ask for. When really, he should have gone to prison. I know that I repeat myself) but they continued on with that sentence. I just couldn't help but continually step in.

'...*insistence on a joint statement which we believe is a folly - as your client is now at risk not only of receiving a far lower sum* (it wasn't ever a factor) *in damages than our client has offered to pay but also of being ordered to pay our client's costs, potentially since October. Your client's offer is conditional upon our clients agreeing to a joint statement. We do not believe that it can offer any potential for costs bonuses. Moreover, it seems relevant now to offer to settle for £250 less than one of our client's existing offer.'* (But remember, they have a confidentiality condition attached to them) and basically said that they '*do not intend to discuss these issues further unless there is some material change of position*'.

They had also stated that if I insist on including the police arrest and caution that he received, they 'would apply for his anonymity'! (This is where I start spitting again! How could he be allowed to be anonymous when what he did was so public? Why would that even be a possibility, that he would be granted identity protection?).

Gervase's analysis came in and two points were highlighted. The court couldn't order a Defendant into entering a Joint Statement in Open Court, as Gabor had already said. So, I could go to trial because Furran refuses to enter into a Joint Statement and because he has refused, if the damages awarded in court are not more than the most recent offer that he made to me, I had a 60% chance of avoiding the usual cost consequences (which would normally follow). It was a benefit but it wasn't certain.

Given that information, I was asked if I wanted to reconsider and if I wanted to progress to trial but the approach of settling by making a new offer of my own to settle, along with applying for a Unilateral Statement in Open Court was a good way forward. I went with that. I really hoped that I was granted one and I explained it in my diary entry:

DIARY ENTRY, 2017: *It's been fourteen months of the litigation and it is now six more days until Christmas and our little chap is bonkers excited. Steve has been absolutely incredible through the litigation, helping me decipher letters and work through my thoughts with me; managing to be so supportive. I often ponder how hard it has been for him. Today's call with Yair and Gabor went really well. I am going to go for a unilateral statement and he can't really contest the words because I will use his witness statement as a guide. It will save time. It is clear that he won't do a Joint Statement. If I insist on a trial, the costs could be horrendous to me and we need to tie things up. The courts might not order enough for me to cover the costs incurred, so it's huge.*

The only downside is that if we went to trial, we could have insisted on Gabor's time being awarded and that money would go in the pot to help someone else on a Pro Bono basis. If they are resistant to my next offer, then I can insist on a trial. The other option was to make him admit to things that he is denying and lay the pressure on. Things like the hacking. Gabor mentioned that I would need to be ready for the cross-examination and it will be with great scrutiny.

So, I am now offering them a chance to settle with no conditions. The Unilateral has nothing to do with them, so they can't argue about it but if we run it alongside his admissions, then they have less to object to. It could be a day of debating if my statement words are not what they agree with and that eats up court time. I wrote to Ames today and talked about the possibility of helping others through Pro Bono if it went to trial, for I am wouldn't be here without it; without Gabor picking it up. END OF DIARY ENTRY.

Ames: '*Do not insist on going to court. You are the most selfless person and the fact that you are not berating yourself because of the possibility of helping through this foundation is predictable. But not rational. They have always said this case is pro bono. They've done all the work on it with the understanding without thought of getting the money back that was spent on it paid back. That's why the foundation is there. You would be foolish to risk your own financial*

future on the hopes of doing for others. While it's in your nature it is
probably difficult to resist, you need to settle and move on. You've al-
ready made up the generosity of this Pro Bono case with the way you
pay it forward every day, with helping everyone and it's not your re-
sponsibility to do any more than take care of yourself and get past this
horrendous experience. Put Linz first, the rest will work out later.'

CHAPTER SIXTY FIVE
A Light Christmas

Christmas 2017 and I have to say that it was the lightest Christmas, in terms of weights lifted in 12 years. The online creations were gone, he had been brought to accountability, we were possibly half way through the trial, I was more in control and Furran may be out of my life this time next year.

I had made him an offer to settle, which was around half of my original statement and less than he had offered to me. His had the silence money caveat attached. Mine had no conditions. To give a very clear message. It was too good of a deal for him to turn down and he had two weeks to respond. Everyone noticed. We had Mama, a dear friend and one of my brothers over for Christmas and my other brother and nephews came for New Year. A gaggle of gorgeous people.

Although cautious because it wasn't quite over and who knew what could happen, I knew that if anyone searched my name, they would be met with nothing about me. Nothing. It felt like I had been cleared of a huge injustice and I hadn't done anything, of course, but the persecution that I always consciously tried to shirk when the laughter died down, was lifted. I was all sorts of giddy - and everyone noticed.

January 2018 - An email to Ames: *'Tomorrow is the date when the Defendant needs to reply to my offer, Ames. We haven't heard anything. I am surprised. I seriously thought that they'd jump at it because there isn't a Joint Statement condition attached. My doing a Unilateral, one by myself, has got nothing to do with them, so they don't have to approve (per se). It's just a money offer to settle out of court and it's less than they offered me, to speed things up. I seriously don't know what they're thinking at this point (unless they want trial and think the court will offer less). If he doesn't respond though, we go to trial. He has until 5pm tomorrow. I will email you as soon as.'*

An email a week later - '*I haven't heard, Ames. I felt de-jected all weekend. It has certainly heightened my anxiety. Gabor sent us a long email on Monday. He suggested that Yair call the defen-dant's counsel directly to see why they hadn't replied and their reply was apologetic and it was because of Christmas. Wimpy excuse. It is the third week into January. Don't you think they should have sent a one liner last week to say they will be delayed? That was it. No date given. Disrespectful. I cannot wait for the next step.*'

An email to Ames later that day: '*I have just found out that the first stage is over. He's agreed to settle out of court and pay the costs. I feel stunned! I feel like it's a great day and I want to jump and scream but I am holding it together because it's what I am good at! Smiley face. Also, it hasn't happened yet, has it? The letter says some rubbish about this client reserving the right to contest this and have his fees paid for but has decided to stop the litigation, which could have been stopped a long time ago...blah de blah de blah blah. We are not over, of course, because we now prepare for a hearing for the Unilat-eral Statement and in the meantime, I feel like I want to cry but I can't. It's stuck. The money thing was hanging over me, even though I know it wouldn't be right if I had to pay the costs but you hear all sorts of things. I am grateful that we heard today. I felt all sorts of tummy churning with not having a response. Today is a good day. I have a ton of people still to tell. I need to drink this gin and then have another one!*'.

January, 2018. Email to Ames: '*Yair hasn't called yet be-cause he is in hearings all day. You know, Ames, I cannot tell you how many times I have yearned for my own business under lindseygoldrick or linzigoldrick.com All of them taken by him and no, I don't want to spend good energy now being taken up with anger about how he messed up my career and how I've lost the verve I once had but I need a change; something for myself. I have felt stagnant for years. If I don't do something now, another year will go by. Prior to Gabor call-ing 14 months ago, I really did start to wonder what the hell I was going to do before I went mad. 13 years ago, I was fired up, you will remember; full of ideas, having a pick and choose of offers and his do-*

ings just got worse and bigger and bigger. I thought a year of it would have been horrendous but it would stop then but it didn't. I have that freedom almost, so I definitely need change. I need to see that signature, Ames. Oh, but doesn't it feel like forever when you have to wait for important things? I cannot wait to thank Gabor, Yair, Gervase and Filiz personally'.

Spring 2018 - The money came through and after I had paid off debts that I had incurred due to reducing my hours at work through stress, it allowed me to take the summer off to be with Rex and not worry about juggling time. As long as I was frugal, I could take the time that I felt like I needed just to acknowledge and finish my drafts and get it completely off my chest.

I sat down and wrote a list of the pros and cons about giving up work for a few months and talked about it with Steve. It felt immensely important to do. I could explore myself again, having felt stifled and silenced for so long, with my name splashed in a negative way, all over the world wide web. I can break free. Steve reminded me about my age (I love being reminded of my age!) and that I haven't been doing anything that I have wanted to do on a career front since the US when I was a project manager for a film company.

It felt luxurious to not be working and to stop and think and breathe but I knew that I had to. The money wouldn't last long but it was there. So, I handed in a couple of months notice at work. I am endeared to the lovely chap and his wife that I worked for and I still see them in passing. And the great thing for my conscience is, I know I worked so hard for them and conscientiously, despite feeling terrorised for the whole 12 years I was with them. It seems incredible to think that I could cover it for so long but I was always taught to keep things close to my chest and not air my linen in public! Look what I am doing now!

I was still anxious about court. For a good six months of the year, everything that I had planned, felt like it may be cut short and I took clothes for court, wherever I went and a winter outfit was returned for a spring outfit which then got ditched for a summer outfit. I still had an apprehension that I wouldn't get the decent ending. So hyped up with nervous energy, I needed a project.

Digging soil always sorts me out but I didn't have the allotment anymore. The smell of earth, though - it calms me down. The intensity of the smell in the rain, too. Grounding. So I dug a seating area out in the garden - a project that everyone said was impossible, in the never ending wet days that followed, for weeks.

As I dug, the pent up feelings of accumulated despair and annoyance that seemed to be enshrouding me, going through what had happened was releasing. The rain symbolic of tears. Unlocking and unblocking. Pent up feelings of loss of control, loss of feeling safe, loss of career, loss of freedom…

With every spade slice into the ground, I thought about his relentless intent to bring me down over rejection. Digging over. Burying. Digging over. Burying. Unearthing. When weeks later I sat in my new seating area sanctuary surrounded by hollyhocks and lavender, I knew that I could now begin to really acknowledge and heal.

I thought about the pleasure of the success of achieving my goal in the garden when everyone said it was impossible. And after great determination and persistence, I felt grateful for my strength because it turned out wonderfully in the end. Thoughts that ran parallel with the case.

Then, a letter came from Furran's lawyer threatening that they would seek costs if I pursued the hearing! How dare they threaten me. I deserved the hearing and I deserved the statement to be read out in court.

The High Court judges had decided that I was entitled to that, so that is exactly what I was doing.

CHAPTER SIXTY SIX
My insurance policy

I kept everyone informed of the trial and wrote to Ames in length about how I was feeling: *'Thirteen years, Ames! All of that time going back and forth to the police and them not being able to do anything. Thirteen years of stress juxtaposed with 9 years of feeling joyous over Rex. Adventures and travels with the amazing people in my life. Feeling utmost pleasure pitted with the evil stuff on the biggest media platform, for everyone to see, all in the same moment. It crushed me.*

I am glad that I pretended nothing was happening and I am glad that anyone's energy was not spent on talking about it, thinking about it, enquiring and feeling sorry for me, etc. The continual acts of contacting Google and other search engines and hosts and domain sites, over and over. The burden over being impersonated on Twitter. These are only things I know about, for goodness sake.

The noises in the night, thinking that it was him, along with worrying about Steve. Oh Ames, I remember the thudding of my heart and the lack of sleep, while I lay at the side of Rex with something heavy in my hand because every single noise was footsteps on the stairs.

I recognise paranoia now but there was nothing I could do to convince myself that there wasn't a chance that he would come close. He is mad and who knows what he is capable of. My tummy flips when I think of him following Ethne from Mama's. Talking to everyone is really helping. What would I do without you all? Goodness, what a long time, though.

We went through a horrendously scary patch with money, too and Rex only started sleeping through the night when he was 6 years old but that has to be because I induced that with on-demand feeding and then not being able to sleep. He must have picked up on my constant checking on him. Hopefully, nothing else.

No, he didn't. He is such an even-keeled, happy boy. No wonder I look old, though. I will focus on looking and feeling better now, though. I wonder if I can work miracles? Ha ha'.

Furran's lawyer then, on learning that I was going to have my Statement read out in court asked me to change *'dated 4 times'* to *'having a relationship with'* on my statement. I agreed because it's hard to define relationships. One person's idea is not another and I didn't want to argue in court. The tactics to embarrass me into not making a statement in court were not going to work. Neither would the patronising and the bullying. Whether I did fall for him or whether I didn't - what he did was wrong.

They tried every way in which to stop that Unilateral Statement being read out at the High Court of Justice. Having said that a public apology really mattered to me, it was clear that he didn't feel sorry.

By this time, after absorbing his Witness Statement and so on, the public apology didn't mean as much to me as having a public statement by myself, awarded by High Court judges that agreed that I was entitled to one. I figured Furran would never acknowledge, and feel genuinely sorry for what he did and it wouldn't have been genuine. What actually happened was a good depiction of the truth. He didn't feel remorse. He had had no intention to stop. Furran not wanting to take ownership, accept responsibility or apologise in public, for what he had done, is the truth.

I was in control now and I had won the battle with the monster. The tug of war was over. He was on the floor. No amount of words printed would ever be as powerful as karma and as powerful as making him stop. Drawing a line under it was being in control.

So, this is what transpired: He had to promise not to do any of it ever again and leave me alone, pay the legal fees and pay some damages to me and hand over ownership of everything that pertained to me - his creations, as well as the passwords to the websites that were still registered, and emails that he had attained, used and embellished were sent on a USB stick. Along with any other little mementoes or keepsakes about me that he had taken when I wasn't looking, as part of the 'delivery up' on the Consent Order.

He had to confirm that no copies were made of these, either and that I would own everything, which gives me peace of mind. The websites were not live on the web but they were still registered until 2020 so even as I write this, I was waiting for the expiry of one. I am so, so, so relieved that none of my Yahoo contacts' private information was ever revealed. Phew.

If Furran breaches this settlement order, then it will be prison. I was happy with this. There is reassurance there. Like Yair had stated, sometimes being hit in the pocket is enough to make people stop and I had got the impression from the very first emails from Furran that he didn't have much. So, being sued and prison are good deterrents in this case. Like I stated, nothing will really ever feel like justice for what he did.

The USB with the material that he acquired and embellished on, were sent to me via my Lawyer with a letter from his lawyers (and bear in mind that an offer had been made and accepted and he had finally admitted it all and agreed to give all of his creations about me for my sole ownership) with the following sentence: *'Not to embarrass your client but it seemed more like a passionate relationship (or similar) than she has claimed'*.

This was not being disputed and it was unnecessary for them to state anything else at this stage. I agree. I was not embarrassed by my gushy emails with bits of poetry on. It is who I am. On email, we had both created the perfect person. In reality, it was not to be. We ended. Well, I had hoped and intended it to be that way, let's say.

What did them saying that have to do with anything? Did this warrant his behaviour? I wasn't disputing the level of romantic emails because again, it would be hard to define whether they were or weren't. A kiss at the bottom of a message could be passionate to one person and just a regular warm sign-off to some. Were they saying that I deserved it? Were they saying that he should be excused or mitigated for this behaviour?

I was disputing the fact that he stalked and harassed me online and offline for 12 years and counting. Didn't matter what our email exchange had been like or for how long. I wasn't embarrassed and what did they think writing that would achieve, especially at that stage when he had accepted my offer and it was almost over? It was not the point. The statement felt weighted. The last word. Unnecessary. Yet, they felt it was necessary to point out.

His Solicitors really made the process quite stressful. It was an extremely unnecessary statement and I wonder if he would have stated it, had they had the upper hand? It had a playground tone to it. Their bullyboy, patronising way was the worst part of the litigation process. Not the reliving of memories or the comprehensive search for evidence. It was their manipulative approach, their pejorative insinuations and their bullying letters.

Yes, they were defending their clients but they removed the fact that I was a human being that had been harassed by their client, fearing for my life and family's safety and being oppressed by the revolting creations of their client since the beginning of 2005 and it was over now.

They contributed and joined him in the bullying, reinforcing his belief according to his witness statement that I was to blame, to the very end and I shall not forget that. I wonder how they would feel if it was their wife, daughter, mother, aunty, friend, grandma, sister that had been subjected to it? Or really, anyone that they loved? I felt like I had another case on my hands. It was just too much.

Summer, 2018.

Opening the usb with all of his creations and embellishments on, with trepidation; afraid of what I would find, I pondered not carrying through with it. Was it a pointless exercise? It wouldn't change the sequence of events, nor settle me to know more. It was an eerie, ominous feeling that I will never get used to but experienced so many times over the years.

I just didn't know what I was going to see. I must have sat at the laptop for ages, pondering whether to click on any files. Opening up what seemed to be hundreds of files devoted to obsession, after 13 years being splashed all over the web with the continual reminder that he had more up his sleeve, I knew there would be things I hadn't yet seen.

Clicking on the files, not knowing what I would come across, was like playing some sort of roulette. Again, the moments it took for files to open felt like an hour. I saw original emails in there with a mix of sentences, different font sizes, crudely put together but also copied images of doves with ribbons, wedding rings, forget me nots and cupids. He had titled some files: Lindsay Face, Lindsay Dance, Lindsay Holiday (not even spelling my name correctly. Got it right on the internet though, didn't he?) and there were images of the beaches I frequented, holiday areas I had been to, the hills I walked and the areas that I visited with my friends, a picture of my car and a street view of Mama's address.

There was a full page of my lipstick blottings and strands of my hair and all the while, naturally thinking, 'What else am I going to find?'. The thudding in my chest!! Goodness. I clicked through, hoping with all of my heart not to see any of my contacts' private information. I had felt fiercely protective over them for all of this time and I can honestly say, that I did not see any. They were all devoted to lucky old me.

Tons and tons of folders lay before my eyes and I decided that I couldn't do it to myself. I did not want to see anymore. I'd had enough!

And I took the USB out of the laptop before I stumbled upon a folder titled 'Lindsay Undressing Videos'. To this day, I do not know what other material is on that USB stick. I haven't felt like looking again. Not yet - but it is my insurance policy.

I will keep the evidence, though. After all, it all had to be handed over to me. No copies. If anything appears in the future that is on there, then Furran is in breach.

I had stumbled upon the file that held the email that was four A4 pages long that I omitted from this, that day and it was still whirring around my head. It sent shivers down my spine and haunted me for a long time, making for restless nights. We were at the tail end now and I was releasing so much of the burden but I couldn't just switch off and feel okay entirely yet.

It was evident in my dreams and I was having the strangest ones. In one nightmare, elements of the very strange long email comes alive:

He is there and he spits at me, 'You even respond to me when you sleep. You are my anam cara!' And then I see his mother chastising him and him cowering in a corner and then see him in the foetus position crying that he is hungry and he was sorry that I had disappointed them with my behaviour. Weird stuff.

Then his Aunt Sarah who is 104 years old comes in with the scratchy see through nighty on, telling me that I lost someone special 'Keep them keen' she says over and over. Then a video appears on national TV - it is my face on someone else's body and he is there, shaving my armpits and taking imprints of my lips and pulling my hair out and his chin looks weaker, so much so that it isn't there and he is rocking his hips back and forth in red underwear.

It's boring hearing about people's dreams, if it isn't your thing, I know, but I state it, to show how deep his weirdness had gotten into my psyche. It is the most bizarre dream and yet it reflects that very strange and obsessive email to me.

He really did say that he wanted the nighty back to post to Aunt Sarah (if I didn't have it in black and white in an email, I would have questioned this memory) and she had actually expressed that he should have treated me mean. I woke up from it and felt disgusting. I showered. I really did curse the day that I met him online. At this point, he had been in my life for 14 years and that was 14 years too long.

I couldn't wait for him not to be in any part of my mind and life.

CHAPTER SIXTY SEVEN
Hold me back

When my legal team emailed me that July 9th had been set for the hearing of the Unilateral Statement at the High Court of Justice in London, I saw the email the moment it came in, as I was lying on the bed, catching up with my emails. I gasped and my stomach rolled. I gave a silent prayer of thanks, emailed a huge thank you wish back. Steve called. He always picked up when he needed to know something important. I let Teen know because she had said she would come with me, and then felt a release of emotions. I closed the laptop. It all seemed surreal. It really was coming to an end.

I remained lying down and stared at the beam in the bedroom. At the part that crosses, that my eyes always gravitate towards; my focus point when I am lying in bed. The piece that I have stared at a million times and mulled thoughts over with, as though it had all the answers and I daren't look away.

The part that I had stared at when I have heard steps coming up the stairs. The focal point that I looked at, as I lay protecting our boy, for he slept with me for safety's sake - with my heart pounding so loudly, as I planned what to do when the door opened. The beam that I thought might be the last beam I ever see! The beam that held my thoughts when I was pulling myself together to get over the negative and seize the day. I felt overwhelmed with emotion and let the tears flow.

I was grateful beyond capacity for explanation for my legal team and the people in my life. I appreciated Steve more, for being genuine and reliable, his unwavering support, his even-keeled and sensible mind. He was sane, untroubled, solid, honest and proud of me. I looked around the bedroom and gave thanks for our cottage. The cottage that kept us safe and warm and well for all of those crazy years. When at times, horror had dared to cross the threshold.

This is the home that looked after us. This home has held the tears of joy and tears of laughter and protected us against it all; keeping us tight. All those years of wondering how it would end and after all of it, I win. Dad would be proud of me too, I thought. And a whiff of a cigar went by and I heard his voice in my head, 'There's no flies on you, my darling Daughter. You're like your Dad. Alright…your gorgeous Mum as well'.

Then the phone rang and it was Debs. I choke out the fantastic news. We had a relief sob together. We talked for a long time, skimming the years; recapping the litigation. I was free. I could talk about whatever I wanted and I was okay to hear whatever she had thought through the years. She had found it hard since I didn't reach out, she said. She knew that the websites were there. There were elephants in rooms and times that I was remote. She had found it hard, knowing what little she did know and wanting to support me more. Her empathy and kindness and our friendship would not allow for switch off. It ascertained what I had dreaded - anyone worrying about me and it made my heart hurt.

'*Timing is perfect*,' she said, '*Nick and Dave have offered us their villa for after it is over. Let's go! Flights are super cheap from Exeter*'. The abundance of generosity and kindness around me, silently cushioning me along the way, was now eliminating what I had been subjected to. Chipping away and discarding and replacing. Rebuilding with an army of love around me. So rich.

Contemplating this, I proceeded to call, text and email everyone to tell them that this was all coming to an end just ten days away.

July 2nd 2018 - Email to Ames: '*My tummy keeps flipping out, Ames. I am keeping up with my meditation. I cannot believe it is a week away. I am so nervous about walking into the High Court of Justice and I hope I don't tumble or bumble but I will have my fabu-*

lous cousin Teen with me. Everybody has offered but I am grateful to have just her. I really do not want a crowd of people.

I know that you offered and I cannot thank you enough and to think that you would come over all the way from the States, as I would for you, just signifies our friendship and I appreciate you so much. Steve was all ready to come, too but I want Rex to have a normal day and go to school and he knows that Teen is the perfect person for me and will keep me grounded. Thank you, Lovey. So much. It is exciting and I am a little nervous.

I am so looking forward to meeting the legal team. It feels surreal. It is nearly over, Ames! I am writing a statement to be read in public, just in case, and am confident about what I have written but am feeling pretty nervous about reading it aloud. What if I am inaudible due to sobbing whilst talking or something? It is so important to me and this is what I need and want to do but I worry that I will be somewhat shaky, completely inaudible and wondered whether I should ask Yair to read it? I don't want to miss the opportunity to state openly exactly what happened. It is the reason why it has got this far. I suppose I am getting my head around it. I have never been up for public speaking. Last minute wobbles and all that'.

An email came flying back from Ames: 'I just got all buttery stomachs when I read this that you may be talking to the press. It is almost there! And of course, you are all worked up! I like the idea of you reading the statement, as nerve wracking as it is. I think that it needs to come from you. Your emotions around it is real and what he has put you through is real. Whoever hears you, needs to see that and hear that and feel that. This is your time. He has stolen so much from you and you are claiming it all back. This is empowerment. This is strength. This signifies you taking it all back - with authority. Own it.

You will have so much energy coming your way when you're there that you will have all you need to make it happen. Don't cower. Don't hide. You've hidden far too long to have a little bit of nerves keep you in hiding. Take it all back, Linz. You've waited 13 years for this.

And I totally get that it's really easy for me to say this, half-way across the world and having not lived it. There is so much emotion surrounding this experience of yours in court that I cannot even begin to grasp it. And the idea of public speaking makes me cringe and cower and want to hide. But you are likely one of the strongest and bravest people I know, having endured the wrath and psychosis of this sick man for so long that I want you to stand tall and face it head on. You have it in you and you'll feel better for it, even if you end up crying or choking up or not doing it as you envision it in your head.

Be your authentic self, Linz. All of it - the fear, the anger, the pain, the same. Let it fly. You've waited 13 years for this. I am off my soapbox now and I so wish I was there. You know I will be as much as I can from thousands of miles away. I will be in that court-room with you, egging you on. Lifting you up. Whispering in your ear that you can do this. That you deserve that stage and you should do with it what you can to get past the horrible experience. Apparently, I wasn't done… but I am now. I swear. So glad your cousin is with you'.

Goodness. So was I.

Looking back at this time, I feel like someone should have kept me home. Intoxicated with the relief that it was almost over had me behaving like a kid that had been sucking on sugar all day. I was at the dental hygienists and she was new at the practice, just a few days before the court. I bounced in there, feeling so high as a kite and she asked me what I was up to. No control over the excitement that I felt, I told her that I was preparing for the High Court and then proceeded to tell her everything. There was no 'off' button. No filter. No control. I hadn't met her before, either.

It felt so surreal and having not talked openly about it for years, suddenly, I wanted people to hear me. Anyone. I had my voice back! I was so elated. She sat, eyes wide, scaler in hand, new client in front of her and just listened. *'You didn't expect that, did you?'*, I laughed.

When my teeth were squeaky clean and I was thoroughly polished, feeling highly emotive, I hugged her so hard before I left. A complete stranger. My new dental hygienist. I made a bet with myself that she would have an assistant with her the next time I went. I have to say that I absolutely appreciated that she didn't shut me up and remind me what I was there for, too.

Oh, but it didn't stop there. I had to pop into the supermarket for some celebratory drinks. I danced up and down the aisles, smiling to myself, smiling at strangers (everyone would argue that this is normal for me), but I was aching for someone else to ask me what I was up to. At the self serve till, I spot a girl that worked there who I always have a little chitchat with.

As she came towards me, to approve the alcohol, I thought she was coming in for a hug and I hugged her so hard. The worse thing was, I got my fingers trapped in her hair and she was trying to escape. '*What are you doing?*', she asked, sounding a little scared. I couldn't believe what I was doing.

I apologised profusely, as I was untangling my fingers and burning up with embarrassment. I cringed as I carried on and I had to find her afterwards and apologise again. She told me not to worry, as she laughed nervously. I told her that I had a spot of good news, so I couldn't help myself wanting to hug the world. Oh my goodness. I often think of her and I haven't seen her since. I think that she put in for a transfer. Look out everybody! I had to get home and strap my arms down.

I was a bundle of nervous energy every day, as the date got closer and when the phone rang, it was usually words of luck being wished. The phone rang and it was Steve. '*There are two more websites up with your name on, Linz,*' and my whole being just deflated and crashed. I had been flying high and I was shot down.

Crushed and astonished, I dropped down on the sofa in disbelief, talking to myself, '*Will he ever, ever stop?*'.

CHAPTER SIXTY EIGHT
Standing up to bullies is important

From feeling elation that the end is close and then the absolute devastation of knowing about more creations in one single moment and the court day hadn't even happened yet, I picked up the phone to call Yair, holding back tears, with the familiar bilious taste in my mouth. Saul Furran is most definitely psychotic.

It was all happening again and it was most definitely not nearly over, at all!

Frenzied, I spoke with Yair, who sounded deflated on the news but as we talked, on finer inspection, the websites didn't have anything in the body of them and seemed to be attached to a bitcoin site. It was just my name. It was enough, though. Yair said that we would start a new claim after this one was over.

As long as they didn't escalate and nothing appeared in the body of the website addresses, I figured that my High Court case would make the news and push them down to the bottom of a Google search and this stifled my anxieties. I couldn't feel like I had been feeling for so many years. Those days are over and I had the best legal team that would help me, should anything else happen.

Buckling now was not an option. I had an influx of calls and messages from my dearest friends and family with terrific words of support. Mama came for hugs. She was proud of my constitution, she said. So many special messages and offers from people to come to court, to show their support but I had them in my heart and my head. As always. My silent support.

July 10th 2018 - The morning after the court day, I gave Rex a staunch hug, his breakfast and he asked me how it went. I tucked his hair behind his ears, over and over, feeling more peaceful than I had done since before he was born, a long time before he was born. I paused and enjoyed the moment. I lamented that I had got the bully to stop and that I had told the world, to make an example of him. '*Mummy feels empowered and even stronger than before*', I told him.

'*Standing up to bullies is important, Rex*', I said, enjoying that he wasn't moving my hand away from curling his hair around his ear. '*It feels good to win. We must always shout out bullies and anyone being unkind to us or our friends and family. As much as we must be cautious to never be a bully. Always be kind, my Love. There may always be someone ready to say mean things. Don't be one of them*'. And just before I lost his interest entirely (if I hadn't already), '*The important thing is to talk, get help and not suffer alone. I couldn't get help for so long but eventually I got it. So much of life requires us to be brave and reaching out for help is being brave*'.

I thanked him for giving me strength, even though he didn't know that he did. He was busy now but he was still in the same room and I carried on, '*You always give me strength, just by thinking about you, Rex. Thinking about anyone you love when you are going through anything is silent, strong support... survival*'. And of course, a lot of that fell on deaf ears but I always figure if I keep repeating myself and be consistent in bite-size pieces (though this time was big chunk-size), eventually it will all be heard.

I then took a strong, black coffee into the garden and sat in my little dig-out, feeling this tidal wave of exhilaration, appreciation and freedom. I left a WhatsApp message for JoJo. It was her Birthday. Too early to call America. Such relief flooded me. It felt hard to imagine that it was done and that the day before was spent in London at the High Court of Justice with my Landmark case, setting a precedent in law.

Teen had been absolutely amazing. Not surprisingly, but she had her own concerns and still came, giving me so much strength and support. She made me eat, she made me laugh, she prepped me for public speaking. We walked, we talked, we

292

laughed, we danced, we visited The comedy Store. Both distracted but together. Both drawing strength from each other.

We were staying in a hotel not far from the High Court of Justice and strolling past there, we glorified in the beauty of the Gothic victorian building, soon to house witness to my vindication statement. Grateful that The Comedy Store entertained and distracted us until late, and after listening to a whole host of fantastic messages on my phone, it was close to midnight.

I lay awake all night long. My stomach churned. Envisaging the day. It was actually the same day in fact at that point, as I watched the hours ticking by. Knowing already that The Times was running the story. Unsure how the day would pan out, despite knowing the outcome, I considered the brevity of life.

A quarter of my life would be summed up publicly this very day. In so little time, I would be discarding perpetual worries and stepping into empowerment.

Because I persisted, stood up to him and won in the end.

CHAPTER SIXTY NINE
My day of Justice

So, this is what my day of justice looks like, I thought, as I looked around the exquisite wood panelled courtroom. It hadn't really sunk in that I was not a spectator at someone else's trial. It would have shocked me if he had turned up because he didn't need to but he wasn't predictable. The only assurance I had was that he fought hard against publicity and was willing to pay for silence.

Gervase representing me, since Gabor was predisposed, reading out the statement: *'unlawful conduct was carried out primarily by means of designing, registering, creating, publishing, owning, maintaining, updating, controlling at least 10 offensive websites....'.* and us all appearing in front of one of the country's most notable, modern and respected Judges. Justice Warby, who was in charge of the Media and Communications List in the Masters Bench in the Queen's Division in the High Court of Justice in London.

This Judge has appeared in many of the key cases in privacy law development and included the Royal Family and other famous people against news groups and so on. It felt like the hugest deal that I, despite not being known, was entitled to a public announcement of privacy invasion and my case was being heard by him. I wanted public acknowledgement of a very public act of targeted crime and this was it.

I looked around and to Teen by my side, appreciating her so much. She matched my smile, sensing how I felt. I thought about everyone that was present with me; strengthening me in spirit; whispering in my ear, lifting me up and to Yair and Filiz and around the room at many different people. Had my legal team not helped me with their tremendous work, where would I be now? This ending far surpassed how I had dreaded.

Gervase continued, *'anxiety…distress…*
embarrassment….' I looked around. A deep intake of breath. Of
those there would be no more. I am not anxious or damaged, I
am fortified. Distressed….no longer. Embarrassment lifted. Having this read out in public felt like I was clearing my name, even
though I hadn't done anything wrong.

There wasn't 'court room' drama. Nothing like I had
expected and I liked the respectful peace. It suited how I felt.
Peaceful. Respected. Entitled to privacy. He was brought to the
High Court of Justice. I gained back full autonomy. Judge Justice
Warby heard. He left. It was over. To end my Landmark case
here gave me closure.

The Unilateral Statement became a public statement
that he was admitting to what he had done. Unfortunately for
him, this was the part that he could have had mutually agreed
wording, apologising as well as admitting. As it was, by not
agreeing, he had admitted but refused to apologise but that
showed what he was made of, as far as I was concerned. I was
fine with that because truly, if there had any been any remorse,
there was plenty of time to have shown that and stopped over the
years.

If he was genuinely apologetic, there would haven't been
blame, disconnection or justification in his Witness Statement.
Too late to backtrack to look better in the public eye and he was
lucky to get the obligatory legal statement of apology. The statement would have looked so different without the omitted important material to avoid court time but I was free to tell the truth.
Furran wouldn't have a criminal record for the crimes that he
committed but he would go to prison if he breached the order.
He's not allowed to get to me, ever again. Anywhere in the world:
close proximity or digitally.

And the internet holds no creations of intentional harm
about me anymore.

It only includes the news about what he did and that I
came out victorious in the end.

Subsequently, I then had a busy time with the media. I could not waste this opportunity but I considered them carefully. The message that it was not about financial gain was important to me, so no offers were attractive that way. It was too important. I could not waste this opportunity to talk.

Nobody should go through anything like that without help and nobody should get away with that behaviour. I wanted to make an example of him publicly because he had hijacked my life for 13 years and he wasn't going to get away with his controlling, bullying and violent conduct lightly.

I also had to give the message to other perpetrators that used the internet to commit crimes that they are not invincible and can be found and that they are not 'hiding' behind the internet, no matter where they lived and how they try to cover up their crime.

I wanted it brought to attention that the police need training for online crimes and dealing with those that have been subjected to harassment and abuse. Because they are the first point of contact and that treatment from the police could save lives. That harassment and abuse will always involve bruising but that mental and physical pain will not be visible.

To have a police constable acknowledging what has happened and not turning someone away saying, 'What do you want me to do?' will make all the difference. There are current applicable laws that cover crimes that are happening on the internet. Offline and online. It doesn't matter where crimes are being committed. A consistent use all across the forces would be great to instil in training courses.

I wanted to highlight that online harassment is not just social media related and there is a misconception there. You can be harassed on the internet even if you have not signed up for an online account, as nobody is immune. If someone wants to commit acts of ugliness and crime, they will do it and use whatever tools they have.

I wanted to highlight that the search engines, web platforms and so on facilitated abuse, by not taking down obvious abuse directed towards me, even after hundreds of pleas, and things need to change.

Also, because he offered me silence money during litigation, to not talk about the case or he would sue me (which enrages me that this is allowed to happen), I wanted to give the message that you cannot always just throw money at a crime to make it go away.

I loved the powerful message of the public acknowledgement at The High Court.

What also felt really powerful and poignant was after my radio interview at LBC, Furran's lawyers called Yair to tell him that I shouldn't have mentioned that Furran was arrested. Yair responded with, '*She can say what the hell she likes. The trial is over.*' Those words just made me feel jubilant:

I can say what the hell I like because the trial is over.

My mind buzzed: Empowerment. My strength prevailing in the end. Contribution to change. Exposure. Example. I had to be brave. Telling the story publicly and relinquishing these oppressive feelings. Good had to come of it and that good was going to be felt by others, too. I had to just do it.

People are shocked to hear how private I am, considering my public appearances after the trial but I couldn't waste the opportunity to help one person. Not doing it would have bothered me forever. This moment would be gone and it would be too late. I had to step through feeling petrified in order to pay it forward.

It all felt so cathartic. Seeing the internet flooded with the good news as opposed to his horrible creations, had me full of euphoria. A wondrous sight for sore, tired eyes!

A lot of people wanted to see what he looked like and of course, he had wiped the internet clean of any information about himself and his family, prior to the court day but I am glad, really.

His face would have been forever attached to mine on the internet and that would have given me nightmares!

The perpetrator's name was such a common name that when his name was splashed all over the media as being the perpetrator, his picture wasn't attached. I could imagine all the panics and worries of people that knew people with the same name; husbands, sons, brothers, fathers, cousins, partners and friends. I felt so sorry for them because he had wiped the internet clean of himself long before, in preparation.

I vowed to set the record straight as soon as I could and when I was interviewed for the BBC, I stated it was the Saul Furran that was from blah blah, the Saul Furran that had a company Furran Consulting Ltd, it was the Saul Furran that now lived in blah or blah blah and was married and whose birthdate was blah blah blah…..and I suppose it was overkill but I was thinking about all of the doubts and panics going around on poor, innocent people. I hadn't thought about it then because it was others that I was thinking of but I wonder if there was also a subconscious part of me that felt that he shouldn't have the luxury of being anonymised by not having his picture online, and having been given the opportunity to remove his picture. As many people commented online: *'Why are we only seeing her and not who did it?'*

Teen texted me after the radio interview: *'If they didn't know who he was before, they certainly do now!'*

CHAPTER SEVENTY
Euphoria

I claimed my name on Twitter and had the tagline: '*I haven't had a voice for 13 years. Hello.*' Receiving words of support from all around the world and also being able to offer my support to others felt so good. This was what I had wanted - turning it into something good.

I wrote to police stations across the counties asking how they would treat someone that came to them with online abuse and got a handful of replies that were concerning. I wrote to the Avon and Somerset Police Commissioner and got the same response. I wrote to our Prime Minster at Number 10, by way of the Digital, Cultural, Media and Sports Department, highlighting my case and saying it wasn't social media, etc (and you know the story) but what were they doing about online harassment, going forward? I got a letter back that told me about '*investing 4.6 million into funding police-led programmes to effectively police a digital age and protect victims of digital crime from the Police Transformation Fund in 2016/17*' and stated that '*there will be something published for online safety legislation as a joint paper with the Home Office as a precursor to bringing forward online safety legislation*'... and I started to zone out.

It felt like an arduous task to even contemplate where to begin to respond and then do something more. A well-written paper for the files is just not good enough. What is going to be done? Immediate action is needed. Not debates. Not spending money on people writing action proposals that don't materialise but look good on paper. An unsatisfactory response. By the time something actually changes, how many lives have been affected?

I had a meeting with my local Member of Parliament who wrote to them on my behalf and I called for followups and followups take time until I felt like I was chasing around for questions that couldn't ever be answered. I was too used to being fobbed off and turned away. I could see that there would be urgent change needed in the future, as more and more people were being harassed online and where was I going to get by myself? That is when I just knew that I needed a bit of a break. I took a break from Twitter. I knew that I didn't have it in me to start up another big case on my own. Yet.

I was, in all honesty, elated but exhausted. I needed to heal and do everything that I could that would involve invoking peace in every part of me, first. Peace and quiet. I could sit in silence and smile because when I closed my eyes, all there was, was love and calm. Oh, how sweet that felt!

I kept an eye on the two new websites and they soon disappeared. Most likely generated by the internet and by bitcoin and not Furran, after all. I have hope.

Debs and I went to our very kind friends' dreamy home in the mountains in Mallorca. Steve and Rex had their boy time again. Our little yellow car was so much fun, tootling along the olive grove-lined roads, winding up the hills. Chasing the cerulean skies. The landscape dry and honey coloured. Sweet candy for the eyes. A festival met us in Valldemossa square. Music, laughter, dancing. Setting the theme. Rejoice. Celebration. Fear no more. I cried on a rock in Deia, as Debs jumped into the Balearic. Splashes of sea met the salty tears running down my cheeks. I had checked my emails on my phone and a lady who had won a major landmark cyberbullying case in the US, had taken the time out to write a thoughtful, supportive email to me and it moved me. Healing. Hell, I was loving this. Heaven. My new friend called Freedom had joined us. All those years. Pent up. Release.

The sun was hot, penetrating our bones. I sank into therapy. We slept. Morning sun streamed through the windows. The terrace held our laughter. Silly dancing witnessed by sunset and then the moon. Stories. Memories. Books unread. We walked. We talked. I had a fantastic listener and talker by my side. A precious friend who had offered herself as a pillar throughout the years. Here we were together, in a stunning part of the world. No place in my body occupied by fear. No place in my head held hostage by angst. We had no place to be but there. Peace took over the turmoil. Harmony shifted the fears that had taken up camp in my mind. A sanctuary built in place. Empowerment took over loss. I had gained. He had lost.

So the responses that I gave to interviewers in the early days, when I felt euphoric about the outcome were borne of that: Ecstatic relief. I realised that as I got this all off my chest. So many people asked me what it was really like and I couldn't go there in my mind. I was enjoying this freedom. I almost felt numb and devoid of remembering what it actually was like. I blocked it at that time, through the desire for respite and revelling in the freedom of deep calm; a harmonic balance.

No churning, no frazzled nerves, no clumsy falls, no darting my eyes around, no roll of dread when I went on the internet. No sinking when someone looked at me twice. So many things were unfolding but until I wrote this, I enjoyed the space in my mind that didn't contain anything worrying about what had happened.

It was weeks afterwards, when I was under an umbrella of euphoria still, I was asked by an interviewer, '*How do you feel about him now?*'

'*The truth is,*' I told them, '*I feel nothing about him. I don't ever want to feel anything because having any type of feelings for him would keep him in my life and I didn't want him to be there anymore. He doesn't deserve any of my headspace and he has been there for way too long already. That is all in the past now.*'

I believed it when I said it but it is not so easy to do in truth, further down the line.

I knew that the time would come where I had to look at it in more detail, in order to move forward and heal.

There had to be some sort of acknowledgement and nurturing work-through and that is why, because I love writing, this has been extremely cathartic and good for me. Steve had talked about suppressed anger, which actually came out during writing and it surprised me, after refusing to let anger into my life for so long.

By the third or fourth draft, more anger came out, especially when presented with Furran's responses in his statement. It reminded me of when Gabor had asked me to write my witness statement. Each draft contained more and more of the word 'fear'.

By writing it all down, I have found it incredibly worthwhile and I appreciate that may not sound enough but I feel that I am going in the right direction. There was something else though that I couldn't quite pinpoint until the final draft. It was within me already and it finally occurred in the next chapter.

CHAPTER SEVENTY ONE
Autonomy - at last

We took a camping holiday, Steve, Rex and I to Polzeath in Cornwall and a journalist contacted me whilst there. She asked me how do I feel now on my first family holiday afterwards? Sitting on the beach, watching my boys surf the waves, I took a huge suck of sea air in and felt it. *'Absolute joy'*, was my reply.

'Joy that doesn't stop when everyone else has gone to bed. I go to bed with joy in my heart, knowing that I will experience freedom in my mind when I wake up from now on. Not that I took it for granted before, but I feel it now, too. We are all having the most freeing holiday', I responded.

We finished our conversation and the boys headed back to me. Rex distracted by a game of football nearby. It was just over 9 years that he had been born. Steve and I lamented about how we kept our beady eyes on him still, vigilantly and how unrelaxed and overprotective we must appear to be to others. We wondered if we would have been different had Saul Furran not affected our lives in the way that he had. Because in that moment, we both could feel the consequences, when everything else had stripped away.

I presume that we wouldn't have been so hyper-vigilant but who can really tell? Saul Furran's actions that have spanned over 13 years had cemented deep protection and strong fear in both of us. Not just me. Steve revealed his worries of us back home when he wasn't here. He wondered whether we were safe and he couldn't do anything about it, if we weren't. It was paramount on his mind but he couldn't voice it, he said. He felt so helpless.

We, as a unit, are stronger than ever now but it occurred to me that Steve hasn't really known me without having someone else committing crimes on me the whole time I have known him. That would have been difficult for anyone to contend with.

Asking him how he felt over those years, he said, '*I think I felt exactly like you did!*' And it surprised me and brought tears to both of our eyes. He didn't know half of what was happening because I was protecting him from that. But how did I know that him not knowing and only imagining what I was going through, and him not being able to be here to protect us, wasn't just the same?

Not long after, we went on another camping trip in South Devon in a farmer's field that we favoured. Early misty mornings as the sun rose up from the water, cast a warmth and brightness over our large plot in a farmer's field. Burgh Island in our sight. Coffee pot on the fire. Blankets wrapped around us. Playing Exploding Kittens. Extra special moments together. No phone signal. No internet connection. Precious times reading in the dark with torches, the three of us. Cooking something on the fire and snuggling in the tent. Going to bed early and waking at dawn to birdsong. Nothing else on my mind. No clocks to know the time. Nothing to monitor or think about. No worries. Bliss. We had brought our kayaks and paddle boards and played on the water, in the water and chased a wave. Meandering down the lanes, floating on rivers, paddling up stream. The sound of seagulls, reminding me about ice cream and sand. Tranquility. Deep sighs of relief. Laughter. Calm.

As Steve fitted us out with our safety jackets, buoyancy aids, id tags and phone numbers on everything, to send us off down the river, I watched him. He was fixed on sorting us out, taking care to see that we were both safe and that we had everything we needed should we come into danger. That is what he does; that is what he likes to do. Making sure that we are absolutely safe. Watching him buckle us up and buckle us in, I thought I might burst with love.

Watching him in that role of care taker for us, lulled me for a moment, for it had been taken away from him for so long. As the days went by, I caught him with a very different look in his eyes when he looked at me and I asked him what it was and he said, '*Pride. I am proud of you*'.

Time together now had a lightness, a brightness and not tinged with frustration or an ominous feeling of danger. I hadn't realised how tense Steve had been until now. It must have been so hard for him. He was calmer, relaxed. He is a natural problem solver. He likes to make sure things are fixed. This had been one hell of a problem that was now fixed. No wonder he looked happier. We all benefited. The three of us. Free to be.

I felt so calm and I wouldn't ever get sick of this feeling. No special effort to compartmentalise those crippling feelings. I acknowledged that it hadn't been a walk in the park, as I tapped away, getting it all off my chest. It almost felt like it was someone else's nightmare, as I expunged it from my mind, expelled it from my body and cast it out to type.

Each day, as I typed more, it got easier and I noticed that things were not such a big deal anymore, such as the blinds were not down in the room where I was and yet it was dark outside. The phone rang and it was an unknown caller and it didn't phase me at all.

I don't feel the unnerve of noises or see shadows at home any more because the shifts and creaks are because it is an old cottage. There is always a shadow, with light and dark. I double check that I have locked the doors - several times, but less so than last month and much less than the month before that.

I still jump a little - or a lot - at people surprising me, but that too is easing. My heart jumps out of my chest for a moment and then I get the pleasure of knowing it was a good surprise. Noises at the door are just that. Noises. I can rationalise those thoughts and am soon settled.

All boxes are still suspect that come to the door and I still gasp when I see that I have missed a parcel. So deeply etched in my mind, no amount of parcels being delivered levy up that feeling of unease but the acrid smoke smell is less strong. In time that will diminish, I know. I mentioned earlier that I still had remnants of the vigilant scanning procedure going on now but now I have less than I did than when I wrote that part.

I still have fleeting memories of not so nice things, like the gloved hand through the letterbox and the lovely thing is that they are exactly that: memories in the past. History now. There is only right now. This moment. This is what I am sure of and… it is really good.

The impact on your mental health, amongst other things, cannot be underestimated, when you have experienced being harassed, abused, bullied and stalked. The fractious experience goes deep but you can work on healing, moving forward. Talking in trusted environments with trusted people is essential in working it through.

Acknowledgement is important. Every day is a brand new day. I am sleeping deeply now, so calm do I feel. The contrast is astounding.

Rather than worrying if he is around the corner, I am excited to see what is there now. I am not changed but I am. I am stronger, more assertive; empowered.

After all, I met someone and it didn't work out. It's life. Nothing justifies what he did to me but that is his issue, not mine.

The very tool that he used to commit those crimes on me - the internet - will not forget what he did. With each refreshing page daily, as it embeds deeper in the index of the internet, he is the most notorious longest perpetrator of online harassment to date.

Luckily for him, he has a common name and he had wiped his image off the internet. It is only possibly on his conscience. He can't escape from the internet. I remember that feeling, once upon a time. I would not wish it on anyone.

I remember feeling glad that his image was not attached to mine and to not be connected somehow.

That is why, at this point at the end of the book in the final draft, it hit me what I hadn't been able to pinpoint. It was to do with connection.

In order to truly disconnect from him, I had to forgive. I had to forgive him so that I can genuinely detach. Had I not written this, it might have taken me longer to get there. Without the anger, I wouldn't have realised what he had taken from me. Without that, I wouldn't have known what to address; what I needed to give comfort to. In order to give true comfort, I needed to release my feelings.

I am not saying: 'It's okay', I am saying 'I am okay'. I will never, ever excuse what he did and I won't seek him down to tell him. That is not what forgiveness is.

I include the true definition of forgiveness:

A conscious, deliberate decision to release feelings of resentment or vengeance toward a person who has harmed you, regardless of whether they actually deserve your forgiveness. Forgiveness does not mean condoning or excusing offences.

I am forgiving because if I don't, some precious mind space would be taken up entangled with negativity that would negate enriching, important emotional healing, peace and harmony. I would lose out if I didn't forgive because I had won, control had shifted and it wouldn't feel complete. It was an important part of the process.

It is possible that Furran does not feel remorse or any responsibility about what he did, and I certainly cannot change what he did do but I wasn't going to be stuck because of what cannot be changed. What he did was all about him, not me.

My forgiveness is important for my heart, my family and my going forward.

Through this evolving process, I am no longer connected with him. Through forgiveness, I am freeing myself of him.

CHAPTER SEVENTY TWO
Final thoughts (and I did not expect this)

This piece makes me uncomfortable but so much of my journey was doing something uncomfortable and about having my own voice and about speaking the truth. Ames was curious about wondering whether I was still the same 'Linz that lit up a room'. We haven't seen each other for 20 years but of course, we have been in contact the whole time.

We had a holiday planned in Portugal in 2020 but I don't need to explain why that didn't happen. It had me curious, though. Was I the same person? I had often wondered it myself and had presumed not, despite being adamant that he wouldn't change me.

I thought back to my coping strategy and the inbuilt childhood lessons.

My parents had taught my brothers and I the power of gratitude and the power of forgiveness. They had taught us how to live in the moment and enjoy and appreciate everything that you have and not want things that you cannot. They taught us to be cheerful. They told us to focus on being kind and helping others and to imagine what it would be like walking in someone else's shoes; to be compassionate and not make judgements.

They taught us to let things go and not carry ill feelings but to always stick up for ourselves. To nurture strength of spirit in times of challenges. To concentrate on the best things in life, for there is beauty everywhere and so much goodness around us. There is always something to be grateful for. There are always people that are worse off and that we were loved. Not everyone is, and that love is powerful and love is healing.

I had fought ferociously for the ordeal to not damage me and take away any of the valuable teachings from my Mama and Dad by my mantras and my gratitude rituals.

And Amy's question had me pondering. I wanted to know if the mechanisms had been effective, since it would definitely help with my healing process. It was important to me what others thought about me now, that have known me since I was born, throughout childhood, my teens, my twenties, my early thirties, throughout the ordeal and dear lovely friends that I have been lucky to become close to in the past few years.

So, I decided to go out of my comfort zone and ask them to give me a word or two to describe me. And while I am not good at hearing praise or receiving compliments, it was part of my process for healing.

I was encouraged to put the responses in to highlight how effective my resolve to keep my spirit and keep my head.

They were incredible and generous and were similar, saying: kind, compassionate, joyful, positive and vivacious. Some mentioned my being warm and lighting up a room (no wonder people invite me camping and welcome me in a power cut!). Thank you, everyone. It was so humbling, more than I expected, and a real boost.

It highlighted that it all had worked. He didn't get to me. I had won. I didn't change. That is proof. Coming from the people that I trust and love the most.

And it is because of everyone being in my life that I was able to cope. So, thank you to all of my treasured family and friends, for the richness you give my life. In you, I am with 'someone like-minded'.

I am smiling now and proud of myself because despite everything, and despite robbing me of privacy and time, he didn't break my spirit, and that acknowledgement only makes me feel even stronger.

I am empowered
I kept my head up
I kept smiling
I kept loving
I kept finding humour

309

I kept turning up
I stayed strong
I remain mostly healthy
I exercised
I kept being kind to myself, too
I am emotionally balanced
I am always grateful
I kept being me and I am still me. Just even stronger.
I kept the faith that it will be over one day...and it is!

Also, it has helped me break down some personal barriers. For instance, I am still precious about my privacy and I was going to keep this as my own cathartic private writing. I pondered it for a long time, feeling so vulnerable about laying it all out. Steve reminded me that I may regret it. Regret meant it was 'too late' and 'disappointment'. That would have felt so much worse than being afraid of how this would be received.

I decided to share.

What I write - what I put out there, could potentially do more good. Sharing can create change; give hope. I like that.

I took the leap! More growth!

As the years passed and my continuous imploring was unheeded, the familiar words of, 'What do you want me to do?' condemned me to diminished expectations and hope. The case was getting more complex by the day.

So, when Gabor, Gervase and Yair said that they would work for me (for so many thousands of hours) without payment because they believed that I needed help (and they knew what to do to make him stop), it restored my faith in humanity.

Kindness, knowledge and faith prevails ultimately. I am forever grateful for their assistance.

I tell myself that the past has no power on me being fully present now and I have full autonomy over my life; my body and my mind. I am free.

The End.

Finally, I am pleased to say that I have created what would have given me what I needed: a forum. A trusted, safe, anonymous, monitored space online devoted to anyone directly and indirectly involved with internet harassment in all of its forms.

With more knowledge about applicable laws as well as emotional understanding, I am confident to share what I can on the forum. In the hope that people will not feel so isolated and that through the forum, they will feel armed with tools and information that will help them.

I hope that people that can support people will join it, as well as the people that need it. People with good intentions are really welcome to join: forum.lindseygoldrickdean.com. Let's help each other, look out for each other and be kind to one another, as we are all immersed in the digital world.

Thank you to everyone that encouraged me to write about this experience. By doing so, I truly feel that I have addressed it and drawn a line under it. I will keep myself in check about that but I am concentrating on the present and the future now.

Thank you to Ames, who helped me do some final edits on this book (by listening to it, I might add. She wouldn't want to feel responsible for any typos!).

Eternal gratitude to my parents, who gave me all the tools and for my smile. Thank you to my son who gives me the reason. Thank you to my husband who is incredibly, incredibly supportive.

Infinite gratitude to Aunty Maggie and Uncle Bob.

Thank you to Teen. For everything.

Thank you to everyone in my life, making it richer and for being so fantastic. I am a lucky lass.

Indelible gratitude again - to those that didn't ask, 'What do you want me to do?'.

And I thank you, for reading this.

Printed in Great Britain
by Amazon